Critical Muslim 9

The Maghreb

Editors: Ziauddin Sardar and Robin Yassin-Kassab

Deputy Editor: Samia Rahman

Senior Editors: Aamer Hussein, Ehsan Masood, Ebrahim Moosa

Publisher: Michael Dwyer

Managing Editor: (Hurst Publishers): Daisy Leitch

Cover Design: Fatima Jamadar

Associate Editors: Alev Adil, Merryl Wyn Davies, Abdulwahhab El-Affendi, Nader Hashemi, Vinay Lal, Hassan Mahamdallie, Iftikhar Malik, Shanon Shah, Boyd Tonkin

International Advisory Board: Waqar Ahmad, Karen Armstrong, William Dalrymple, Farid Esack, Anwar Ibrahim, Robert Irwin, Bruce Lawrence, Ashis Nandy, Ruth Padel, Bhikhu Parekh, Barnaby Rogerson, Malise Ruthven

Critical Muslim is published quarterly by C. Hurst & Co. (Publishers) Ltd. on behalf of and in conjunction with Critical Muslim Ltd. and the Muslim Institute, London.

All correspondence to Muslim Institute, CAN Mezzanine, 49-51 East Road, London N1 6AH, United Kingdom

e-mail for editorial: editorial@criticalmuslim.com

C. Hurst & Co (Publishers) Ltd.,41 Great Russell Street, London WC1B 3PL

ISBN: 978-1-84904-394-6 ISSN: 2048-8475

To subscribe or place an order by credit/debit card or cheque (pound sterling only) please contact Kathleen May at the Hurst address above or e-mail kathleen@hurstpub.co.uk

Tel: 020 7255 2201

A one year subscription, inclusive of postage (four issues), costs £50 (UK), £65 (Europe) and £75 (rest of the world).

The British Museum

Discover the Islamic World

From early scientific
instruments to
contemporary art,
explore how Islam
has shaped our
world through objects
for centuries

Great Russell Street,
London WC1B 3DG
⊖ Tottenham Court Road,
Holborn, Russell Square
britishmuseum.org

Mosque lamp. Enamelled glass.
Syria, c. AD 1330–1345.

Wider Concerns of Halal

You think you know what is *halal*?

It's not just about '*halal* meat' and '*halal* food'.

In fact, *halal* is one of the most sophisticated concepts of Islam. It is best translated as 'praiseworthy' and has a direct relationship to public interest, environment, business ethics and moral behaviour. During the 'Golden Age of Islam', the concept of *halal* was used to generate policy and legislation for city planning, protection of flora and fauna, trade and commerce and was a driving force behind social and cultural productions of Muslim civilisation.

We aim to advance a more holistic understanding of what is *halal* and what it means to lead an ethical, socially responsible life in the twenty-first century.

Look out for our workshops, seminars and school visits.

Halal Food Foundation is a charitable arm of Halal Food Authority.

Halal Food Foundation

109 Fulham Palace Road, London W6 8JA, UK
Registered Charity Number: 1139457
Website: www.halalfoodauthority.com
E-mail: info@halalfoodauthority.com

The Barbary Figs

by

Rashid Boudjedra

Translated by
André Naffis-Sahely

Buy a copy of Rashid Boudjedra's *The Barbary Figs* at
www.hauspublishing.com or by calling +44(0)20 7838 9055
and a recieve a copy of Khaled al-Berry's memoir
Life is More Beautiful than Paradise free.

RASHID AND OMAR are cousins who find themselves side by side on a flight from Algiers to Constantine. During the hour-long journey, the pair will exhume their past, their boyhood in French Algeria during the 1940s and their teenage years fighting in the bush during the revolution. Rashid, the narrator, has always resented Omar, who despite all his worldly successes, has been on the run from the ghosts of his past, ghosts that Rashid has set himself the task of exorcising. Rashid peppers his account with chilling episodes from Algerian history, from the savageries of the French invasion in the 1830s, to the repressive regime that is in place today.

RASHID BOUDJEDRA has routinely been called one of North Africa's leading writers since his debut, *La Répudiation*, was published in 1969, earning the author the first of many fatwas. While he wrote his first six novels in French, Boudjedra switched to Arabic in 1982 and wrote another six novels in the language before returning to French in 1994. *The Barbary Figs* was awarded the Prix du Roman Arabe 2010.

CONTENTS

ET CETERA

Subscribe to Critical Muslim

Now in its second year, *Critical Muslim* is the only publication of its kind, giving voice to the diversity and plurality of Muslim reporting, creative writing, poetry and scholarship.

Subscribe now to receive each issue of Critical Muslim direct to your door and save money on the cover price of each issue.

Subscriptions are available at the following prices, inclusive of postage. Subscribe for two years and save 10%!

	ONE YEAR (4 Issues)	TWO YEARS (8 Issues)
UK	£50	£90
Europe	£65	£117
Rest of World	£75	£135

TO SUBSCRIBE:

CRITICALMUSLIM.HURSTPUBLISHERS.COM

41 GREAT RUSSELL ST, LONDON WC1B 3PL
WWW.HURSTPUBLISHERS.COM
WWW.FBOOK.COM/HURSTPUBLISHERS
020 7255 2201

THE MAGHREB

DUSKLANDS

Robin Yassin-Kassab

Morocco's Arabic name, 'al-Maghreb', emerges from the root gh-r-b, which denotes concepts including the west, distance, and alienation. 'Ghareeb' means strange. 'Ightirab' means living outside the Arab world, whether in the west or the east. 'Maghreb' also means sunset, dusk, the evening prayer, the time at which the daily fast is broken. Al-Maghreb al-Arabi refers to the entire Arab west – Libya, Algeria, Tunisia, Mauritania, the Western Sahara – but Morocco has no other name. It is al-Maghreb al-Aqsa, the furthest west, the strangest.

The ancient Egyptians believed they spent the afterlife wandering 'the Western Lands'. William Burroughs, who lived in Tangier, wrote a novel inspired by the notion. When I lived in Morocco, teaching English at the turn of the century, a Syrian woman of my acquaintance used to play on the word like this: *la tustughreb, anta fil-maghreb* or, Don't be shocked, you're in Morocco! On this return visit I heard the same phrase from the mouth of a Moroccan man in a train.

But shocked I was, a little bit, twelve years ago.

I'd been living in the *mashreq*, the Arab east, before I arrived, and (foolishly) I expected the maghreb to be similar. I found a much more liberal place, one much less subject to taboo. For instance, depending on class and region, a Moroccan girl with a boyfriend is not quite the social catastrophe it would be further east. Moroccan sleaze is not hidden away (which is perhaps, overall, a good thing). I once almost pushed my son in his pushchair past men engaged in a sexual act, not in a dark basement but among the trees at the side of a main road. Several times I walked past the same exhibitionist in central Rabat. There were police nearby but they ignored him. And I frequently saw ragged street children sniffing glue-soaked rags, more of a South American scene than an Arab one. (I didn't see that on this recent trip). In addition to public taboos, Moroccans lack the softness and eloquence, the courtliness, of the eastern

Arabs. But they also lack the airs and graces, the intense class resentments, the hypocrisies. You don't feel everyone is judging everyone else as you can do in the east, at least not in the same way, not to the same extent.

Then there were the contradictions, or perhaps the diversity, better put, of language, ethnicity, culture and, most of all, class. Parts of the big cities were comparable to Europe in their lifestyles and aspirations. Some of my students went to French-language schools, spent their holidays in Europe, and spoke French at home. Meanwhile much of the countryside was consigned to illiteracy and grinding poverty. There was almost no modern infrastructure out there. The people didn't speak French. Some didn't speak Arabic either.

I return twelve years later to Rabat, once my home, a handsome capital surrounded by red walls and built in that distinctive architectural style which connects Andalusia to West Africa. Rabat's 'new city' contains tree-lined boulevards, embassies and white villas, and the enormous Makhzen (royal court) compound. The *madina al-qadima* (old city) and *kasbah* (fortified settlement) are to the west. A necropolis lies west of the madina. Then comes the beach and its piers, the crab-crawling rocks, and the cold Atlantic. The madina is neither traditional nor modern: it's contemporary, and Moroccan traditions are an integrated part of contemporary life. The glossy-artisanal rue des Consuls is designed to serve foreigners, in the past and the present, but it's by no means an over-touristed souq. The flea market in the *mellah* (what used to be the Jewish quarter) deals in antiques, broken office machines, and books – classics and curiosities in Arabic, French and English.

My visit comes in Ramadan, whose rhythm has overtaken the madina. This means quiet mornings and bustling afternoons. As the maghreb prayer calls, the sunset is dispersed by light Atlantic cloud, then the streets empty and silence reigns while the fast is broken. A fat moon rises. An hour later boys are sitting on the steps of the kasbah beating drums and singing traditional songs, not for show but to amuse themselves. A couple break into dance as they walk past. More drums and picnics down on the beach. The mosques are full (of both men and women) for Ramadan *taraweeh* prayers, and the markets are crammed until two in the morning.

Outside the city walls, the Chellah, once a Phoenician, then a Roman settlement, is a suitable location for historical musings. Morocco's first Islamic rulers were the Idrissis, Zaydi-Shia, and like the current monarchs, descendants of Ali and Fatima. They built Fez and founded its great religious institutions. Then the *murabitoon* (Almoravids) of the Sanhaja tribe swept from Senegal and Mauritania as far as Spain. The greatest and most tolerant Almoravid sultan, Yusuf bin Tachfin (reigned 1061–1106), founded Marrakesh and ruled from Ghana to Lisbon. Later, by Khaldunian process, urbane decline set in, and the Almoravids were swept aside by the *muwahidoon* (Almohads), a new set of puritanical nomads who first burnt then refurbished Fez and Marrakesh. Next came the Merenids of the Anti-Atlas Zenata tribe, but in the fourteenth century Bubonic Plague and chronic infighting splintered the polity, and Portuguese soldier-traders took over the coastal ports. The Saadi dynasty pushed back foreign encroachment, and in the seventeenth century the Alawi dynasty took over. It still rules today.

'Khaldunian process' refers to the theory of Tunis-born ibn Khaldun (1332–1406), the historian and founder of sociology, that dynastic rule works by a cycle whereby a new and innovative group strengthened by tight social cohesion, *asabiyya* in ibn Khaldun's word, defeats the old rulers, then in victory becomes urbanely civilised, then decadent, and eventually loses power to a new, highly coherent group. 'So it is', writes Robert Irwin in this issue, 'that the wild and sometimes fanatical tribesmen are able to defeat and conquer empires and cities and go on to create new states.' As Irwin notes, ibn Khaldun, who emphasised the decisive role of social and economic forces, saw 'urban life as leading to degeneracy' and looked at luxury with disdain. The great historian is regarded as an objective, neutral scholar. But Irwin throws fresh light on ibn Khaldun, arguing that he had strong Sufi tendencies.

The most intact building inside the Chellah's walls is an elegant Merenid mosque with a patchily blue-tiled minaret. (Moroccan minarets, ancient or modern, are not the cones or needles of the east, but rectangular towers. They look like the church towers of Spain.) On the slope above the ancient foundations and the mosque, whitewashed cubes topped by octagonal domes contain the remains of holy men – *marabouts*. Trees fill the gaps: bananas and olives, palms and figs, bamboo, baobabs and firs. Storks (onomatopoeiacally named *laq-laq* in Arabic) make that deep repetitive click with their beaks. They are huge birds, almost humanoid as they step the corridors between the trees, giants as they flap overhead. Their nests look like giant rings on finger-like trunks in the near distance. Beneath the walls a woman tends her field of greens enwalled by high bullrushes. She wears a broad straw sun hat from the Rif. And beyond her, the flood plain of the Bou Regreg, the river separating Rabat from Salé.

Salé was once a pirating capital. Between the seventeenth and nineteenth centuries the north African maritime economy was dominated by corsairs (from the Arabic *qursaan*). The original pirates were Moriscos who'd been first forcibly converted to Christianity, then driven out of Spain. They understood their work not as mere piracy but as an effort to rebalance power in the Mediterranean. At that stage Christian sailors north of the sea were as keen on slaving as the Muslims. It was a very lucrative business. Captives of high birth could be ransomed; those of education could earn their freedom. One well-known slave was Miguel de Cervantes (1547–1616), author of *Don Quixote*, ransomed by his parents after five years of captivity. The Sally Rovers, as Salé's corsairs were known in English chronicles, roved as far as Cornwall to snatch hostages.

Earlier in its history, Salé was the upper limit of the Barghawata confederation, which ruled its own coastal state from the eighth to the eleventh centuries. Barghawata's syncretic religion of Sunni, Shii and Khariji Islam alongside Amazigh traditions and perhaps Judaism, boasted a king-prophet, Salih ibn Tarif, who produced his own eighty-sura Amazigh 'Quran'. Alongside pockets of Shiism, Barghawata's influence persisted in the mountains until it was finally eliminated by the rigidly orthodox Almoravids, castigators of heresy in al-Andalus too. Today the entire region is Sunni, of the Maliki school.

More recently, the city has provided an illusion for the screen. When I lived in Rabat I sometimes saw helicopters hovering over the beach across the river. *Black Hawk Down* (2001) was being filmed. Salé was pretending to be Somalia. The cinema and other forms of shadow-play make a constant Moroccan theme, as we shall see.

After a week spent in Rabat and nearby Casablanca, meeting Moroccans and indulging in nostalgia, I headed down the Atlantic coast. If I'd made a different journey this narrative would have taken a different route, but I wanted to go somewhere I hadn't been before. Twelve years ago I visited the northern coast, Asilah and Tangier and the beautiful village of Chefchaouen in the Rif. I saw the imperial cities of Meknes and Fez (the latter absolutely central to Moroccan history, and boasting – now Aleppo's been half destroyed – the most intact medieval Arab-Islamic city in the world), the nearby Roman ruins of Volubilis, the shrine town of Moulay Idrees, and Middle Atlas towns like Sefrou. I wandered the High Atlas, and climbed Jebel Toubkal, north Africa's highest mountain. I clambered through the Todra Gorges and followed the desert trails as far as M'hameed. I explored the vast caverns near Taza and sojourned in Oujda on the (closed) Algerian border. So: been there. Done that. (Of course all I did was cover roads, lines on the map. I'd actually seen far less than one per cent of the country.)

But this time I made a journey south down the Atlantic coast, then inland to Taroudannt and Marrakesh on my way back to the airport at Casablanca. I justified the route like this: most Moroccans live on the coasts; the coasts have determined Morocco's economy and foreign relations; I was aiming for *al-maghreb al-aqsa*, the Furthest West; finally, on the coast in this Ramadan July it should be cool enough to think.

The Atlantic Coast

First stop was el-Jadida, then further south, passing Safi where your sardines are packed, to Essaouira, an exhilarating place with its huge doors, high ramparts and constant wind.

El-Jadida has a full complement of Moroccan summer tourists, but no foreigners; Essaouira, on the other hand, is one of the most (foreign) touristed spots in the country, and Ramadan here exists in parallel to holiday world – but these aren't package tourists, and the place hasn't been squashed by them. In fact, a positive cross-fertilisation is apparent in the art, craft and fashion on sale.

The Atlantic isn't gentle like the Mediterranean. It raises powerful waves to crash against the shore. It's cold, and there are perilous undertows. Surfing is a more popular pursuit than swimming, though there are swimmers, sometimes women as well as men.

In both towns, late afternoon fishermen are joined by footballers, walkers and runners. And these people are fasting. The day I met the cinema critic Adile Semmar, he'd been swimming because 'I was too tired to either work or read.' The option of going to sleep in the weak hours seemed not to occur to him. This is a million miles from Saudi Arabia.

Both towns were shaped by the Portuguese, although Mogador Island (actually two islands) off Essaouira, a purple production centre under the

Phoenicians, has ancient origins. In 1764, with the Portuguese expelled, Sultan Muhammad ibn Abdullah (1710–1790) hired the French military architect Theodore Cornut to rebuild the city, like so many Moroccan cities a happy accommodation of European, Arab and African influences. El-Jadida, called Mazagan, remained in Portuguese hands for another two centuries. It finally earned its name el-Jadida – the New – when Jews from nearby Azzemour were settled here in the nineteenth century. Unlike in other cities, el-Jadida's Jews were not confined to a *mellah*.

The *mellah* first appeared in 1438. As Louis Proyect notes in his contribution to this issue, 'the Sultan created a *mellah* near the palace after a number of Jews were killed in the aftermath of a rumour that they had placed wine in the mosques of Fez, a city with a large Jewish population'. Ostensibly, they 'made the Jewish communities appear as outcasts, isolated from the wider society' but in fact 'the Jewish quarters were quite porous. Jews were able to move in and out of the *mellah* and even settle in other cities where there were none'. The *mellah* constituted a 'Jewish space' within rather than an isolated part of the city. 'It was a locale from which the Jewish community interacted with the city as a whole, and with the wider world.' However, there were some 'ridiculous laws' that 'required Jewish women to wear shoes of different colours, one white and one black, as well as the code that prevented Jews from riding horses'. But Jews never faced an 'existential threat' in the Maghreb.

Back in the fifteenth and sixteenth centuries Portugal, formerly Muslim-ruled, was expanding aggressively, its focus on naval routes and its deployment of advanced military technology setting the pattern for later, further-flung European conquests. El-Jadida was founded in 1506 under the name Mogador, and the commercial fortress colony rapidly became one of the most important entrepots in the country.

Both towns reminded me of the other side of the continent, the Indian Ocean, where Arabs and Africans, Islam and the Portuguese, also collided and intermingled. Here too there's the legacy of a slave trade, and multilingualism, and whitewashed box houses on a sparkling sea. Architecturally, these ports bear resemblance to Muscat and the Gulf ports, the surviving old quarters at least, and to the ports of east Africa and western India. El-Jadida's 'Portuguese City' reminded me specifically of Galle in Sri Lanka.

European encroachment intensified dramatically in the nineteenth century. In the seventy years before the French Protectorate, Morocco was constantly harrassed but, unlike its Algerian neighbour, was not swallowed up. It therefore had some time to respond to the challenge by means of indigenous reform.

In this period the monarchy often worked as hard as any contemporary presidential candidate, travelling the national territory not only to gather taxes but to establish economic, political and military alliances with tribal chiefs and warlords, more closely integrating the national space. And there were other attempts to catch up. In 1865, for instance, Sultan Muhammad IV (1802–1873) introduced a state-sponsored printing press.

But the European tide was unstoppable. Military and economic pressure steadily undermined the reforming state. Its authority was eaten away by the 'Protections', whereby first Europeans, then any Moroccan working for or associated with Europeans (eventually including even aristocrats and ministers), were granted immunity from Moroccan law. The International Zone based on Tangier and guaranteed by Britain and Germany was a geographical extension of the Protection concept, and another blatant invasion of Moroccan sovereignty. The final collapse was brought nearer by the disastrous reign of Sultan Abd al-Aziz (ruled 1894–1908), more noted for amusements than concrete achievements. His palace hosted firework displays, a cinema, and photographic equipment grazed over by sheep. Meanwhile overspending, debt and lawlessness increased, and rural rebellions erupted.

Yet, then as now, civil society flourished and even to an extent repaired the damage to the social fabric done by the monarchy and foreign encroachment. Muhammad al-Kattani (1858–1927) head of a *zawiya* (Sufi lodge) in Fez, called for Islamic revival through *ijtihad* and resistance to European penetration. This late companion to Muhammad Abduh (1849–1905), the Mufti of Egypt, and similar mashreqi reformers founded a newspaper and issued mass-produced pamphlets. A very political player, when the traditional ulema accused him of heresy he cultivated an alliance with Sultan Abd al-Aziz, then supported the successful take-over by Abd al-Hafeez, Abd al-Aziz's brother. But this was his undoing: fearful of al-Kattani's rising popularity, the new sultan had him beaten to death in front of his wives and children.

Wherever I travel in this country, I can't escape the cinema. There's an Orson Welles Square in Essaouira. The city ramparts provided the setting for the opening scene of the great director's *Othello* (1954) – the Moor, after all. The Portuguese Cistern in el-Jadida was used for the film's riot scene. Nor can I escape the strong Moroccan aesthetic, which in recent years has neither withered nor been consigned to the dread realms of 'folklore', but on the contrary has adapted and flourished under contemporary pressures. The country's current mass architecture uses 'modern' materials yet remains entirely and distinctively Moroccan because of the colour schemes, the large doors and balconies, the roof terraces, and structurally, the upper stories jutting out into the street. These houses are brightly and individually painted, which means cityscapes here are seldom grey or monotonous. On the shore south of Essaouira, surrounded by curious goats, I realised something obvious: the primary colours of the Moroccan aesthetic are taken from the environment – pure shades of blue from sky and sea, ochre from the sand, the greens of the trees, the pinks and reds of the mountains.

Morocco's sustained and successful artisanal culture seems even healthier now than when I lived here. Indeed, its painted wooden furniture, leatherwork, silver jewellery, and clothes, have carved out a global niche. Moroccan clothes, constantly changing and relentlessly fashionable, have influenced Western designers since the 1960s. Off the catwalks, Moroccans easily and elegantly combine Western casual with revived Arab and African styles to synthesise their own: a mix of *djellabas* and tunics, tracksuits and burnouses. In general, they look good. The women look very good.

Then there's the ubiquitous visual art, paintings for sale or on the walls of private homes, particularly art naif and abstract works referencing the Berber motifs traditionally patterned into carpets. Marrakesh is not the only city to boast several galleries of high-quality contemporary art. Contemporary Moroccan literary production includes novels and memoirs, both gritty realist and magical romantic. As Marcia Lynx Qualey's essay demonstrates, the region is steeped in poetry which often represents and serves as the 'voice of dissent' (not necessarily political). The great living poets of the Maghreb, Qualey informs us, craft their work in 'many interconnected tongues', including modern standard Arabic, Darija or Moroccan Arabic, Tamazight, and French. And Anita Hunt describes Mauritania as the 'land of a thousand poets', often-overlooked but remarkably diverse and creative.

Food is another manifestation of the aesthetic, for alongside Syrian-Lebanese cuisine, Morocco's is the richest and most idiosyncratic in the Arab world. Friday couscous is still served in homes, mosques and restaurants. For the rest of the week there's a range of tagines and pastillas flavoured with cumin, saffron and mint, merguez sausage and grilled fish or *fruits de mer*, flavoured breads and perhaps the world's best olives, tongue-curling sweet things, snails-in-pepper-soup, and orange juice on every corner. Most often of all, harira soup – tomatoes, meat and lentils – its bubbling odour omnipresently teasing throughout the long Ramadan days. And mint tea, of course, which brings with it its own serving rituals and a whole other branch of artisanry – the teapots and glasses which are now as popular in bourgeois west London as in a Moroccan café.

It's a fine environment to travel through, and now I make a meditative focus on the basics of movement: locating the train, coach or grand taxi station (demoting in this order as I move south); finding accommodation and food. There's enough to think about getting from A to B. In each place I concentrate on finding my bearings, making a map, saying hello. I sniff the air and taste the mood. Then I leave.

But before I arrive at my next destination, allow me to remember Casablanca, the country's largest city and industrial heart, and setting for the famous Bogart-Bergman film (1942) – though that was actually shot at the Warner Brothers studios in Burbank, California. For much of its history, Casa was a small pirate port. Its dramatic growth spurt occurred in the twentieth century as a direct result of colonialism. Before building, however, the foreigners destroyed. In 1907, following the murder of eight Europeans, a French gunboat levelled parts of the city.

Morocco finally lost its independence to the Protectorate in August 1912 when Sultan Abd al-Hafeez (the killer of Muhammad al-Kattani) was forced to resign; he was replaced by the much more pliable Mawlay Yusuf (1881–1927). French Resident-General Lyautey moved in to establish 'indirect rule', a theatrical system of dual government in which the Makhzan's ritual pageantry was preserved or increased while its actual power diminished to (partial) authority over religion, culture and education (90% of Moroccans were illiterate when the French left: a result of the apartheid system in which Europeans, Jews, Amazigh and Arabs were educated separately, and the last two categories barely at all). The French technocratic bureaucracy, meanwhile, made all the important practical decisions concerning the law, the economy, and infrastructural development.

This shadow play covered the nakedness of both the monarchy and the occupation, but didn't fool the countryside. Foreign rule was fiercely resisted by the Zayan confederation in the Middle Atlas and by Abd al-Kareem (1882– 1963) in the Rif mountains (Abd al-Kareem's main target was the Spanish, who had occupied the north). It took the imperial powers several years and many dead soldiers to put down these challenges. The French employed a scorched earth policy to defeat the insurgents.

Then they turned to developing 'Le Maroc Utile' – the central Atlantic coast and the wheat fields of the adjoining plains. Architect Henri Prost's modernist and 'neo-Mauresque' 'new cities' appeared next to the 'old'. The zoning of old and new, and Lyautey's romantic respect for defanged 'tradition', saved the old. Moroccan madinas are still whole and entire; they avoid the savage interruptions (by motorway, car park or Stalinist towerblock) of Cairo, Damascus or Baghdad.

The new cities are often very pleasant too, but were clearly not built for Moroccans. One sign of this is Casablanca's central Sacre Coeur, a huge, useless cathedral in white concrete (but I'm too harsh: now desacralised, it has found a use as an occasional venue for arts events, and also sheltered a pregnant dog when I visited). There's a good view of the city from its birdshit-spattered tower, including across to the almost equally arrogant Hassan II mosque, third largest in the world, with a laser aimed at Mecca, much resented by Moroccan interlocutors who wish the garish thing were named 'the Moroccan People's Mosque', seeing as the Moroccan people paid for it.

Scorched earth and better conditions in the new cities sparked a rural exodus and a population explosion, resulting in shanty towns or *bidonvilles* sprouting on the urban outskirts. French rule also catalysed an independence movement spurred on by soldiers and migrant workers returning from France, where exposure to racism, poor work conditions, and to the citizens of other colonised countries, expanded leftist and anti-imperialist political awareness. Nationalist intellectuals established 'free schools' and cultural and literary associations – another of the recurrent episodes of civil society stepping in to repair the damage done by sultans and imperialists.

The Amazigh

My hotel in Taroudannt is outside the walls, not far from the first fields, but can't be described as quiet because it's right next to a mosque, a sand red one with a cream stripe, Maghrebi crenellations and a keyhole window on each side of the minaret. The loudspeakers are directed right at my room, so I hear *taraweeh* and *qiyam al-lail* as if on a soundsystem at the Notting Hill Carnival. Fortunately the *qari*'s recitation is beautiful. So too is the collective voice of the distinctively Moroccan *tahaleel* chanted after dawn, and the *tarteel* after the *asr* (afternoon) prayer.

Taroudannt is the commercial and artisanal capital (there's no industry) of the Souss valley, a wide plain between the High Atlas and the Anti-Atlas crammed with argan trees and citrus groves. Its streets are cluttered with bicycles and motorbikes (women ride here too, although it's a somewhat more conservative place than the coastal cities), and horse-drawn carriages, which create a traditional odour of straw and dung. The town is much more populated than last time I was here, twenty years ago with friends escaping a package holiday in Agadir. We stopped for the night in Taroudannt on the way to Marrakesh. I remember a freezing dawn waiting for the bus to pass through, a few men hunched against a wall, heads hidden in their pointed hoods. This time it's hot. I try to write on the hotel's roof terrace but I drop too much sweat on the page. A pink gecko regards me wearily from a wall. So I give up and sweat in the streets instead. In the main square stalls sell grilled prawns, figs, enormous melons. A crowd of storks dances overhead. Most people here are Shleuh Berbers. Tashelhit is spoken alongside Arabic.

Up to 45 per cent of Moroccans speak a Berber (more properly, Amazigh) language: Tashelhit in the south, Tamazight in the Centre, Tamarif in the north. Almost all of the remaining 55 per cent (except perhaps for the speakers of Arabic's Hassaniya dialect, found in small southern and eastern settlements) are of partly Amazigh ancestry. Morocco's most widely spoken language is Durija, Moroccan Arabic, which, by its music, vocabulary and grammatical peculiarities, is Arabic mapped onto an Amazigh base. It has a distinctive rhythm in which a phrase sounds like a shrug; its vowels are either elided (so *Kareem* becomes *Krim*) or lengthened (so *Mohsin* becomes *Mohseen*). There is a case to be made that Classical Arabic (or its Modern Standard version) is an elite language in Morocco, one that preserves elite power, that it's even perhaps in some way a little 'foreign' – but Durija is as Moroccan as couscous. Those Arab nationalists crazed by the homogenising urge (an impulse which has wrecked Islamism too) worry about the 'purity' of Durija, but people who understand Arabism as a cultural reality, a powerful set of linguistic, social and political relationships between diverse peoples, celebrate Durija as an example of the tremendous breadth and possibility of the language.

Arabism is a matter of civilisation, not of race, and without the Berbers, Arab civilisation would have had no Tariq ibn Ziyad (who led the Muslim armies into Spain in 711), no ibn Battuta (the great travel writer; 1304–1369), and no al-Idrisi (the geographer and cartographer; 1099–1166). From this perspective, the Amazigh like the Kurds and Nubians are an essential component of the Arab collectivity.

French orientalists, however, with their racial theory and divide-and-rule strategy, categorised Arabs and Berbers as separate races. The nationalist backlash to colonialism then emphasised the language of national unity (or homogeneity) and sought to erase difference. Amazigh language and identity was too often regarded as an embarrassment, even as a threat.

In recent decades there's been a backlash against the backlash, a Berber Pride movement which in its most extreme forms has used terms such as 'invasion' to describe the slow Arabisation of north Africa. According to Adnane Addioui, the head of Enactus, an organisation of students, academics and business leaders committed to 'entrepreneurial action to transform lives and shape a better more sustainable world', and a welcoming host in his Salé home, this is a line taken by those with an extremist secularist agenda which rejects Islam as 'foreign', though it arrived in Morocco long before Christianity took root in England, and most of its fiercest propagators were Berbers. 'I'm a proud Amazighi,' Adnane declares, 'but I don't consider that my people were colonised by Arabs.'

Indeed they weren't. After the Umayyad general Uqba ibn al-Nafi' (622–683) rode his horse into the Atlantic, swearing that he'd conquered all the land there was to conquer, he was driven back to what is now Libya by the Amazigh queen Kahina. The indigenous population rejected Arab conquest but welcomed Islam. The Bani Hilal migrations in later centuries did much more damage, and did alter demographics, but the Arabisation of the region occurred primarily as a result of trade, intermarriage, and the influence of itinerant scholars and mystics.

In the words of cinema critic Adil Semmar: 'No Moroccan can claim to be 100% Berber, and no-one can claim to be 100% Arab.' In 'racial' terms, positing a distinction between Arabs and Amazigh is as absurd as distinguishing Celts from Anglo-Saxons in England. Yet when I met Hafida Elbaz of the Association Solidarité Feminine, who prefers to speak French, she was at pains to emphasise that 'there are hardly any Arabs' in the country, that most 'Arabs' are in fact Andalusans. By this narrow ethnic reckoning, there are hardly any Arabs in Syria or Egypt either.

Adil Semmar, who I met in a Rabat café, believes the Amazigh pride campaign, at least in its more extreme and anti-Arab manifestations, is not a popular movement but an elite concern of limited relevance. Yes, there's a small autonomy movement in the Rif. This is what happens when 'people lose faith in institutions but, thinking locally, they don't take on the whole system'.

But the fact remains that some rural Moroccans can't speak (and certainly can't read) Arabic. As a result they are at a disadvantage in the state's courtrooms, even in hospitals. This problem is finally being remedied. 'Now our children can learn to write the language at school,' Said Dafyollah, hotelier and mountain guide (he's in my guidebook), told me proudly.

The language is now being written and taught using the ancient hieroglyphs of the Tifinagh alphabet (official signs are now trilingual – French, Arabic, Amazighi). Adil Semmar describes the choice of this third alphabet (after the Arabic and the Roman) as mere 'political correctness'. After all, English use of Roman script does not entail submission to Rome, and bringing yet another script into areas of high illiteracy will not necessarily prove empowering. Said agrees Arabic script might have been more practical.

Amazigh-language radio and television broadcasts are now an integral element of Moroccan media, and the state no longer prevents parents from naming their children with Amazigh names. But are these language rights enough? 'No, not yet enough,' says Said. 'We sometimes feel the Arabs have marginalised us.' (The examples he gives are economic, and relate to the urban-rural divide.) 'But we are taking our rights little by little.'

In conversation Said also makes such statements as 'Our Arabic culture is beautiful,' which seems to prove Adil and Adnane's point that the issue is not one of starkly delineated ethnic groups in conflict, but of establishing rights for people excluded by illiteracy and poverty as much as by language. Unlike in Algeria or Libya, where Amazigh populations and cultures have been more brutally suppressed, the Moroccan king (and therefore state) has welcomed (or perhaps co-opted) the Amazigh movement. It is unlikely, therefore, that Arab-Amazigh tensions will expand.

Said takes me to Tioute, a village at the foot of the Anti Atlas. The road would pass through desert were it not for the ubiquitous argan trees, which can survive in temperatures of up to 50 degrees. The fruit is bitter – believe me, I've tasted it. But the crushed nut produces a vitamin E-rich oil with a host of cosmetic and culinary functions. The Tioute palmerie contains 3,000 trees and makes very pleasant walking. The village's ruined kasbah, however, is doubly ruined by the monstrous incongruity of a garish new restaurant (no customers inside). Before the restaurant, part of *Ali Baba and the Forty Thieves* (1944) was filmed here. Further east, the crumbling kasbah of Ait Benhaddou has provided the setting for tens of films, including *Jesus of Nazareth* (1977), *Time Bandits* (1981), and *Gladiator* (2000). While we're on the topic, the 'Lebanese' scenes of George Clooney's *Syriana* (2005) were shot, very obviously, in Morocco, featuring Moroccan clothes, Moroccan houses, Moroccan faces, and Durija. Clearly, for Hollywood, one Arab location is as good as another.

Tioute's kasbah was once owned by the Glawi clan, a family counted among the 'Lords of the Atlas', brutal warlords whom the French subcontracted to keep order in the High Atlas and the south.

'Are the family still around?' I ask.

'A few are in Taroudant,' says Said with a wave of the hand and an audible sneer.

'They're the ones who helped the French.'

'That's right.' He purses his lips and raises his brow.

In 1953 Thami al-Glawi, pasha of Marrakesh, conspired with the French to depose Sultan Muhammad V (1909–1961) in favour of his uncle. The sultan had become increasingly uncooperative with his colonial overlords. During World War II he refused to implement Vichy orders to detain and deport Morocco's quarter of a million Jews. In the post-war years he entered an uneasy alliance with the nationalists who would form the Istiqlal or Independence Party. Istiqlal's intellectual leadership calculated that it needed the symbolic value of the Sultanate on its side, something comprehensible to the country's illiterate, pre-nationalist majority. In 1947 Muhammad broke publicly with the Protectorate by affirming Morocco's 'Arab-Islamic destiny', and was rewarded by a wave of popular devotion. By 1953, when the Glawis helped the French depose him and he was exiled to Madagascar, his figure had become a symbol of national suffering under colonialism. In the frequently insurgent north, a Moroccan Army of Liberation launched attacks against the Spanish and French occupiers. Meanwhile the Istiqlal's 1944 Manifesto of Independence called for a democratic constitutional monarchy.

Morocco achieved independence in 1956, but the monarchy never became constitutional, nor the state democratic. In stages the sultan, now styling himself 'king', seized control of the army and security services, the Interior Ministry and Justice Ministry. Instead of redistributing land deserted by the colonists, he bought it up himself.

Tyranny and Civil Society

I came to Tarroudant from Sidi Ifni, several hundred kilometres down the coast from Essaouira, both the furthest south and the furthest west that I've been in Morocco. Such are the microclimates on the journey, trapped between the ocean, the mountain ranges and the desert, that a twist of the road is enough to throw the environment from lush tropical to alpine forest to baked bare rock. I'd been in keen travel mode, but now in Sidi Ifni time seemed to readjust in the drizzle-thick mist which coats the back of your throat and sometimes tastes of seaweed. Even when the weather clears, as it did on the day I walked north amid soft, wild, crumbled sandstone boulders and brilliant moss cascading from the cliffs, there's still an eery mix of mist and sunshine, no line between sea and sky. My hotel hung above a house that looks like a ship, which hangs above the beach. After *maghreb* there's a competition here between drums and amplified *rai* from a water-front restaurant, and camels looming hugely through the fog, and the relentless crash of waves.

It's a wonderful place to visit, but perhaps not so wonderful to live in. If you look up 'Sidi Ifni 2008' on YouTube you'll find scenes of large, angry crowds, and police kicking down doors, dragging men from their homes, administering savage beatings. The protestors and rioters were demanding work opportunities and better transport links.

Sidi Ifni was a Spanish possession from 1859 until 1969; Spain still holds two enclaves on the Mediterranean coast – Ceuta and Melilla. The Spanish built the Saharan/art deco fusion centre in the 1930s, the Plaza d'Espagne (now predictably renamed Place Hassan II) and its fairyland municipal buildings around a tiny park of conifers and palms. Throughout the town, blocks of housing are integrated so simply and elegantly into the scrub hills that the place feels like a dream, but the Plaza d'Espagne in particular seems unreal, like a perfect North American suburb about to be visited by a Stephen King horror. But it's much more unbuttoned, laidback, than American suburbia. Perhaps the air is Latin American, with Tuareg turbans added. Paella is served alongside tagine. The lamp-posts are blue.

Not very far away, as borderless as the ocean's horizon, lies the sparsely-populated and phosphate-rich Western Sahara, in dispute since Spain pulled out in 1975. Moroccan maps incorporate it into the national territory. The UN disagrees, holding that tenuous Moroccan historical ties to the area do not justify its annexation. But the 'Moroccanness' of the Western Sahara is a populist cause adopted by Hassan II (ruled 1961–1999) after a series of coup attempts revealed his vulnerability. He mobilised the 1975 'Green March' of hundreds of thousands of Moroccans into the southern desert, whipping up petty nationalism and deflecting attention from his economic and political failures. The result was a grievously expensive war with the indigenous independence movement and its armed wing, the Polisario. A large section of the Saharan population has been languishing for decades in Algerian refugee camps. Sand berms scar the desert. The UN has called for a referendum, whose implementation in the face of Moroccan obstructions is as likely to happen as a two-state solution in Palestine. In any case, demographics are being altered by the state's sponsorship of immigrant Moroccans. The territory remains tense, closed to journalists. In recent years there's been an upsurge of protest and corresponding repression in the Saharan city of Layoune.

Most damagingly, opposing positions on the Sahara have kept Morocco and Algeria at loggerheads, their borders closed, killing commerce in border communities and ruining any hope of a Greater Maghreb economic zone. According to Adnane Addioui, 'Morocco and Algeria both produce propaganda to make our people hate each other. But we have the same make-up, the same challenges, the same resources. This region won't be a rising force unless we're together.'

The king's firm alignment with the West helped shield Morocco from effective international action over the Sahara. A still more crucial monarchical alignment was the one begun by Muhammad V and developed by Hassan II – the alliance with the same rural elite which had served the French. This relationship – which made it possible to ignore the urban political classes – is one of two key factors behind the state's abject failure to develop the countryside. It's not so much that the notion of building a modern social infrastructure didn't occur to Hassan II; his deliberate policy was against such development, not only because it would unsettle his rural friends, but also because, like the French before him, he feared that education would translate into militancy. Responding on television to student protests in 1965, the king expressed himself thus: 'Allow me to tell you, there is no greater danger to the state than the so-called intellectual; it would have been better for you to be illiterate.'

Illiteracy, and its correlation with poverty, Berberism and rural abandonment, is perhaps Morocco's most important social and political fact. Twelve years ago, a Rabati student who worked for the Makhzan answered my question on what to do about the illiterate classes with this simple sentence: 'They will die.' He wasn't the monster his statement suggests. What he meant was the proportion of illiterates would decline as the old died and the young went to school. But his optimistic prediction has not worked out. The adult literacy rate today is only 56 per cent.

Despite illiteracy and diversions in the Sahara, the monarchy has had to meet several waves of mass resistance. The largest were the protests and riots involving students and workers in Casablanca in 1965, savagely put down (hundreds killed) by General Oufkir (later shot for his part in a failed coup d'etat). Throughout the seventies and eighties state repression intensified through the disappearances of dissidents (most famously, the leftist politician Mahdi Ben Barka; political imprisonments, and a 'state of emergency', into what became known as the 'Years of Lead'.

Once again, it was civil society which brought the country through this grim period and into the new century, ameliorating the monarchy's oppression and neglect. Morocco has an effective National Human Rights Council. In rural areas, women's cooperatives have expanded social and economic opportunities (tourists are advised to buy their craft souvenirs, or argan oil products, directly from such organisations). In several cases, NGOs run their own literacy programmes.

Some groups provide support to victims of marital violence. Some lobby against the employment of child maids (a practice much reduced since I lived here). There are organisations which work with abused and sometimes drug-addicted street children. Hafida Elbaz's Association Solidarite Feminine works to prevent unwanted children being thrown on the streets in the first place, or being cooped in orphanages which she describes as 'as bad as Ceaucescu's'. The Association does this by counselling unmarried mothers, teaching them their rights, attempting family reconciliation, and helping them find work which offers childcare facilities.

I walked to meet a couple I knew when I lived here, a couple who happen to be gay. They are a rarity, two men living together. They know of no other case. Their gay friends with education and means have left the country; those without have married. Homosexual lovemaking can have you jailed for three months. The law is sometimes applied. Amongst the urbane classes, meanwhile, the king's sexuality is an open secret (of course he has married and produced an heir).

In Casablanca I met Karima Zoubir, a prize-winning director whose latest film is *Camera / Woman*, a documentary about a divorced woman and family breadwinner who works as a videographer of weddings. Female videographers are preferred to men as they film uncovered women at weddings, but covering the parties means working at night, which results in social opprobrium.

Morocco has been at the vanguard of north African cinema as it achieves world standing. As Jamal Bahmad writes in his essay on Maghrebi films for this issue:

Over the last few decades, this cinema has offered a realist critique of the neoliberal present and a critical repertory of ordinary subjects' small acts of resistance against daily regimes of oppression. Cinema is thus one of the contemporary Maghreb's compelling postcolonial archives and, in decades to come, a source of social history and perhaps lessons and seeds for change at the hands of a people yet to come.

According to Rabat-based film critic Adil Semmar, film production has jumped from an annual four or five films a decade ago to twenty features a year today, two or three of which are of the highest quality. He recommends two in particular: *Death for Sale* (2011) and *Sur la Planche* (On the Edge, 2012). Fashionable subject matter over the last ten years has included first women's issues, then migration issues, and now terrorism. Cinema has benefited from state support, though Kareema complains that it rarely disburses funding for documentaries. The television channel 2M, however, is now promoting investigative documentary films.

On the subject of women, Kareema makes the obvious but worth-repeating statement: 'Morocco isn't one thing; it's a lot of things.' She's from Safi, where there's no segregation and wedding parties are mixed. In Amazigh cultures, she says, women have often played prominent roles. On the other hand, in parts of the Rif a woman is forced to remain unmarried if her family can't find her a cousin as a spouse.

In this field, the monarchy has been a progressive force. Muhammad V's daughter Lalla Aisha was an early unveiled woman active in the public sphere, and something of a national role model. And Muhammad VI, the current ruler, was responsible for pushing through the progressive 2003 family law code, or *Mudawwana*, which sets the marriage age at eighteen, allows a wife to initiate divorce, considers husband and wife as equals before the law, and constrains polygamy (a practice which was already dying out). The king encouraged it, but it was left to women's groups to publicise it in Durija and the Amazigh languages. Even after their work, Karima says, 'the Mudawwana hasn't done much at all to change life in rural areas, because rural women aren't aware of it.' Which brings us back to illiteracy. In a country which offers itself as a screen for Hollywood's high-tech, half the population can't read the daily newspaper.

For those who can, Morocco's press is brave and lively; journalists have sought to expose corruption and abuse, and have paid the price, often in prison cells. In the 1990s a 'Years of Lead' literature emerged, books and magazine features detailing the abuse of former political prisoners and their families. But press freedom has actually declined under the new king. Papers such as *Le Journal*, *Demain* and *Doumane* have been repeatedly censored and fined. Many of the best journalists give up and look for work abroad. During my trip, an edition of the French paper *Le Monde* was swept from the newsstands because it had covered furious protests against the royal pardon of a Spanish paedophile.

The Simulacrum

Muhammad VI succeeded his father in 1999, a couple of months before I arrived to live in Rabat. His almost immediate sacking of Driss Basri, his father's dread interior minister, raised popular expectations. In 2003 the young king set up the Equity and Reconciliation Commission (ERC) to compensate the victims of the Years of Lead and to allow a public airing of their stories. The rules of the game: abusers weren't named and Hassan II wasn't criticised. The recommendation for judicial reform in the ERC's final report (2005) was ignored. Still, in the grim Arab context the experiment represented a refreshing openness as well as great political intelligence, a willingness to compromise, to play for hearts and minds, the better to keep hold of the reigns of power.

Defanged, surviving leftists returned home from exile or their desert cells, but starting in 2001 the radical Islamist threat rationalised a new bout of repression bluntly aimed at supporters and associates of the al-Qa'ida-linked Salafiyya Jihadiya. This group was responsible for the 2003 suicide bombings in Casablanca which killed forty-five people. The bombers lived in Casablanca's *bidonvilles*, which now contain between a quarter and a third of the city's population.

Morocco has a private media, a parliament and a prime minister. From a certain perspective, through a certain blur, it looks like a functioning democracy. But Muhammad VI's relationship with parliament is very similar to the French Protectorate's relationship with Muhammad's tame forebears. It's equally theatrical, just as much a shadowplay, an illusion. The king divides and rules the political class through a multi-party system (over forty parties) carefully calibrated so that no party can ever exercise real power. In the words of journalist and blogger Ahmed Benchemsi, 'Freedom at the polls coexists with a structurally rigged electoral system.' The parliament, like the Protectorate's Makhzen, is an empty symbol, a simulacrum, a screen.

Abysmally low voting rates suggest the people understand the game. The king, meanwhile, stands at the apex of a business empire as deeply sunk into the Moroccan economy as the military empires are sunk into Egypt and Pakistan. He's the country's biggest landowner and banker, he controls the market in basic foodstuffs, and his family owns Morocco's largest conglomerate, the SNI group. Forbes magazine estimates

Muhammad VI's personal wealth at $2.5 billion, making him five times richer than Britain's Elizabeth.

Put beside that, this statistic: five million Moroccans live abroad, not counting illegal migrants – far more than Egyptians or Turks, although those countries have double Morocco's population. The largest expatriate population is in France. (In this issue of *Critical Muslim*, Suhel Ahmed reviews the French prison film *A Prophet*, an important take on the condition of *les beurs*, French people of Maghrebi origin.) A recent survey says 70 per cent of Moroccans would like to leave the country. By now we are desensitised to photographs of Moroccan bodies washed up on the shores of southern Spain. We don't think much about the fact that some Moroccans readily risk death to escape economic and developmental stagnation.

In 2011, influenced by the revolutions to the east, a massive rally for reform in Rabat kicked off the youth-led 20th February Movement (see Cecile Oumhani's 'Diaries of a Revolution' for background on the uprisings in Tunisia and Libya, and their aftermaths). Demonstrations erupted in all major Moroccan cities, cohering around slogans such as 'Down with Autocracy'. The king responded almost immediately. On 9th March he announced a commission to draft a new constitution, and on 12th June interpreted the draft to a television audience. On 1st July, after a mere fortnight of debate, the constitution was approved by 98.5 per cent of voters, a suspiciously high rate given that the 20th February Movement had rejected the document. And the fortnight between the constitution's appearance and the referendum was hardly characterised by 'debate'. According to Adnane Addioui, a critical Muslim if ever I've met one, imams dedicated their Friday sermons to describing a no vote as a vote against Islam. The word 'YES' was pasted up in the streets and inside taxi cabs.

The constitution supposedly ensures 'the rule of law', an 'independent judiciary', and an 'elected government that reflects the will of the people, through the ballot box'. But the reality is once again very different from the appearance, once again a shadow play, a rhetorical sleight of hand in which the noble sentiments of one passage are undermined by the details of another. Nothing much changed, but the monarch's carefully stage-managed manoeuvring (assisted by the New York PR firm Beckerman) took the wind out of the Moroccan spring's sails.

And as the sails slumped, repression intensified. The state refrained from gunning people down, but three protesters died from beatings, and many were imprisoned on trumped-up charges. The protest rapper Mouad el-Haked has been imprisoned since September 2011 on the very questionable basis of assaulting and 'insulting the police'.

What to do now? When Adnane Addioui welcomed me for *iftar*, he stressed the necessity of the people owning and responding to their own problems, not waiting for the theatrical state to wave its wand. He drove the point home with a blizzard of Durija proverbs: 'Break it and the state will pay'; 'to rent is not to own'; 'the shared face is never washed'. He prefers 'empowerment' to charity, because 'charity is an institutional method for keeping people in their place'. The organisation he heads in Morocco, Enactus, works with more than 2,000 students and over forty colleges and universities. One of its many recent projects has been to assist deaf people in the Salé region to set up an e-learning and media facility, creating four jobs.

Adnane sees what he calls 'social entrepreneurship' as a necessary complement to political process. As the revolutions further east are demonstrating, a leadership, indeed an entire social structure, is required to fill the gaps vacated by a challenged or failing state. It's not enough to overthrow; we must, simultaneously, build.

He loves the Arab revolutions, despite the mounting losses. He points out that Egyptians, Libyans and Tunisians, unlike Moroccans, are returning home from abroad to try to shape their societies. He calls for radical change: 'Chemotherapy is no good; excision is necessary!' I'm surprised he speaks so openly. Others have asked me not to go on record with their criticisms of the monarchy. 'But I don't have an issue with the monarchy!' he responds. 'I have an issue with a mindset, with an unaccountable system. A transparent, constitutional monarchy would be perfect.' So this engaged radical is not asking for more than what Muhammad V seemed to agree to in the forties and fifties when he joined forces with the Istiqlal to seek national independence.

In the meantime, what is it that keeps the monarchy going? What saves the state from revolution?

'Why is Morocco peaceful?' A young man pulled on his iftar spliff and returned the question to me. 'Because of this, the hashish! This is why Moroccans say 'everything's fine'. And you've seen the state of Morocco...' Of course, most Moroccans make no closer approach to hashish than catching a nose-full as they pass street corner smokers, so this explanation works only as a metaphor for wilful disengagement. (Naguib Mahfouz's wonderful novel *Adrift on the Nile* uses this symbolism. The dramatic final frames of the film version show the anti-hero stumbling between gutted buildings screaming 'Don't smoke hashish!')

Among the non-narcotic reasons for Morocco's apparent stability is, first, the monarchy's intelligent statecraft. In this respect, it's more of an institution, and a frequently meritocratic one, than a one-man show. The king's advisers, business partners and international friends work hard to anticipate, respond to, and defuse unrest. Again and again the monarchy has reinvented itself, adapting to colonialism and anti-colonialism, the Strong Man Age and the Liberal Age, Arabism and Amazigh Pride. Like a professional actress it rushes through the dressing room and appears a moment later as an entirely different character. There's no comparison with the clumsy savagery of a Qaddafi or an Assad. Nor with the amateurish gangsterism of a Bin Ali or a Mubarak, upstart plunderers arrived late on the scene.

And here is the second reason for the monarchy's longevity: its deep-rootedness, which means that when the monarchy is thuggish, it hides itself under a mystical curtain. Even if its failures helped to open the country to foreign penetration, even if it collaborated with colonialism, it still predates colonialism. The king is of the Alawi family, descended from Ali, bearing the Prophet's blood, and among his official titles is *ameer al-momineen*, Commander of the Faithful. Temporal and spiritual authority are united in his person. For all the simulacrum of liberal democratic modernity – again the theatre, the silvered screen – state propaganda makes it very clear indeed that the king's semi-sacred presence is the real source of power. As in the old dictatorships, pictures of the boss grace almost every public wall. In cafés he's portrayed drinking tea; in cake shops he eats cake; in toy shops he kisses children. God, Country and King is written in whitewashed stone on the hills watching over towns. Cloth slogans draped across streets repeat state TV rhetoric: love and sacrifice for the Giver and Builder, Commander of the Faithful, King Muhammad VI.

The third and related reason for the monarchy's stability is the innate conservatism which is persistent and widespread in the Arab world, despite the revolutionary surges. It was well articulated by Fou'ad, a middle-aged man who worked in my Essaouira hotel, and who walked his bike alongside as I made my way to the bus station. Working from the same mentality which blames women when men beat them, he blamed 'the youth' for starting the trouble in Syria, Egypt and Tunisia. When I told him about the Syrian regime's systematic employment of rape and torture, its constant massacres and its ethnic cleansing (this was a few weeks before the massive poison gas attacks in Damascus), he shrugged and conceded that every leader makes mistakes, or his hangers-on make mistakes behind his back, but still he must be obeyed. (This position – loyalty to the *wali al-amr*, even if he's unjust – is in fact the traditional quietist position of the Sunni ulema. Syria's Shaikh Ramadan Bouti destroyed his reputation by clinging to it until his assassination in March 2013. The uselessness of this traditional position in the face of vast injustice is one factor contributing to the spread of radical Salafism.) In fact, Fou'ad continued, it would be best if every country had a king, like Morocco. Then there'd be peace and stability everywhere. It was noticeable, after all, that not one monarchy had collapsed into revolution. His analysis, of course, ignores the Bahraini monarchy, as well as the oil wealth factor which allows Gulf monarchies – for now – to soothe their people's frustrations with cash, but it does betray the traditional Arab desire for a strong man leader, a father figure, a hero – a desire which Egypt's General Sisi is exploiting as I write.

Fourthly, the deliberate delaying of development turns out to have been a clever Machiavellian policy. The republics to the east rushed to distribute land, to nationalise foreign and domestic industry, to build hospitals, schools and universities. They did it badly, corruptly, but still they did it. And the unemployed graduates produced by these regimes became their nemesis, the urban foot soldiers of revolutionary activism. In Morocco too, protesting unemployed graduates have been a common sight for two decades, but they haven't yet reached a critical mass. The real critical mass is the one which still can't read. And the mystique of the Sharifian ruler has a longer shelf life amongst the illiterate.

Finally, the terrifying examples of the Arab countries currently undergoing revolution and counter-revolution strike silence into many a Moroccan heart. I was in el-Jadida when Tunisian leftist Muhammad Ibrahimi was assassinated, sparking another round of protests and strikes. Liberals and secularists were threatening to launch a campaign against the ruling Nahda Party to mirror the *tamarrod* campaign which precipitated a military coup and mass slaughter in Egypt. Libya was violently unstable, perhaps chronically so. The Syrian death toll averaged between one and two hundred a day.

But the story isn't over. Morocco's social problems are persistent; its economic problems are increasing. After 2011 the public space is forever changed. Adnane Addioui again: 'However limited, 20 February was a real revolution. The proof of that is that people are talking now. People are criticising the king on TV. The taboo has gone.' And Adil Semmar: '20th February never existed as an organised movement, but the spirit is still there. It's not going away.'

Marrakesh is a good place to end. Specifically, the central Djemaa al-Fnaa, or Gathering Place of Extinction, so-called because it once hosted executions. Now it hosts foreign visitors and Moroccans in all their diversity, as well as sorcerers, snake charmers, storytellers, henna patterners, monkey-masters, Gnawa drummers, acrobats and dancers. As dusk falls, the food stalls open, displaying a panoply of food and drink, an interlocking nexus of aromas and flavours.

This Maghreb issue of *Critical Muslim* aims to offer a banquet as varied as the one displayed in the Djemaa al-Fnaa, a topical and geographical breadth to mirror (or at least hint at) the vastness and complexity of the region. As well as the essays on Maghrebi politics, history and culture already mentioned, we have outsider perspectives. Julia Melcher analyses Tangier's 'Interzone' as experienced by foreign (and alienated) writers such as William Burroughs and the Bowles couple, deliberate strangers who helped construct our contemporary Anglo-Saxon vision of north Africa. And John Liechty's amusing, irascible and perceptive piece recounts the attitudinal idiocies and bureaucratic malice suffered by an American married to a Moroccan. The issue also contains Maghreb-influenced short poems from George Szirtes and (the half-Tunisian) Sarra Hennigan.

Meanwhile in Marrakesh, prices are up to tourist levels. I'm not resentful. The city deserves to spoil itself, being, as it is, a location on the circuit for the rich and beautiful of the world. Sean Connery and (ex-con) Jimmie Boyle are just two Scottish examples of those who've bought riyads in the Marrakesh palmerie. An *Absolutely Fabulous* episode was shot here. The place is famous. And it's beautiful – its elegant Koutubiya mosque, its palaces and surrounding walls, its splendid souqs.

It touches 47 degrees in the early afternoon. Then black clouds thicken, red dust sheets drape the sky, thunder cracks, and rain falls in fat splotches. From the roof terrace I make out a rainbow plunging down to tall trees and red houses, all against the wall of the rearing High Atlas.

MYSTICAL IBN KHALDUN

Robert Irwin

The fourteenth-century Maghrebi philosopher of history Wali al-Din 'Abd al-Rahman Ibn Khaldun (1332–1406) has been thought by many to be the most profound thinker Islam has ever produced. The nineteenth-century pioneers of Islamic modernism Jamal al-Din al-Afghani and Muhammad 'Abduh made a close study of Ibn Khaldun's masterpiece, the *Muqaddima* (The Prolegomena) and taught from it. Taha Husayn, in his lifetime Egypt's leading man of letters, wrote a thesis at the Sorbonne in 1917 on Ibn Khaldun that was subsequently published in French and Arabic. Later Ibn Khaldun's ideas about the decay and collapse of empires were studied by the Islamic activist Sayyid Qutb.

The world historian Arnold Toynbee, who produced a ten-volume study of the rise and fall of civilisations, described the *Muqaddima* as 'undoubtedly the greatest work of its kind that has ever been created by any mind in any time or place'. According to the philosopher, sociologist and anthropologist Ernest Gellner, Ibn Khaldun was 'a superb inductive sociologist, a practitioner, long before the term was invented, of ideal types, a brilliant account of *one* extremely important kind of society'. Gellner presented him as a value-free sociologist whose theoretical models were relevant for the modern Middle East. Ibn Khaldun's ideas were cited with approval in Bruce Chatwin's novel *Songlines* and they underpinned the *Dune* cycle of science fiction novels produced by Frank Herbert.

Much of the *Muqaddima* was written in 1375 in a remote castle in north-west Algeria, but Ibn Khaldun continued to revise it almost until his death in Egypt in 1404. The *Muqaddima*, which began as a preface to a history of the Berbers, occupies three fat volumes in its English translation, while the standard Arabic edition of the chronicle itself, the *Kitab al-'Ibar*, is in seven volumes. It is on the *Muqddima* that Ibn Khaldun's chief claim to fame rests, rather than on the *'Ibar*. The *Muqaddima* is divided into six parts: 1. human society in general;

2. nomadic society; 3. states, caliphs, kings; 4. civilised society, towns; 5. trade, ways of earning a livelihood; 6. sciences and arts. Because the book is so long, it has been selectively read and selectively abridged. By the time readers of the *Muqaddima* get to volume three they are apparently fagged out and one consequence of this is that they miss the importance of divination and occultism more generally in Ibn Khaldun's thinking.

The first question Ibn Khaldun asked himself was why do historians make mistakes? Three things lead to error in writing history. Firstly, partisanship; secondly, gullibility; thirdly, ignorance of what is intrinsically possible. It is this third issue that he mostly sought to address, for inferior historians are ignorant of the general laws that govern the formation and dissolution of human societies. They have not studied the underlying laws of history, but are only the compilers of events. Ibn Khaldun scrutinised accounts of past events and sought to assess them on the grounds of plausibility. One needed to take account of cause and effect, then of how things work when the situations are similar and then of how things work when the situations are dissimilar. This was an unusual thing for an Islamic historian to do.

The most famous and perhaps the central thesis of the *Muqaddima* is that in the harsh conditions of desert life tribal groups necessarily develop a special kind of group solidarity, which Ibn Khaldun called *'asabiyya*. This cohesion, together with the nomadic tribes' hardihood and courage, gives those who possess it a military advantage – an advantage which is further reinforced if a religion acts as an additional binding force. So it is that the wild and sometimes fanatical tribesmen are able to defeat and conquer empires and cities and go on to create new states. But within a few generations, perhaps three, maybe four, these conquering tribesmen lose their *'asabiyya* and become civilised. They succumb to luxury, extravagance and leisure. The ruler who can no longer rely on fierce tribal warriors for his defence has to raise extortionate taxes in order to pay for mercenaries or slave soldiers and this in turn will lead to further problems. The ruler is vulnerable when his government is seen as corrupt and extravagant, and his rule is finally doomed when it is seen as impious. His regime will fall to the next assault by a new army of puritanical tribesmen from the desert. So his city will fall to new men and the cycle will recommence.

Religion was a desirable supplement to *'asabiyya* for tribal conquerors who aimed to set up a state. The first Arab tribal conquerors could never have established an empire without the additional unifying bond of Islam. There is a moralistic feel to Ibn Khaldun's rags-to-riches-to-rags-in-three-or-four-generations syndrome. He saw urban life as leading to degeneracy and he was unreasonably prejudiced against luxury. Yet there was a Qur'anic and traditional background to this sort of prejudice. 'When we desire to destroy a village, we order those of its inhabitants who live in luxury to act wickedly within. Thus the word becomes true for it, and we destroy it.' (Qur'an 17:16) Moreover Arab historians of the early Islamic conquests made much of the uncouth and raggedly Spartan quality of the Arab warriors. The philosopher Ibn Rushd's commentary on Plato's *Republic* may also have had some influence on the *Muqaddima*, for Ibn Rushd's book also stressed the solvent role of luxury.

Ibn Khaldun's concept of cultural mimesis has also attracted attention among modern Western thinkers. 'The vanquished always want to imitate the victor in his distinctive marks, his dress, his occupation, and all his other conditions and customs.' He instanced as an example the Muslims living under Christian rule in Spain. Among other things, they even had frescoes painted inside and outside their houses.

Ibn Khaldun consistently emphasised the decisive role of broad social and economic forces. For example, he argued that, though a rise in tax rates immediately brought in extra revenue, in the long run the state's revenues from taxation were diminished as producers were discouraged from producing by the high rate of taxation. Today this phenomenon is known as the Laffer curve, and in a well-known speech Ronald Regan quoted Ibn Khaldun to this effect: 'In the beginning of empire tax rates were low and revenue was high. At the end of empire tax rates were high and revenue was low.'

Ibn Khaldun had originally intended that these prolegomena should serve as an introduction to a history of the Berber dynasties of North Africa – the rise of the Almoravids (drawn from Sanhaja Berber tribesmen) in the eleventh century and their fall in the twelfth century; the rise of the Almohads (from the Masmuda Berbers) in the twelfth century and their fall in the thirteenth century; and the rise of the Merinids (from the Zanata Berbers) in the thirteenth century and their slow decline beginning in the fourteenth century. But as time passed and his intellectual horizons widened, he set himself to write a universal history. The result was the *Kitab al-'Ibar*, a work which despite its global pretensions, focuses mostly on North Africa and the Middle East, for it contains little on Europe, the Mongols, China or India. The title suggests that Ibn Khaldun intended that his book should have a moral and even religious purpose, for *'Ibar* is the plural of *'ibra* and *'ibra* means admonition, warning, example, or advice. The word and similar words derived from the same trilateral root feature prominently in the Qur'an. For example:

'Surely in that is an example for men possessed of eyes.' (Quran 3:13)
'In their story was a warning for those with understanding'. (Qur'an 12:11)
'So take warning, you who have sight.' (Qur'an 59:2)

Though the events chronicled were intended to deliver warnings to the book's readers, by common consent, the chronicle is less interesting than its theoretical precursor, the *Muqaddima*.

Ibn Khaldun and his history were the product of 'interesting times' (as the old Chinese curse has it). He was born in 1332 in Hafsid Tunis.

Throughout his life he was stalked by tragedies. The first of these occurred in 1348 when the Black Death reached North Africa and he lost his parents as well as many of his teachers and friends. He was seventeen when this happened. In the *Muqaddima*, he wrote as follows:

Civilisation both in the East and the West was visited by a destructive plague which devastated nations and caused populations to vanish. It swallowed up many of the good things of civilisation and wiped them out. It overtook the dynasties at the time of their senility, when they had reached the limit of their duration. It lessened their power and curtailed their influence. It weakened their authority. Their situation approached the point of annihilation and dissolution. Civilisation decreased with the decrease of mankind. Cities and buildings were laid waste, roads and way signs were obliterated, settlements and mansions became empty, dynasties and tribes grew weak. The entire inhabited world changed. The East, it seems was similarly visited though in accordance with and in proportion to [the East's more affluent] civilisation. It was as if the voice of existence in the world had called out for oblivion and restriction, and the world responded to its call. God inherits the earth and whoever is upon it.

Ibn Khaldun declared that the reason for writing his history was that the Black Death and political turmoil had wrought such vast changes that a new kind of history, one that did not follow the model provided by the tenth-century 'Abbasid historian's al-Mas'udi's *Muruj al-Dhahab* (Meadows of Gold), was called for.

One consequence of the pestilence was that the Merinid ruler Abu'l-Hasan, who had briefly occupied Tunis, was obliged to retreat with his courtiers and army back to his capital, Fez. North African politics at this time was dominated by a prolonged and inconclusive struggle for dominance over the Maghreb between the Merinids of Fez, the Hafsids of Bougie and Tunis and the 'Abd al-Wadids (or Ziyanids) of Tlemcen. But what should have been a relatively simple three-cornered struggle, or 'Game of Kings', was made more complicated by the fact there were often rival claimants for these thrones within the ruling families. And across the straits of Gibraltar on the edge of this struggle, the Nasrids of Granada also meddled in North African politics. Ibn Khaldun moved from city to city and ruler to ruler, serving in various administrative and scribal capacities. At times he seemed on the verge of becoming the power behind a throne, but at other times he ended up in prison or in flight. He was a kind of bureaucratic *condottiere* and he operated in dangerous waters in which death was commonly the penalty for political failure. His own brother Yayha, who also entered politics, was murdered in Tlemcen and Ibn Khaldun's great friend Ibn al-Khatib (on whom more shortly) was executed in prison in Fez. Ibn Khaldun's intrigues were successful only in the sense that, at the end of them all, he was still alive. Shuttling backwards and forwards between the Merinids, the Hafsids and the Nasrids, he moved from Bougie to Fez, to Granada, then Bougie, Fez again, Granada again, Tlemcen, Tunis and Cairo. The historian who wrote so much about nomads was himself a nomad.

Though it would be wearisome to follow Ibn Khaldun's political career in any detail, it is worth lingering over his association with the Nasrid ruler of Granada Muhammad V and his vizier Lisan al-Din ibn al-Khatib. This began in 1359 when the ruler and his vizier were ousted from Granada by a palace coup and went into temporary exile in Morocco. Ibn Khaldun, who at that time held an important administrative post in Fez, was instrumental in securing their welcome by the Merinid ruler and he befriended Ibn al-Khatib. In 1362 Muhammad V and his vizier returned in triumph to Granada and Ibn al-Khatib set about expanding the palace of the Alhambra and specifically designing the Court of the Lions. That same year Ibn Khaldun, whose career in Fez had not been prospering as much as he thought it should, was allowed to join his friends in Granada.

Ibn al-Khatib (1313–74) was the single most influential person in Ibn Khaldun's life. In his lifetime Ibn al-Khatib was more famous, more powerful and more productive than Ibn Khaldun, and for centuries his fame would outshine that of his younger contemporary. During his temporary retirement in Morocco, Ibn al-Khatib had written books and sat at the feet of a Sufi master. He wrote history in the flowery style that was so admired at the time and his chronicles were peppered with poetry. A gloomy and arrogant aristocrat, Ibn al-Khatib regarded the masses with disgust. He wrote that all dynasties were in the long run doomed by corruption, greed and ambition. History was a vicious circle of usurpations and depositions. A couple of lines from a Victorian hymn by H.F. Lyte might serve to describe his world view:

Change and decay in all around I see;

O Thou, who changes not, abide with me.

Apart from his chronicles, Ibn al-Khatib produced approximately sixty other books, including a Sufi treatise, *The Garden of Instruction in Noble Love*. In Ibn Khaldun's so-called autobiography, the *Ta'rif*, Ibn al-Khatib was described as 'one of the miracles of God in the areas of poetry, prose, knowledge and culture'.

In 1364 Ibn Khaldun served the Nasirid Sultan by going on a diplomatic mission to Pedro the Cruel in Seville. The mission was successful and Muhammad V looked on Ibn Khaldun with favour. But it was precisely his successes in Andalusia that put him in peril, as the hitherto friendly Ibn al-Khatib seems to have become suspicious that Ibn Khaldun wanted to replace him as vizier as well as Andalusia's top intellectual.

Judging it better not to face Ibn al-Khatib's outright enmity, Ibn Khaldun left Andalusia in 1371 and went back to re-engage in the dangerous game of North African politics. But in 1375 he took a kind of sabbatical and retired to Qal'at ibn Salama, a castle in the region of Tlemcen which was put at his disposal by a friendly Arab tribe. It was here, in this remote castle that serious work on the *Muqaddima* and the *'Ibar* began: 'I completed its introduction in that remarkable manner to which I was inspired by that retreat, with words and ideas pouring into my head like cream into a churn, until the finished product was ready.'

In 1378 he emerged from his scholarly retreat and returned to Tunis and to politicking, though without any sustained success, and in 1382 he moved to Egypt. In doing so, he escaped from the North African backwater, since Mamluk Cairo was the intellectual and cultural capital of the Islamic world in the fourteenth century. In the *Ta'rif*, his so-called autobiography, he wrote that Cairo was 'the capital of the world, garden of the universe, forum for the gathering of peoples... palace of Islam, throne of power, a city embellished with palaces and mansions, ornamented with colleges and schools, its scholars are like shining stars.... One could not stop speaking of this city, of its high degree of civilisation. Of its prosperity.'

1382 was also the year that the Circassian Mamluk Barquq became Sultan of Egypt and Syria. Ibn Khaldun swiftly won the new Sultan's favour and Barquq gave him several profitable administrative and teaching posts and repeatedly appointed him as Maliki Chief Qadi (though Ibn Khaldun's arrogance and the severity of his judgements earned him the jealous enmity of Egyptian *ulama* and hence he was repeatedly deposed). Eventually Ibn Khaldun was successful in getting permission for his wife, children and precious library to join him in Egypt. But the boat bringing them from Tunis to Egypt sank off the Egyptian coast and all were lost. This was neither the first nor the last of the tragedies that Ibn Khaldun had to undergo.

In 1399 Barquq died and he was succeeded as sultan by his son Faraj.

At this point Timur (also known as Tamerlane), the leader of a Turko-Mongol horde composed mostly of Chagatai Turks and a would-be world conqueror, seeing that Faraj was newly and only precariously established on his throne, decided to invade Mamluk Syria and advance on its capital, Damascus. Ibn Khaldun had travelled with Faraj and the Mamluk army to Damascus, but when Faraj decided to retreat back into Egypt, the historian remained in the city and was part of the delegation of citizens that went out to negotiate terms for the surrender of the city to Timur's besieging army. Timur, who was fond of historians (though they seem to have been a lot less fond of him), was most impressed by Ibn Khaldun and summoned him day after day to debate the great political and religious issues of the age. It was a confrontation that can be compared to the meeting of Aristotle and Alexander or Napoleon and Goethe. On the other hand, Ibn Khaldun, who was so fascinated by nomadic warriors like the Banu Chagatai and their leaders, may have looked on Timur in much the same way as an experimental scientist looks on a newly acquired laboratory rat.

Eventually Ibn Khaldun was successful in persuading Timur to let him return to Egypt and hence Ibn Khaldun avoided the subsequent sack and massacre that took place in Damascus. Yet tragedy continued to stalk him, for on his way back he was attacked by brigands and stripped of everything he had including the clothes on his back. Ibn Khaldun described his encounter with Timur and much else in his *Al-Ta'rif bi Ibn Khaldun wa Rihlatihi Sharqan wa Gharban (Presenting Ibn Khaldun and His Journeys in the East and the West)*. Yet, though the *Ta'rif* is conventionally described as an autobiography, it is a remarkably reticent one, revealing little or nothing about his personal feelings and tastes, his family life or his working methods. It is really more of a curriculum vitae tacked on to a chronicle of public events.

Ibn Khaldun died in 1406. During his lifetime and in the centuries that immediately followed, his philosophical approach to history had little impact. Robert Brunschvig, a historian of the medieval Maghreb, commented: 'the systematic lack of comprehension and the resolute hostility which this nonconformist thinker of genius encountered among his own people forms one of the most moving dramas, one of the saddest and most significant pages in the history of Muslim culture.'

Antoine Isaac Silvestre de Sacy and Joseph von Hammer Purgstall first made the West aware of the genius of Ibn Khaldun in the opening decades of the nineteenth century. An edition of the *Muqaddima* by De Sacy's student Etienne Quatremère was posthumously published in 1859, and another student of De Sacy, the Baron de Slane, translated it into French in 1867. Much later, in 1958, an English translation by Franz Rosenthal appeared.

The *Muqaddima* is a very long book (1,676 pages in Rosenthal's three-volume translation) and it seems that the book's readers have been able to take what they wanted from it. Ibn Khaldun has been variously compared to Machiavelli, Vico, Montesquieu, Durkheim and Marx. He was judged to be the world's first sociologist, or rather, he was perhaps the first cultural historian. Readers interpreted the *Muqaddima* as foreshadowing positivism, nationalism, rationalism or empiricism. Taha Husayn was sure that Ibn Khaldun was a covert atheist. Less anachronistically, twentieth-century Arabists tried to present his thought as drawing chiefly on the principles and methodology of Islamic jurisprudence (Hamilton Gibb), or as being a belated representative of the tradition of *falsafa*, the Hellenistically derived philosophy of which Ibn Sina and al-Farabi were earlier representatives. At least two scholars, Muhsin Mahdi and Patricia Crone, suggested that the *Muqaddima* was in large part an attempt by Ibn Khaldun to understand why he had been a political failure.

The keenness of modern Western Christian or secular thinkers to legitimate their thinking by drawing on the writings of a fourteenth-century strict Muslim is most curious. It reminds one of a couplet from Omar Khayyam's *Ruba'iyat* (as translated by Edward Fitzgerald):

Myself when young did eagerly frequent
Doctor and Saint, and heard great Argument
About it and about: but evermore
Came out by the same Door as in I went.

In 2010 Allen Fromherz published a biography, *Ibn Khaldun: Life and Times,* in which he argued for the importance of Sufism in Ibn Khaldun's life and its role in shaping his philosophy of history. 'Ibn Khaldun's description of "awakening" to the hidden truth [of history], of finding meaning behind the surface of events, had parallels in the Sufism or Islamic mysticism that so inspired Ibn Khaldun's grandfather, father, and undoubtedly Ibn Khaldun himself.' As Fromherz sees it, the historical process of cyclical dissolution and rebirth, outlined by Ibn Khaldun, echoed on a macroscopic scale the individual path of a mystical disciple who 'died' in the hands of his master and then was reborn. Ibn Khaldun was led through Sufism to realise the futility of material power and possessions. Crucially it was Sufism which led him to look beyond the *zahir* (external appearance) of historical events and intuit the *batin* (hidden truth) of the inner laws that determined those events.

One's first response to the above must be that, if this is so obvious, why has no one seen it before? And 'undoubtedly' does not seem quite right. If Ibn Khaldun was a Sufi, what kind of Sufi was he? Who was his *murshid* (spiritual master)? Which *tariqa* (Sufi order) did he belong to? Why does he not mention any personal mystical experiences in either the *Muqaddima* or the 'autobiography'? Moreover, none of his contemporaries described him as a Sufi, nor are they on record as detecting a Sufi message in the *Muqaddima*.

Nothing in the ups and downs of his career in Egypt suggests that he had given up on power and material possessions.

These are all legitimate reasons for doubt. Nevertheless, I believe that it is almost certain that Ibn Khaldun was a Sufi. First, he lived in an era when Sufism was becoming institutionalised and *zawiyas* (Sufi hospices) and *tariqas* (Sufi orders) were being formed. In fourteenth-century North Africa, Sufism was so very popular in the cities and in the countryside among both the elite and the masses that it would have been strange if Ibn Khaldun had not become a Sufi.

Then, although Ibn Khaldun does not confess to being a Sufi in the *Muqaddima*, the book does contain two extensive discussions of Sufism and Ibn Khaldun's treatment of the subject is overwhelmingly favourable:

Sufism belongs to the sciences of the religious law that originated in Islam. It is based on the assumption that the practice of its adherents had always been consid-ered by the important early Muslims, the men around Muhammad and the men of the second generation, as well as those who came after them, as the path of truth and right guidance. The Sufi approach is based upon constant application to divine worship, complete devotion to God, aversion to the false splendour of the world, abstinence from the pleasure, property, and position to which the great mass aspire, and retirement from the world into solitude for divine worship. These things were general among the men around Muhammad and the early Muslims. Then worldly aspirations increased in the second [eighth] century and after. At that time, the special name of Sufis was given to those who aspired to divine worship.

Ibn Khaldun supported the practice of the *dhikr* (incessant repetition of words or formulas in praise of God), which removes the veil of sensual perception and then the Sufi beholds divine worlds. 'It is like food to make the spirit grow.' It makes the spirit ready for 'holy gifts'. That Sufi saints could work *karamat* (miracles) was an undeniable truth. Sufism, unlike theology or philosophy, led to happiness. The writings of Abu Hamid Muhammad al-Ghazali (1058–1111) had a huge influence on Ibn Khaldun and they are much quoted in the *Muqaddima*. Al-Ghazali, a very grand and influential thinker, espoused a moderate Sufism which he was able to reconcile with strict Islamic Sunni orthodoxy, though he argued that literal interpretations of spiritual truths sufficed for the masses and that more esoteric interpretations should be reserved for the elite.

Ibn Khaldun made it plain that the Sufi path led to God and that Sufis were a force for good in the world. Although, influenced here perhaps by al-Ghazali, he had reservations about certain famous (or perhaps that should be notorious) Sufis who had fallen prone to heresy, occult practices and syncretism, including al-Hallaj (857–922), Ibn Sabin (1217–68) and Ibn al-'Arabi (1165–1240). Suspicious of some of the more speculative doctrines and provocative utterances of such Sufis, Ibn Khaldun favoured a simpler ascetic and devotional mysticism.

Not only did Ibn Khaldun write about Sufism at length in the *Muqaddima*, but in the 1370s he produced a short treatise *Shifa' al-Sa'il li-tadhib al-masa'il*, ('The Cure of the Questioner through the Clarification of the Problems'). In it he addressed the then controversial question of whether it was necessary for someone on the Sufi path to place himself in the hands of a *murshid* (spiritual master) or whether it was possible and safe to make progress on the path by reading books. Ibn Khaldun discussed the history of Sufism and its elaborate technical vocabulary before concluding that the guidance of a *murshid* was necessary if heresy was to be avoided. According to the Sufi Abu Yazid al-Bistami, 'He who has no shaykh has Satan as his shaykh.' Ibn al-Khatib's treatise on Sufi love, *Rawdat al-ta'rif,* has been mentioned. Ibn Khaldun studied it and quoted from it approvingly in his *Shifa'*.

Later in Egypt he issued a fatwa in which he again denounced speculative and heterodox Sufis. Since they were guilty of *bid'a* (innovation), their books should be burnt. He did not think that speculative Sufism was merely intellectually dangerous. Rather he feared that it might produce social unrest, since millenarian movements led by self-professed Mahdis or Imams might be stirred up by esoteric Sufi writings in which Shi'ite doctrine and occult prophecies were combined. There was a danger that Sufism, which had had its golden age in the ninth and tenth centuries but which more recently had been infected by heresy, was in decline.

At the end of his life Ibn Khaldun was buried in the Sufi cemetery in Cairo. So it is all but certain that Ibn Khaldun was a Sufi, though not an uncritical one. But this does not mean that he necessarily produced a distinctively Sufi philosophy of history. An intellectual is not a kind of sausage machine in which everything that enters his mind is processed to come out again in his writings. Wittgenstein loved cowboy films, yet they did not, I think, influence his philosophy in any way. Becoming a good Sufi does not turn one into an inspired social historian. Moreover, Sufis did not monopolise the concepts of *zahir* and *batin*. The tenth- or eleventh-century *Ikhwan al-Safa'* (Brethren of Purity), the mysterious compilers of an early encyclopedia, relied heavily on the concepts of the veiled and the external. So did medieval occultists such as Jabir ibn Hayyan, pseudo-al-Majriti and al-Buni. There is nothing very mystical in seeing hidden forces at work in history, otherwise we might have to regard Oswald Spengler and Eric Hobsbawm as crypto-Sufis.

Looking at it from another angle, no other medieval Sufi seems to have been inspired by his mysticism to write a mystical version of history. Fromherz's suggestion that Ibn Khaldun's theory of the death and rebirth of civilisations was inspired by the metaphorical death and rebirth of the Sufi disciple will not do, since for the Sufi disciple there can be no rebirth in the manner of Osiris or Adonis. Rather the disciple remains bound in corpse-like obedience to his *murshid*. The disciple's pact with his master must not be confused with a spring vegetation ritual. Moreover, when one dynasty perishes, it does not get reborn; instead it is replaced by another one.

The real sources of Ibn Khaldun's theoretical approach to history are probably less exciting. His methodology was explicitly modelled on *'usul al-fiqh* (the principles of jurisprudence), and in particular on consensus and reasoning by analogy. Despite his frequent criticisms of al-Mas'udi, Ibn Khaldun did have lot of respect for this historian of the 'Abbasid period and was strongly influenced by the man he called the 'imam of historians'. Al-Mas'udi's writings were wide-ranging and digressive and they revealed a sharp awareness both of the mutability of societies and the relativity of cultures. Finally, the ups and downs of Ibn Khaldun's career coupled with an immersion in Ibn al-Khatib's elitist and gloomy writings gave Ibn Khaldun's version of history its pessimistic spin.

DIARIES OF A REVOLUTION

Cécile Oumhani

Paris

December 2010

Days are wrapped up in the cold darkness long after sunrise. I fumble around in the kitchen to get myself a cup of tea, as B. listens to the news. A young street-vendor has set himself afire in a remote underprivileged part of Tunisia because the police would not let him sell his fruit. Hundreds of protestors are now taking to the streets. They will be crushed in a matter of days, we know… The brutal repression that followed the 2008 revolt in the mining area of Gafsa is at the back of our minds. We still dare not imagine that the impossible could come true. For years, B. has kept telling me: 'I don't think I will see democracy in Tunisia or any other Arab country in my lifetime.'

January 2011

As time goes by, protests spread irresistibly to the coastal regions and the capital. Our hearts are in our mouths. The regime has set out to quash the protesters and the count of the dead keeps rising as security forces shoot indiscriminately. They shoot them as they walk out into the streets. They shoot them just because they are in the street, no matter if they are just going to work. They even shoot them as they walk to the cemetery to bury their dead. In some places, hospitals cannot cope with the number of casualties. Hospital staff members break down, so unprepared and horrified are they.

Everywhere TVs, radios and computers are now on almost day and night, eclipsing any other interests. Facebook pages, videos on mobile phones, Twitter messages capture our whole attention. More than ever before, I realise that new technologies have introduced different approaches to events, new ways of perceiving them, of experiencing them. They have turned us into first-hand witnesses. They have given us new responsibilities. I had not used Facebook much before the Tunisian Revolution, but I start doing so now, to follow what is going on as closely as possible. At the same time, I notice established newspapers are posting on their sites the messages, the videos they receive, thus acknowledging that protesters are also becoming the reporters and journalists of what we still daren't call a Revolution.

12 January 2011
Around noon, one of my Facebook friends posts on my wall: 'I don't know how I am going to get home for lunch. They are gunning down people in the streets. I am afraid....' Comfortably seated in Paris, I read her message, overwhelmed by a sense of helplessness. It takes me a few minutes before I can type one or two lines of support. 'Hold on, we are all thinking of you!' This is so little and there is so much I would like to be able to tell her, to do, to help. Several hours later, in the evening, I read on Facebook that another of my friends has directly experienced the cruelty of the regime. Her cousin was shot dead in cold blood as he walked home from the hotel where he worked as a receptionist. He was married, with young children.

13 January 2011
If only we could bridge distances. If only it were just a matter of smashing the computer screen. If this could be enough to give flesh to your voices... We have been talking to you on the phone almost every night since December. So much emotion as events seem be moving at an ever faster pace... As always, we have been very careful not to speak openly. We never mention the protests, we only ask about the weather, the cold, the rain, anything plausibly unrelated to what we are all concerned about, even in our sleep. For decades, restraint had become a second nature for us, and on either side of our conversations. We had all become experts at using coded references.

Tonight we speak, you speak about the country erupting in massive protests, the people who have been brutally killed. As openly as if we were sitting in the same room... For the first time in ages... As if we already knew what was about to happen. Or had we perhaps suddenly got beyond the point of caring, of feeling frightened? Could we possibly know that it was now a matter of hours before the regime fell?

The dictator starts delivering his last speech. *Fahimtkum*... I have understood you. *Yezzi min el kartouch*... Enough violence, he drawls. Hardly has he finished when dozens of cars filled with members of his clique start parading and honking down the capital's main avenue to express their support.

14 January 2011

We sit down in front of our TV and computer screens, both overcome by a sense of expectancy and paralysed by the prospect of more violence against the people. Protests have been scheduled opposite the Ministry of Interior, a place of sinister memory. This is where opponents of the regime were detained and tortured. Crowds of demonstrators have gathered on Tunis's main avenue opposite the building. Women and men of all ages, all walks of life, calm, determined. I skip from one media site to another, trying to keep track of the messages and videos posted by demonstrators and journalists. It is difficult to form an accurate idea of what is happening. As the afternoon goes by, tension rises to a climax. Streets are now empty because of the curfew. Journalists say an important government statement is about to be made. The army has taken hold of the airport. No plane can take off or land. Horrendous visions run through my mind. More killing… Martial law… Anything but what is finally announced by the Prime Minister. Ben Ali has left the country.

Tunis

End of January 2011

The man briskly walks away, holding *Le Canard enchaîné* under his arm. He has just purchased a copy of the French satirical paper at a newsstand on Tunis's main avenue. He is beaming with joy and willingly stops to answer the journalist's questions about the Tunisian Revolution.

'I have never been able to buy *Le Canard enchaîné* in Tunis before; this is the first time, he exclaims. Can you imagine?'

His voice breaks.

'You are crying, sir,' observes the journalist.

'Yes, I am crying,' the man replies, moved beyond words by such a significant, palpable sign of change in his everyday life.

People now line up at newsstands, as determined as if they were buying bread, eager to read what they were denied for decades.

Not so long ago, only weeks back, some papers just were not available.

'No copies of *Le Monde* today.'

We all knew what it meant. We all knew better than to ask what it meant. A look or a faint smile was the only way we could share what it meant.

The Tunisian satirical paper *El Gattous*, the cat, was still to be born. In August 2011.

Paris

20 February 2011

The landscape at the window fades into icy greyness. I barely give it a glance. It is two months since the difference between day and night has vanished, replaced by one long wake. Nothing matters but all the people gathering by tens of thousands, hour by hour, here, there. Voices chanting the same words, fearless, relentless... *It was like a mantra,* my poet friend in Tunis will tell me, months later. Faces and voices that belied certainties and defeats, instilling in the world the unheard-of, the undreamt-of.... After Tunisia, Egypt, and last week, Libya...

The man's voice on the internet sounds very close. His anxiety seems to pour into the room. It splashes around the carpet before it takes hold of me. *A massacre is taking place in Benghazi. A massacre... Worse than anything you can imagine... Bombs, not bullets... Anti-aircraft weapons against civilians... Please forward my message. The whole world must be informed of what is going on in Libya, in Benghazi. In other cities, like Misrata, they are demonstrating.* A faceless, nameless voice... Pain's burning lava...

I still haven't met Najat, a resident of Misrata; I will meet her in September, in a Tunis clinic, where war casualties are treated. I don't know what Najat is doing on Sunday, 20th February 2011. I am only aware that protests are going on in Misrata. Is her fifteen-year-old son in the street too, with the four members of her family who will die, arms in hand, between February and September? So many unknown faces... They crowd here, there. I stare at them. I listen to them. I hear the faceless voice. It breaks. Breaks the glass between people. Breaks what separates them. Then the wave rushes in.

21 February 2011

At the Fontaine des Innocents Square, a light rain is falling from the sooty sky... About a hundred people have gathered, holding up flags and photos of bodies torn to pieces. The night lights of the city keep dancing on the protesters and their banners. One of the rally organizers takes the floor.

Anonymous, we know you are here tonight and we thank you for your support. I look around. Where is 'Anonymous'? Are they wearing the Guy Fawkes mask that has become their emblem for the occasion? But this would be an immediate identifying feature and then they would no longer be anonymous. There's no better way to remain unknown than to merge into the crowd without a mask. Already last January, they were noted for siding with the Tunisians through their cyber attacks on the former government.

A few steps from me, a young man slips his mobile phone into his pocket. His shoulders fall and he breaks into tears, sitting on the pavement. His head tilted forward in the darkness, he starts sobbing uncontrollably. *A phone call from home in Libya* someone says next to me, before a circle forms around him.

Dam echchouhada ma yemchich ila lhiba.

The blood of the martyrs will not be poured in vain.

The clamour rises again and again. Like a roaring sea… Waves crashing on the sand burn our eyes and blur our vision. Words, names all seem to melt into one big scream.

Wahid. Wahid. Min el Maghreb ilal Bahrein.

United. United. From the Maghreb to Bahrain…

Eyes search for each other in the darkness. They shine with the emotion shared in the syllables chanted in unison. Moments ago, we were perfect strangers.

Tunisia

19 March 2011

The November 7 Boulevard, a formerly omnipresent tribute to the dictator's coup in 1987, has been renamed Mohammed Bouazizi Boulevard. In other places, it has become Revolution Boulevard and leads to territories left unchartered for decades. They only existed on the forbidden world maps of secret dreams. The walls of every town and village have become the pages of a book thousands of anonymous hands are now writing passionately. *Power to the people…We want a free press… Bread and water, yes, Ben Ali, no… Where there is a will, there is a way… Hasta la victoria siempre! Liberta!* New words ring out everywhere; they suffuse the landscapes, transform perspectives, as far as the eye can see. What are the shepherds thinking of, as they quietly wait by their sheep or their goats, on grassy hillocks? What new world is the fisherman searching for, as he unfolds his nets on the wooden jetty that creaks and sways in the wind? What chords is the barber-musician playing on his lute in his empty shop? The jeweller, scared by a time of uncertainty, has put away all his necklaces, bracelets and earrings; the model's busts at his window all sit bare, not far from a building torched because its owner was a *qawwed,* one of Ben Ali's informers and supporters. At the optician's, not a single customer will fail to give his opinion to the lady who still does not know which glasses frame suits her best. Does it look better with or without rhinestones? What she will choose has become everyone else's business.

Mustapha, you show us a house in the middle of an orange grove. Its shattered windows have turned it into a contorted face, its large empty eyes staring at us from among the trees. *A gift from the dictator to one of his courtiers...* You tell us about the parties they would have at weekends with people from the palace as their regular guests. The owner treated his farm hands brutally. Armed at all hours... Any of them that showed the least sign of resistance, was promptly taken to the police station to be beaten up all night and fired the next morning. How angry the people were with him, with the police commissioner, when the regime fell... I notice the impish look on your face, after too much suppressed resentment, when you mention the police commissioner running away through a back door under the protection of huntsmen with their rifles. You describe his wife's underwear stolen from the terrace and hung out at the police station's door for the crowd to see.

We drive through Bou Charray, where Slim Chiboub, one of the dictator's son-in-laws, had a stud farm. You tell us stories of racehorses fed on pistachios and honey. *Imagine, pistachios and honey...* Of course, they would not eat the hay the horse thieves gave them. Very soon they had to let go of their booty and leave them by the side of the road, rumours say. What else could they have fed them?

13 March 2011

A dull flapping sound rises in the early morning, louder as it draws near. The helicopter rotors hiss above the street, above our houses; their heavy chop fills the air. The wings of a huge brown insect hovering over the ground beneath... 'What is this?' I ask you. *Nothing. It's just the army. They come and patrol from time to time.* Looking for members of the former militias, escaped prisoners, still at large. Papers have widely published a call from the Ministry of Justice urging common-law detainees to report to authorities and regularise their situation.

The chairs at the café down the street squeak on the tiling. Squeezed in your parkas, you sit down to have an espresso or a café crème. Cups clatter and spoons clank for a while. This has become your debating club. *We are now free to say whatever we want at the café or at our friends'. No one will tell the police.* Today you are concerned about the Libyan Revolution. What if it failed, while everyone is so busy talking at the Arab League and in the West, with still no prospect of any agreement? The tyrant's victory would be horrendous for the Libyans. It would also be a threat to the Tunisians. The question of the transitory committee that will replace the city council and the mayor comes up. Then the conversation shifts, driven by the passion and exhilaration of change. The physician who was trained in the former USSR reads out a Latin quotation. *Homo locum ornat, non hominem locus.* It's not the place that makes the people, but the people who make the place. You write the sentence down for me on a page of your notebook. The freshness of March has made your cheeks rosy and your eyes are shining when you proudly present it to me. A beautiful comment on the citizen's role in his country… And you go on, saying that there are no longer any subjects here. They have become full and equal citizens. Concerned and involved in all city affairs.

14 March 2011

Soumaya, there is a tremor in your voice when you remember the fifteen nights your husband and your son spent watching at the end of the street with the neighbourhood committee. The dictator's militias terrorized everyone all over the country in the aftermath of 14 January. A young man was shot dead as the neighbourhood watch stopped what turned out to be a false ambulance with three men of the former regime hiding inside. You knew about such stories. You had heard them. At regular intervals, you would brew some tea and take it to the watchmen. The black marks of the fires they lit to fight the cold and the fear are still visible on the asphalt.

You hold out the history book your ten-year-old pupils have been using. Indignant, you leaf through it, pointing out what must now be rewritten, all these chapters with no other aim than to celebrate the former regime. *Now we have the right to say no!* Your eyes light up as the prospect of boundless horizons to explore makes you dizzy. You tell me how happy you feel when you read "Freedom", Éluard's poem, with your pupils. *I was born / To give you your name / Freedom....*

On television, the nurse in the Tunisian spot writes 14 January 2011 with a pen on the plastic bracelet she slips around the tiny leg of a newborn baby. *I have opened my eyes in a world where human beings have won their freedom through the sheer power of words,* says a voiceover. She takes the child in her arms, swaddled in a blanket, carries it all the way to its mother, through corridors where women and men, young and old, are seated along benches, waiting. The multiple faces of a new Tunisia... *This world I had not imagined, where we would all share the same hopes, where the student would thirst for knowledge, where the patient would give his blood, where justice would exist.* On the TV news, gone is the time when the dictator's actions of the day were recounted with solemn music in the background. The refugees from Libya are flooding into the camps that have been set up in the south of the country. People are demonstrating. People are speaking, expressing themselves. Everyday, ordinary citizens...

15 March 2011

Jihen, you come from the suburbs of Tunis to visit us. You tell me how you stayed on your own with your little girls when the airport closed. It was impossible for H. to come back or for you to leave and join him in Algiers. The ceaseless sound of helicopters and the thick clouds of teargas....Through the shutters, you could see figures running, jumping from one terrace onto another. You and the girls slept in the same bed, your heart in your mouth. They could not wait for the curfew. Only then did the street become silent. You explain that you had stored food so that you would not have to go out, except once when you had to get medication to soothe Y's sore throat. It was one of your neighbours who helped you. How frustrated you were not to go and demonstrate on Bourguiba Avenue! Who would have looked after your daughters?

You take us to a seaside resort, enjoying what is your first outing in weeks. People are still reluctant to go out for walks or drive after sunset. There are rumours of cars held up for a necklace or a handbag, former RCD members or militias in hiding in the countryside and false roadblocks. At the table beside us, four young men, two young girls, their heads covered with grey cotton... Are they brothers and sisters? Or cousins? They obviously belong to the same family. Libyans who have come by car... If I were a Libyan mother, I would do everything I could to protect my children from the madness of the tyrant. It is 1500 kilometres from Tripoli to where we are, with the border crossing point in Ras El Jedir, where thousands of migrant workers are fleeing the violence in Libya, unsure how they will be able to go back to their countries.

Inscriptions are visible everywhere on the walls, on the doors of some villas. *Honour to our brave martyrs... The truth has come out and injustice has been defeated... Home returned to its owners...* Slim Chiboub, the stud farm owner whose racehorses were fed on pistachios and honey, also owned a luxurious villa here.

16 March 2011

Nabeul... I search the streets for traces of winter, eager to decipher on the façades the narrative of what we did not see, because we were still on the other side of the Mediterranean. The post-office has burned down. The doors to the bank have been hastily boarded up. The smashed Monoprix windows have been walled with bricks. A schoolboy is walking along the street, down to a bookshop and stationer, perhaps looking for new copybooks in which to write history in the making. At the entrance to the medina, I stumble upon the dark line of eyes staring from a street café. Images of sharp glass... Did they take part? And what scenes still haunt them as they sit in the afternoon sun? The murmurs of the city encircle me, a wall where I still hope to make out the recent past.

How many steps till we can bridge the gap with the days when we were not here? From the soles of our shoes on the pavement ring all kinds of echoes. They rise in the street all around us.

Is it on the same day? Saif el Islam Qadhafi vowing to a crowd of supporters waving green Jamahariya flags that the Libyan rebellion will be quashed in no time... Forty-eight hours at most. 'Libya is not a piece of cake and we are not Mickey Mouse.' His father murderously yelling that the whole Mediterranean has become a war-zone and that no place in the area is off limits for him...

17 March 2011

We are driving towards El Haouaria, at the far north of Cap Bon. As in other towns and even the smallest of villages, walls only speak about the Revolution. *Power to the people! RCD get out!* The charred ruins of the local office of the

RCD party and the police station are a testament to the crowd's anger. Military vehicles are patrolling on the coastal road.

The purity of the sky will not alleviate the anxiety weighing on us. Over there, east from where we are, another massacre is about to take place, in Benghazi. The anxiety flows in our veins like molten metal. At the restaurant, all eyes at all tables are riveted to the news on al-Jazeera. Conversations have stopped.

Hours go by as we drive along green hillocks and olive groves. I obstinately look east, as if towards a door I cannot wait to see open. At the café in Kelibia, lovers are whispering, not far from where we sit. How can one admire the beauty of the sea or think of romance when the worst has already started a few hundred miles from here? Tonight twilight only conjures up visions of death and deluges of fire devastating the population. B. arrives, rushing up the stairs after a conversation with the waiter who has been watching TV. He has just heard that a resolution may be voted on tonight. Against all expectations... He pauses for breath. The flow of unknown faces over there in the besieged city suddenly seem to be bathed in light. The worst could still be avoided.

20 March 2011

The sky looks like freshly washed clothes hung out to dry on the terrace. Khadija stands at the sink, a tall slim figure in her bronze velvet dress. She tells me about her daughters. She explains how she would go and wait for them every evening outside the factory gates. She did not want them to go to the demonstrations. 'They are all I have.... I was too scared they would be killed.' Her husband works as a night watchman. She remembers how she would block her door during the night and sleep with a knife under her pillow and a long stick beside her. Just in case.

She adjusts her beige headscarf with a wrinkled hand. A twinkle comes to her eyes. '*Erhal kulhum*!' she exclaims. *Let them all get out!* She bursts out laughing. There is not the faintest shadow of a cloud in the pure morning azure.

Paris

19 April 2011

A solidarity rally at the Trocadéro Human Rights Plaza... A young Syrian holds out a flag for me to carry.

Zenga zenga dar dar erhal erhal ya Bashaar!

Alley to alley, house to house – in mockery of one of Qadhafi's speeches – get out, get out Bashaar!

Slogans burst forth with the jubilation born of hope. They ring high up in the spring sky; they reverberate against the Palais de Chaillot façade in rhythmical echoes. The sunshine floods into the sea of flags where the TNC colours blend in as the crowd makes way to welcome the Libyan rally.

Echchaâb yurid isqat ennidhâm!

The people want the fall of the regime.

The same slogans ring from Tunis to Cairo, from Benghazi to Damascus and Sanaa. With a difference of one word or two… The wave is breaking, irresistible. No matter the price to pay.

Houria! Karama!

Freedom! Dignity!

La Goulette, north of Tunis

September 2011

After dark, the main street is aglow with lights and the decorative chains hanging from the terraces of the numerous popular eateries, fish restaurants and ice cream parlours. September is a hot month. Tunisians call this period *quweïl errumman,* the pomegranate siestas. Then the heat typically comes back with a vengeance, just when the fruit is ripe enough to be picked. Whole families, husbands and wives rolling buggies or holding their toddlers by the hand, strolling up and down, young men hanging out together, are all enjoying the festive atmosphere. After the months when unprecedented events began to unfold, they are going out to take in the new scenes of their lives, to keep track of the prospects looming at the horizon, or simply unwind.

On the ochre walls of the old karaka, not far from the harbour, traces of the spring exhibition remain. Photos of ordinary, everyday citizens were posted on many public buildings to emphasise that the formerly omnipresent portraits of the dictator were gone; the focus was now on the Tunisians. Wedding feasts are in full swing in the neighbouring reception halls, with loud rhythmical music playing late into the night. Ramadan was in August this year. Schools are starting very soon and time is running short to celebrate the newly-weds. Boys are merrily diving from the bridge into the canal, with loud splashes, not far from a wall, adorned with brightly coloured revolutionary graffiti. The fishermen will return at dawn and seize upon the momentary pause to try and catch their prey.

Tunis

4 September 2011

We go through the Belvedere park, then up the hill to Montfleury to visit M. at a clinic. Members of the staff are urgently calling for new donors to give blood. With the war casualties in Libya, supplies are running low. Najat walks into the room, a light figure in her loose black gown, passionate and eager to share her experiences. Her husband is here for treatment he could not have received in war-torn Libya. Fear overpowered her as they drove all the way here from Misrata. The journey was long, arduous and uncertain. Relief only came after they managed to cross the border point. Outside I can see several cars with Libyan plates stationed in the streets around the clinic building, some with the thick white pillows used to carry the injured still visible on the seats. Four members of her family have died as *chababs.* She remembers how all offices and businesses closed in February, when the revolt started. No salaries have been paid since then, but solidarity has worked and people have helped each other. She pauses in mid-sentence, as she invokes her fifteen-year-old son. The brilliant high-school student had never held a gun or a knife before. But he went out to fight, like the other men.

More and more cars, carrying TNC stickers or flags blowing in the wind from their windows, pass by everywhere in Tunis and in the suburbs. Thousands of people are entering the country every day, for medical reasons, or simply because of their fatigue and a need for a break after weeks of war.

6 September 2011

The word *thawra*, revolution, is omnipresent in the old medina. It is painted on the vividly coloured canvasses exhibited in a *madrasa* that has been turned into a cultural centre. It appears on bracelets of all styles and shades displayed for sale in an art gallery set up in one of the medina's old palaces. Che Guevara T-shirts are sold beside *kachabias* and *gandouras* in the souk. Crowds cheerfully jostle their way through the narrow alleys. A picket line bars all access to the Café M'rabet. A man tells us that they have been on strike for months but their boss will not hear of any dialogue. Then he kindly takes us to a carpet merchant's, where we walk up the stairs to the terraced roof. The view over the white-washed houses of Tunis under the noon sky is breathtaking. A clamour can soon be heard rising nearby, somewhere around the Kasbah. A demonstration... The police are holding a sit-in and protesting. *Tanjah etthawra...* Success to the Revolution, they are chanting. What were they doing during the Ben Ali years?

La Goulette, the Port of Tunis

9 September 2011

B. and the children arrive with fresh bread from the baker's round the corner, sobered after having seen a group of Salafis. Not a word was exchanged as the men passed with a self-righteous frown. The children now comment on their unfamiliar attire. Men simply did not grow beards before. Neither could women wear a *hijab*, let alone a *niqab,* to go to university or work. Recent glimpses of women wrapped up in thick black veils – previously unseen – wearing black gloves in the stifling heat, come to mind. Furtive visions... These are new sights for us.

In the afternoon, we sit under the shade of the tall, ageless eucalyptus trees at a café in La Marsa. The Beys used to have one of their residences here at the time of Ottoman rule. My friend E. mentions fears shared by some that the Islamist party is going to win the October election. It seems improbable to me. Islamists were so conspicuously absent from the streets last winter. Everyone spoke of a young generation of protesters claiming no connection with religious parties. On the other hand, the prospect of so many political parties running makes such a victory less unlikely. Over a hundred have emerged on the political scene in the past few months.

October 2011

Ever since January, we have looked forward to a different future, we have hoped for a new and better world, confident it was in the making. Liberty, dignity... We are swept along by a general sense of euphoria. Somehow we feel all this is bound to continue. How could it be otherwise?

The cartoonist 'Willis From Tunis' has drawn dozens of cats joyfully jumping into a big ballot box. Election day is drawing near. I print her cartoon and put it on my desk.

After the election.
Is this the end of a dream?

The victory of the Islamist party has left us disappointed, quite stunned. We sit by the window beside our laptops and the papers on the sofa. B. turns off the radio. Ever since the results were announced, he has kept bravely pointing out that those are the rules of democracy. It is now the opposition's responsibility to start preparing for the next elections, he says. 'What was the fuss all about?' E. moans. 'I suppose that's what a majority of people want and we have to accept it.' She goes on to express her anxiety about the future, democracy, and the status of women.

Paris

5 February 2013

1846, abolition of slavery… 1857, *Ahd el Aman* – the Pledge of Security – the rights of the citizen… 1861, the first written constitution… Pioneering dates. I read my notes for a talk on the Tunisian Revolution I am giving tomorrow in Montélimar, in the south of France.

I have searched the past for what could be a signal for hope, desperately trying to clear up the uncertainties now weighing upon us. Anything to obliterate the present, to turn it into a mere parenthesis on the way to democracy…

6 February 2013, 9 o'clock in the morning

I absently open my Facebook page. The words hit me like a slap in the face. I have to read them two or three times before reality sinks in. I immediately switch to Tunisian and French online newspapers. I have now forgotten everything about Montélimar. My notes and clothes are piled on the bed beside an empty suitcase.

Chokri Belaid, a highly respected secular opposition leader, has been assassinated. Shot dead an hour ago. He was leaving home as I was comfortably drinking my morning tea.

In the short distance between his doorstep and his car…

Chokri Belaid had no police protection. He only had his freedom of speech.

What is the use of my notes? What do they mean now? What is the point of going anywhere to talk about the revolution?

Belaid's widow's photo has now been posted on Facebook. The vision of Basma Khelfaoui holding up her arm in a sign of victory, marching in the street, will go round the world in a matter of hours, a symbol of courage and determination. Her pink coat and green scarf seem to defy the anonymous killers. She walks on, holding up her head, bravely looking in front of her.

I hastily slip a copy of Moncef Ouhaibi's 14 January poem in my folder. I will read it tonight in Montelimar in Belaid's memory before I speak about the past two years.

Tunis

8 February 2013

The whole country has ground to a halt after a call for a general strike. Hundreds of thousands of Tunisians take to the streets for Belaid's funeral.

His widow walks alongside his coffin to the cemetery. Thousands of women, some relatives and colleagues, and many ordinary citizens, follow her. Their presence marks a break with tradition. Gone are the days when women stayed away from the cemetery during burial ceremonies. 'This is the true Tunisia,' exclaims a young woman.

Tunisia

February 2013

Days later, everyone is still in shock, struck dumb by what is unprecedented violence. The last time such an event took place was in 1952 when trade union leader Farhat Hached was assassinated.

What has happened to the euphoria of 2011? Where has the enthusiasm gone? Unemployment is as high as ever. Who can afford meat and vegetables? The price of milk has doubled.

Echchaâb sâket, people keep silent… The thick black letters on the walls of the market square seem to blare out. Silent people… Mute, holding their breath, before another social explosion…

Ya hukûmat get ou, government get ou… The last letter is missing, as if the person who painted the slogan were stopped in mid-action. Was he suddenly short of paint or did he need more time to finish?

20 February 2013

You were so cheerful and full of hope, Soumaya. That was over a year ago… You serve us delicious hazelnut tea. You never used to wear a scarf. Over the years, you so often joked about your colleagues insidiously putting pressure on you to cover your head. This, although doing so was against the rules for teachers and those working in state administration… Some headmasters seemed to turn a blind eye. You consistently asserted your independence. You were always so confident. I have rarely if ever seen you with any head covering. This one is of an elegant blue with silver threads. You pause before you explain. 'Dressed as I am, no one will bother me in the street when I go to work.' The threats you leave unsaid, I can guess from your eyes.

You resume the conversation, telling me about the little seven-year-old girl in your class whose eyes look so sad. Her father is a fundamentalist and he will not allow her to attend any music or sports class. Nothing will make him change his mind. Neither you, the headmaster nor the way she turns around, staring at the others preparing to attend their next singing lesson…

21 February 2013

A large weapons cache has been discovered north of Tunis. We sit in front of the TV screen, mesmerised by the pictures, an endless show of all kinds of guns, sabres and knives, not to mention bombs and grenades. The camera stops a while on the black Salafi banners. Not a word to comment on what is shown. Just music, the kind you hear in a horror film… It is played over and over again.

A few days later

Driving across the Cap Bon and its wide expanses of green in springtime has always appealed to me. Every time I wonder about the white hamlets perched uphill, apparently remote from the rest of the world. On our way back, we are stopped at a roadblock as we enter Menzel Temime. Another one is posted outside the town. The police don't keep us waiting for too long. When we reach home, G. tells us a vehicle bearing a French registration plate has been found in the main square of a market town, three miles from here. It was full of weapons.

The following day, the paper runs the whole story. It turned out the owner of the car, a migrant worker who had come from Marseilles on holiday, was a hunter. He had left two or three shotguns on the backseat before going on an errand. On his return, he saw the crowd surrounding his vehicle, got scared and ran away.

23 February 2013

The police control entrances to Hammamet, the renowned seaside resort. They have done so ever since the Revolution. Dusk has fallen when we drive down the streets of what looks like a ghost town. Several hotels have closed because tourists are so scarce. The souvenir-shopkeepers will move mountains to catch the attention of the occasional holidaymakers passing. The restaurant where we stop is empty, except for one other table. Tunisians are philosophical and have a sense of humour. 'If things go on like this, even barbers will have to close down', the waiter comments in a bittersweet tone.

24 February 2013

Almost every evening there are debates on television, interviews of citizens in the streets eager to voice their anger and frustrations, a sign that they are not ready to give up. 'We want a new agenda', says a young woman in sports clothes just before starting her workout. 'Politicians in power keep moving chairs around and we, the people, are caught among the chair-legs', complains an old man. 'We no longer even watch TV', comments a mother and her daughter in unison. 'I am fed up. Fed up', exclaims a middle-aged man. 'And please don't cut what I said', he adds briskly.

In Tunis yesterday, demonstrators rallied after the new prime minister was appointed, chanting *Echchaâb yurîd qâtel Belaïd*... the people want the man who assassinated Belaid, denouncing the slow pace of the police investigation. And they will go on taking to the streets, as long as necessary, everybody tells me. They will go on demanding all the truth about the assassination, checking on the new constitution that is being drafted. They will not relent until the next elections are scheduled.

28 February 2013

One of the independent TV channels, el-Hiwar, has been in serious financial trouble for a while. A solidarity campaign was organised to raise money. Bunches of parsley were sold at 20 Tunisian dinars instead of the normal 350 millimes. People from all social backgrounds, rich and poor, stood in line to buy the precious herbs. The bunches sold out within an hour. A sign of hope.... The Tunisian people are still determined to stand up for their revolution, whatever the difficulties.

Tunis-Carthage International Airport

28 February 2013

In the departure lounge, the old pilgrims on their way to Jeddah have not changed. I have known them for countless years, the white cloths they wrap themselves in, their pensive countenances, and their peaceful smiles.

The young women now going on the pilgrimage have neither faces nor smiles. Not even fingers. They show nothing but cloth and gloves.

The little girl stands in front of her mother. She slightly tilts her head forward so that the woman can unfold a scarf over her tiny face and tie it behind her neck. The child then proudly turns to gaze at the world around her from behind the piece of cloth. Like her mother.

Outside on the tarmac, the planes line up before inscribing their silvery wake in the sky. Insidious changes in ways, manners... History has been on the move for over two years already. And many more will come.

Superb, a man who had just arrived from Libya appeared, a huge TNC flag thrown over his shoulders, one September morning at Carthage airport. Two years ago.

Splendid, two young women draped in one large Tunisian flag wept for joy as they held hands and embraced, on a January Saturday in Paris. Two years ago.

May 2013

Clouds endlessly scuttle across the sky, blown by the wind. Each day brings its lot of contradictory news.

Pictures are shown of the security forces injured while fighting the jihadists entrenched in the Chaambi mountain not far from Kasserine, where the revolution started in December 2010. One had his leg blown off and another lost his eyes. Could we have imagined that violence would erupt again in this way a year and a half ago, oblivious as we were of what could stand in the way of the revolution?

Still, Habib Kazdaghli, the dean of La Manouba Faculty of Arts, has been acquitted this month. In March 2012, he was accused of hitting two veiled students on what were, by all appearances, politically motivated charges. He always stood firm against allowing the *niqab* inside his Faculty, claiming that seeing students' faces was a necessity for pedagogical reasons. Several times the verdict of the trial was delayed. Throughout those months, he received wide support through petitions and rallies. The court's decision has proved that in the end justice can be done.

For over two years we have been living in a state of expectancy, with tension rising further and further towards a climax that seems out of reach. Or have we just behaved as impatient youths, forever obliterating the gap between human time and historical time? Perhaps all revolutions put their citizens on a razor's edge, demanding their constant commitment and vigilance for very long periods.

The Maghreb Since 1800

A Short History

KNUT S. VIKØR

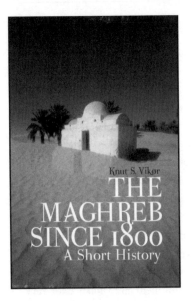

ISBN: 9781849042017
£16.00 / Paperback / 256pp

The Maghreb — the region that today encompasses Morocco, Algeria, Tunisia and Libya — is a region apart within the larger Muslim and Arab world. Today the focus of popular uprisings for democracy and participation, it underwent long periods of colonisation and anti-colonial nationalist resistance, both peaceful and militant. To understand the nature of today's developments in North Africa we need fully to appreciate the tumultuous history of the region and how its four discrete countries followed different trajectories, some marked by a continuity of social and political structures in both the colonial era and as independent states, while others were marked by sharp ruptures and violent struggles. These historical differences are still visible in the current era and tell us much about the societies in question.

This short history of the Maghreb surveys its development from the coming of Islam to the present day, but with greatest emphasis on the modern period from the early nineteenth century onwards. It follows the French protectorates, Morocco and Tunisia, and how their nationalist movements forged the independent states that followed; and it chronicles the wars of resistance and liberation in Algeria and Libya, and how these conflicts also marked their independence, with a long-running civil war in the former and the recent uprising against the Gaddafi regime in the latter.

'This accessible and timely history of the Maghreb offers a concise, readable analysis of key events in Algeria, Libya, Morocco, and Tunisia over the last two centuries. ... The result is a clear, balanced, and thoughtful discussion which adds insight and understanding to our knowledge of the region.'
— Ronald Bruce St John, historian of the Maghreb and author of *Libya: From Colony to Revolution*

WWW.HURSTPUBLISHERS.COM/BOOK/THE-MAGHREB-SINCE-1800

41 GREAT RUSSELL ST, LONDON WC1B 3PL
WWW.HURSTPUBLISHERS.COM
WWW.FBOOK.COM/HURSTPUBLISHERS
020 7255 2201

POETRY IN THE MAGHREB

Marcia Lynx Qualey

In my sleep I speak
a medley of languages
and animal calls
Abdellatif Laâbi, 'In Vain I Migrate', translated by Andre Naffis-Sahely

Great poetry, even when it is beholden to power, is a voice of dissent. This dissent need not be political; indeed, it is more often the dissent of beauty, insanity, individuality, or emotion. But from its place at the margins, poetry can occasionally move into the centre, where it gives voice and dress to the identity of a people. It echoes with particular possibility at times of cultural and political shifts: in 2010 and 2011, Abu al-Qasim al-Shabbi's 'Will to Life' took a prominent place in the public sphere when it shaped the revolutionary hopes of many in Tunisia and beyond. Other poetic expression followed.

But poetry must also grapple, particularly at times of change, with its relationship to power. This relationship does not extend only to the poetry's content, but also to its building blocks. After all, most poetry is made from a particular language, and each language has a relationship to power and dissent, centrality and margin. In the Maghreb, the roles of languages have shifted over time: Latin, Greek, and Phoenician each had their place. Arabic moved through North Africa and Spain as a medium of conquest, science, and art. French was a language of colonial power and visionary anti-colonial literature. Later, Modern Standard Arabic became a language of authentic 'Arab' expression while also being a tool to suppress freedoms for Arabic- and Tamazight-speaking peoples.

None of these languages is wholly distinct. Abdellatif Laâbi, one of the Maghreb's great living poets, crafts his works from several of them. His mother tongue is Moroccan Arabic; he has translated from Modern

Standard Arabic and co-translated from Tamazight; he writes his own poetry and prose in French.

As Laâbi and fellow Moroccan poet Mohammed Bennis have noted, languages are not fixed entities, but instead are live, interpenetrating bodies. In a 2001 interview with *Double Change*, Laâbi said, 'Even when I am writing in French, my Arabic language is there. There is a musicality in Arabic, and these words enter into my French texts.' In an essay from the same year, 'Dans le dialogue,' the Arabophone Bennis said, 'As a modern Arab poet, I am committed to French culture and its modernity. The French language was the home of a poetic revolution and it gave my Arabic language a poetic strength, more valuable than any of the other modern languages.'

Both Laâbi and Bennis chose to write in a language that was not his mother tongue: one in French and the other in Modern Standard Arabic. These choices have faced Maghrebi poets for centuries, as the region has been multilingual for all of written history. Since the end of direct colonial rule – 1951 (Libya), 1956 (Morocco and Tunisia), and 1962 (Algeria) – the Maghreb's four biggest nation-states have taken diverse linguistic paths.

Neither Laâbi nor Bennis chose to write in darija, or Moroccan Arabic. But this can hardly be considered a 'free' choice: the Maghrebi poetry that's canonised is rarely written in the language of everyday use. North Africa's Tamazight population has had an alphabet since at least the third century, but most North African writing has been done in the Punic, Greek, Arabic, and Latin alphabets.

There certainly are benefits to writing in a mother tongue, and many popular poets do compose lyrics and verse in Tamazight or colloquial Arabic. However, there are also ways to resist by moving between languages. Laâbi for one does not regret his chosen language. He said in a 2013 appearance in London that, 'To live in one culture, to speak only one language, is to live in a prison.'

Algeria: poetry and the enemy's tongue

The literary landscape of the Maghreb has long been a site of flux. In the past two thousand years, many different languages have washed over the Maghreb's shores and cities, among them: Greek, Latin, Phoenician, various Arabics, and French. Arabic brought the most significant and long-lasting changes, although French colonial rule also brought powerful change to language and literature, nowhere more than in Algeria.

Of all North Africa, Algeria had the longest and most affecting relationship with colonial Europe. For more than a hundred years, 1830 to 1954, Algeria was 'French Algeria'. The nation was not simply a colony under French rule; it was a 'new world' for hundreds of thousands of European immigrants. While Morocco and Tunisia were able to end direct French rule with relatively little violence, it took eight years of fierce war (1954–1962) to convince the French to end their Algerian occupation.

Before the French occupation, in 1820s Algeria, literacy rates were relatively high. According to Mary-Jane Deeb, writing in Helen Metz's *Algeria: A Country Study*, a French report authored just before the conquest estimated 'that in 1830 the literacy rate in Algeria was 40 per cent'.

Poets in early nineteenth century Algeria, in the final years of Ottoman rule, had many traditions to draw on. Algerian poetry was sometimes composed in Modern Standard Arabic, but also in colloquial Arabic or Tamazight. Authors often drew on Andalusian poetic conventions, and their works were sometimes put to music: hawzi, bedoui, and rai. Thanks to these songs, work by some late-Ottoman poets has remained in circulation, such as the poems composed by Mostefa Ben Brahim (1800–1867). From his 'Saddle Up, O Warrior!':

After I'd sent word to her back.   I saw my messenger come

As I saw the boy from far away   my mind flew off to him—
I lost patience & asked him   to tell his story right away!
He answered saying: 'Yes   I am the one who roams the desert
though yesterday I was heading   to the town when I saw
a crowd of young girls in a garden   who strutted along before me!
They looked like a swarm of doves   nesting on the roof of a palace!

Although the French set up educational and language institutions in the nineteenth century, the establishment of 'French Algeria' did not mean an immediate shift in poetic traditions. Colloquial and classical Arabic poetry remained a literary and cultural force, if a waning one.

But by the 1930s, a hundred years after the invasion, 'a Frenchified urban elite arose in Algeria', Pierre Joris and Habib Tengour write in their *Poems for the Millennium* anthology. The poets of this French-educated elite found new ways to wield the language that was meant to shape them into supportive French subjects. According to Joris and Tengour, Algerian writers in the early twentieth century created a Francophone literature that 'broke with colonial Algerianism to bear witness to the country's deep reality'.

However, this turning towards French also cut Algerian poets off from the larger conversations within Arabic poetry. Algerian poets thus stood 'outside the reworking and rethinking of the language of writing and deconstruction of forms that occurred in the Arab literature of their time', according to Joris and Tengour.

The struggle over an Algerian identity – French, Arab, Tamazight – also meant a struggle over language. During the battle over the fate of their country, many Algerian writers wrote in French. The Francophone poet, novelist, and short-story writer Mohammad Dib was born in Tlemcen in 1920 and published his debut novel in French in 1952. He was expelled by French authorities in 1959, during the French-Algerian war, and chose to spend his life in France. Through all that came later, Dib never released his claim on the French language. In his final interview, he said that 'as a writer, the passage from culture to culture becomes a strength, an advantage, because it sharpens the senses. It forces one to look more deeply into the hell hidden inside man, and that's a gain for literature.'

But Dib could not be called just a Francophone writer. He was raised on Arabo-Andalusian hawzi music, and read in French and English, particularly high modernist works, and the shape of his poetry reflects all of these influences. From his 'Guardian Shadow 1':

Fasten your doors
Women, bitter sleep
Will flow through your nerves,
Water, sand have erased
The trace of your steps,
Nothing belongs to you.

Yet despite the existence of a small Frenchified elite, not many Algerians learned to read and write during the more than 130-year occupation. The

French established schools in Algeria, but these were primarily for European children. When the French finally decamped from Algeria in 1962, the adult Algerian literacy rate had dropped from 40 to around 10 per cent. Most of these adults were now literate not in Arabic, but in French.

By 1962, the French language had penetrated most aspects of Algerian city life. However, Algerian linguist Lameen Souag said in a recent email interview that 'much of the expansion of French among Algerians actually dates to the period immediately after independence' when mass education became a reality. Popular education began in French, he said. This is because 'at independence, most of the small minority of literate people, who would become the teachers, had been educated in French in French schools...and were illiterate in Arabic – thanks to "French Algeria" and its policies'.

In this environment – the end of colonialism and the sudden expansion of French literacy – battles over power played out in battles over the use of language. In the early post-colonial years, a number of authors attempted to stop writing in French. The author Assia Djebar made films for a decade before she returned to French prose. Other writers, such as the poet Malek Haddad, silenced themselves almost entirely.

During the 1960s and 1970s, Algerian language and literature was full of fiery attempts to re-imagine Algerian selfhood. A number of authors were influenced by Malek Haddad's 1969 essay 'Les zéros tournent en rond', in which he discredited creative writing in French. Haddad's essay, together with anti-colonial feeling and the government's Arabisation programme, which privileged Modern Standard Arabic, both improved the position of Arabic and ultimately silenced many authors.

Many Algerians held onto French. Poet, playwright, and novelist Kateb Yacine (1929-1989) claimed his power by claiming the French language, calling it 'war booty'. Yet Yacine did not yoke himself to French. Beginning in the 1970s, he began writing theatre in Algerian Arabic. This tradition has continued, and colloquial theatre in Algeria has been an area of vibrant artistic life.

Yet while culture was officially Arabised, writing in French continued to remain popular among Algerian authors more than anywhere else in the Maghreb. There are many reasons. There were few Arabic-language publishing opportunities within Algeria. The nation was largely cut off from other Arab countries. Modern Standard Arabic was poorly taught in Algerian schools. Also, during the 'Black Decade' of the 1990s, a number of authors were killed or fled Algeria, and had to write in exile.

'Many authors were murdered, many fled', critic Nadia Ghanem said in a recent interview. This 'has created a vacuum, and the transmission of the banner to the next generation has been greatly interrupted. I wonder what effect this has had on the young who perhaps want to publish in the traditional way, but have seen at close quarters that if you write and upset a party you will end up imprisoned, tortured, shot dead, made to disappear.' So French continues to have a large space in Algerian literature. As Ghanem notes, French literature is exportable, and there is 'some money in it and a future for a writer'.

Some Algerian novelists have found Arabic literary audiences outside Algeria – Waciny Laredj, Ahlam Mostaghenmi, Tahar Wattar, Abdelhamid Ben Haddouka, Zohor Wanissi. Some, like Rachid Boujedra, have worked in both French and Arabic. But finding an Arabic audience abroad has been rarer for Algerian poets, and Algerian education has not energised the teaching of Modern Standard Arabic to develop new readers.

Of late, some young authors have found their voice in Tamazight languages. More than a quarter of Algerians are Tamazight speakers, and Tamazight was finally recognized as an official language in 2002. Kabyles represent the largest Tamazight group, and Lameen Souag says that he has noticed 'the presence of a small but rapidly growing Kabyle literature.'

Pierre Joris and Habib Tengour, in *Poems for the Millennium* (2012), saw hopeful signs on the Algerian poetry scene. In particular, they noted a rebirth of public poetry events, which have been 'creating spaces for exchanges beyond language divisions'. These language divisions – the medley of languages – can profit poetry by allowing authors to stand simultaneously outside and inside. But they work only if there is space for poets to write, from the margins, without fear.

Morocco: Interconnected tongues

The landscape of Moroccan poetry also underwent considerable linguistic shifts in the twentieth century. Although French became a serious force, particularly among the elites, Morocco was – unlike Algeria – able to maintain some distance from its colonising power. The country did not become a 'protectorate' until 1912, and even then local elites maintained positions of power. While tens of thousands of European colonists did move to Morocco, this colonial project was not on the same scale as the hundreds of thousands who moved their lives, schools, and businesses to Algeria.

Before European colonialism, Moroccan poets were strongly marked by their proximity to Andalusia and Andalusian poetic traditions. The early twentieth century ruptured some of these traditions, but poetry in French, colloquial Arabic, and in Modern Standard Arabic all developed and grew. Indeed, scholar Claude Reynaud has credited the depth of contemporary Moroccan poetry to the interplay of French, Arabic, Berber, and oral and written forms—but also to a poetry magazine, *Souffles (Breaths)*.

Souffles was founded in 1966 by Abdellatif Laâbi. The magazine was closed in 1972, and Laâbi jailed for nearly a decade. But it was soon followed by Mohammed Bennis's magazine *al-Thaqafa al-Jadida* (*New Culture*) in 1974. These magazines both were formed in the tumultuous years after Morocco's King Hassan II declared, 'there is no danger greater for the State than that of self-styled intellectuals. You would have been better off remaining illiterate.' Although *Souffles* was Francophone, it distanced itself from the Francophone writing that was directed at French readers of the colonial power. *Souffles* influenced many Moroccan writers, including Rachida Madani. Her collection, *Tales of a Severed Head,* speaks directly to the power of words and of authors at the margin:

I am tied in this garden by thousands of vines
by the venomous perfume of lovely sentences
more than by my actions.

According to Bennis and others, the post-colonial state harassed and suffocated the 'self-styled intellectuals' of Moroccan poetry. In a 2007 interview with Camilo Gomez-Rivas, Bennis said that trying to work within the cultural establishment was 'a nightmare'. It was only once he was outside that Bennis was able to found a publishing house, Toubkal, as well as his magazine. Bennis said that he resisted state culture, in part, by preserving language. He told Gomez-Rivas:

The poet is the keeper of what he has received from the old poets, so that their legacy is not lost. Through his work, the poet transmits the poetry to those coming after him. We give him the language for safekeeping so that he preserves it, but not in the traditional meaning of the word. To preserve here means to allow it to live. And he transmits it to those coming after him. By which I don't mean to say that a poem from the time of Abu Tammam or Badr Shakir al-Sayyab stays as it is. No. What must be preserved is the spirit of the poem, the spirit of creativity in the poem.

Poetry, language, and meaning are thus saved. When 'we watch the news', he says, 'all newscasts have the same language, whereas poems do not all have the same language'. In this light, language draws its meaning from its individual forms. But Bennis also laments how Moroccan poetry is split between many languages, and this 'division is multiplied with the role of Tamazight and with the spread of writing in multiple languages in Morocco or by Moroccans abroad, which include English, Italian, and Spanish' and other languages. These divisions create margins upon margins, making it difficult to 'preserve meaning' and to have a national poetic conversation.

Yet each of these languages can be a site of creative resistance. Poet Ali Sadki Azayku published first in French, then later in Tamazight, but in Arabic characters. In his 1978 poem, 'Mother Tongue', he wrote in French:

My tongue is being slowly strangled
To death,
And yet lives on,
Speaks tirelessly to those who cover their ears
So as not to hear.
Thirst should be slaked
Amazigh is my mother tongue
Rejected by everyone.

The poem ends:

Amazigh is my mother tongue
It longs to break the wall of silence
To set hearts ablaze
And make them flame like stars united
In the heavens above.

Thirty-some years after Azayku wrote the poem, Tamazight has become a small but thriving space, particularly since the creation of the Institut Royal de la Culture Amazighe (IRCAM) in 2003.

Although fragmented, the Moroccan poetry scene is vibrant: in Arabics, French, Tamazight, and other languages, in Morocco and abroad. Indeed, Moroccan poets and authors have been producing work of global interest. There is Laâbi, who received the Prix Goncourt in 2009; Francophone Tahar Benjelloun, who is perhaps the most widely read Arab author internationally; Mohammed Bennis, who has won a number of regional and international prizes. There are many more: Charni's *Tales of a Severed Head* was recently translated from French into beautiful English by Marilyn Hacker (2012). Medhi Akhrif received a prize for African poetry in 2011. Fouad Laroui, who writes his poetry in Dutch, won the 2013 Prix Goncourt de la Nouvelle.

There are still divisions between Morocco's several languages, which are also markers of class and power. Yet there is great poetic possibility in this cacophony of margins.

Tunisia: red lines, parallel cultures

Latin and Punic texts from Carthage, now a suburb of Tunis, are among the earliest known works of Maghrebi literature. Although these works had wide influence in North Africa and beyond, twentieth and twenty-first century Tunisian poetry has not had the same international influence.

Tunisia, like other nations of the Maghreb, was part of the Ottoman Empire until its invasion by France. Themes of independence and freedom came to poetry soon after the 1881 invasion. Abu al-Qasim al-Shabbi (1909–1934), who wrote in Modern Standard Arabic, is perhaps the Tunisian poet with the largest reach. Although he died very young, his work resonated and remained popular; one of his poems was turned into the country's national anthem.

As in Morocco and Algeria, a number of Francophone writers came to the fore after World War II, during the fight against colonial France. Poetic revival began at the same time as poets grappled with how to talk about their country. In *Trends and Movements in Modern Arabic Poetry,* Salma Khadra Jayussi suggests that for a while Arabic poetry in Tunisia was at an *impasse*, as education was mostly in French, and Arabic poetry remained stuck in old forms.

But, following Tunisia's independence, schooling improved both in Arabic and in French. There was a rush of experimentation: with colloquial language, with 'nonmetrical and free poetry', and other forms. Salah Garmadi (1933–1982) was one of the experimenters. He published a volume of poems in colloquial Tunisian Arabic, *Living Flesh,* and another in French, *Our Ancestors the Bedouins.* He also wrote in Modern Standard Arabic and translated French poetry into Arabic, and co-founded *Alif* magazine (1970-1982) with Lorand Gaspar. According to Joris and Tengour, Garmadi did not believe in silencing any of the languages; he declared: 'to a deathly silence I prefer the rift, and to the mute mouth, even as little as a murmur'.

In his 'Counsel for My Family After my Death', which Garmadi wrote in Arabic and translated into French, the poet rejoices in living language and shuns the banalities of life:

Should I one day die among you
but will I ever die
do not recite over my corpse
verses from the Qur'an
but leave that to those whose business it is
do not promise me two acres of Paradise
for I was happy on one acre of land

However, the poetic climate had already begun to stagnate under Habib Bourgiba, Tunisia's first post-colonial ruler. When the popular poet Saghir Oulad Ahmed composed his poem 'Nashid al-Ayam al-Sitta' ('The Anthem of the Six Days') in 1984, he was sacked from his job and imprisoned on charges of failing to pay alimony. Oulad Ahmed's first collection was banned under Bourgiba, and wasn't published until 1987, when Zine El Abidine Ben Ali came into power after a coup that ousted Bourgiba. However, any opening in poetic possibilities was short-lived.

'During Ben Ali's time, it didn't matter if you wrote in French or English or Arabic', Tunisian poet Inas Abbassi told me. 'You could not approach red lines, even if you didn't have readers. They would read your work and judge you. I remember one writer used the number seven ironically and as a result he spent a few months in prison.'

During the Ben Ali years, novel-writing grew very quiet, although poets were able to work a little more freely. Oulad Ahmed, writing in Modern Standard Arabic and largely distributing his work informally, struck a popular chord. According to Tunisian critic Mohamed-Salah Omri, Oulad Ahmed was part of a parallel culture, a shadow that existed alongside the official state-sanctioned culture. He was inspired by the *saalik* poetry movement of the sixth century, which championed the rights of the poor over the rich. 'I look for another relationship with language', a sentiment that comes out in 'The Will':

Verily, my nationalism . . .
What a heavy 'verily' to start that Roman sentence!
But you are sentenced to use such words and bother about
grammar, even with your mouth full! Even if you lose a tooth
over them. Even if you stand, screaming in the desert:
'Verily, no reader am I!'

Although there are some Francophone Tunisian poets – among them a number in the diaspora, like Amina Said – most Tunisian poetic production has happened in Arabic. French poetry is decreasing, and what with the youngest up-and-coming poets, there is also a new wave of Tunisian poetry in English. Immediately after Ben Ali stepped down in January 2011, after the country-wide demonstrations that began the 'Arab Spring', there was a wave of straightforward protest poetry. Whether Tunisian poetry can stand on its feet, and develop new and vibrant langauge, will depend on how individual poets can collaborate to share their voices.

Libya: reaching out to the world

Libya, like Tunisia, was one of the literary and scholarly centres of the ancient world. While most of these connections have been ruptured, the country's oral poetic tradition 'stretches back to the beginning of time and it has never stopped nourishing the country's spiritual inclination', according to Libyan-American poet Khaled Mattawa.

Italian colonial rule of Libya was relatively short-lived, but nonetheless physically and morally destructive. After the Italian-Turkish War of 1911–1912, Italy seized control of Libya. In the early decades of colonisation, around 150,000 Italians settled in the country, a population that swelled to about 20 per cent of the nation's total. Meanwhile, many of Libya's Bedouins, about half of the population, were killed either directly or through disease or starvation after they were resettled into camps.

The Italians were strong censors. But nonetheless, in the early twentieth century, Libyans began to gain access to European and contemporary Arabic literature. However, because of colonial-era censorship, most of the great Libyan poets were exiled to Egypt and elsewhere in the Arab world. Beginning in 1943, after a little more than three decades of Italian rule, Libya was placed under Allied control. It was 1947 when Italy officially relinquished its 'claim' to the country and 1951 when Libya became the first North African state to gain its independence. That was when newspapers and other print materials sprang up, through which authors circulated their short stories and poems. The 1960s and early 1970s are seen as the golden age of contemporary Libyan literature.

But things began to change after Moammar Gaddafi took power in 1969. Publishing outlets were shut down. In 1974, newspapers were nationalised. In 1977, all remaining publishers were merged into a single government-owned house. And by 1980, the majority of the country's poets and writers were in prison, although a number of writers were released from prison in 1988. In the early 1990s, there were no independent newspapers or magazines, and books still had to be submitted to a censor prior to publication, but censorship laws were loosened somewhat, leading to a new flowering of poetic expression.

Ashur Etwebi, born in 1952, is one of a few poets who weathered the Gaddafi years in Libya, and one of only a few to have a collection translated and published in English: *Poems from above the Hill: Selected Poems of Ashur Etwebi*. Many of his poems move through nature; the humans are often mute, as for example in 'Of solitude and a few other matters':

A woman without desire
her stone roses, sumptuous
her breasts, two salted rivers

her face, ambiguous cruelty
her belly, planes, horses, and bulls
in her arms the days sleep white
white like the sun
      the white
      sun

Most Libyan poetry that's been written down is in Modern Standard Arabic. But spoken-word poetry is often in colloquial. There is, however, a growing interest in languages other than classical Arabic. 'While collo-quial has been used in Libya for a long time in folk or traditional poetry, which enjoys a huge popularity, English and Tamazight language usage is growing, and the latter is expected to enjoy an interesting revival after decades of being banned by the Gaddafi regime', says Libyan poet, transla-tor, and blogger Ghazi Gheblawi. 'There is also an expectation that more second generation expat Libyans will prefer to write their works in Eng-lish, but this is yet to be seen.'

Already, celebrated poet Khaled Mattawa writes in English. Mattawa has won, among other accolades, an Academy of American Poets award, the PEN Award for Poetry in Translation in 2003 and 2011, and two Pushcart prizes. It was Mattawa who helped organise the first ever Tripoli International Poetry Festival, which took place in April 2012. It was perhaps the first international literary festival to bring important world poets to Libya; hopefully many more such events will follow.

Across the Maghreb, the immediate post-colonial era was a fruitful one for poetry. And the Arab Spring too has had its own impact. In the last two years, a lot of poetry has been written: much of it functional, to express a particular political viewpoint. Some literature has been pulled out of desk drawers – like that of International Prize for Arabic Fiction-shortlisted Tunisian novelist Houcine El Oued – and more is being written daily and shared in newspapers and online. Perhaps what will matter for poetry's development as much as the climate for free speech is finding places to share it. Print magazines – like *Souffles* – are not likely to rise again in the same way. But finding spaces to develop and share words, such as Morocco's Dar Al-Ma'mûn, a heaven for poets and translators located near Marrakesh, will be necessary for poetry's future.

Politics and Power in the Maghreb

Algeria, Tunisia and Morocco from Independence to the Arab Spring

MICHAEL J. WILLIS

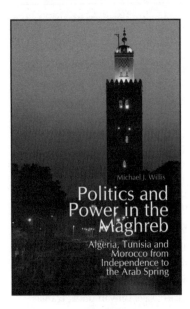

ISBN: 9781849042000

£29.99 / Hardback / 320pp

The overthrow of the regime of President Ben Ali in Tunisia on 14 January 2011 took the world by surprise. The popular revolt in this small Arab country and the effect it had on the wider Arab world prompted questions as to why there had been so little awareness of it up until that point. It also revealed a more general lack of knowledge about the surrounding western part of the Arab world, or the Maghreb, which had long attracted a tiny fraction of the outside interest shown in the eastern Arab world of Egypt, the Levant and the Gulf.

This book examines the politics of the three states of the central Maghreb — Algeria, Tunisia and Morocco — since their achievement of independence from European colonial rule in the 1950s and 1960s. It explains the political dynamics of the region by looking at the roles played by various actors such as the military, political parties and Islamist movements and addresses issues such as Berber identity and the role played by economics, as well as how the states of the region interact with each other and with the wider world.

'History, culture and geography have set North Africa apart from the rest of the Arab and Mediterranean worlds. Yet it would be difficult to find three more different countries than Morocco, the conservative monarchy, "revolutionary" Algeria, and "moderate" Tunisia — particularly in light of the Arab Spring of 2011. Drawing on more than two decades of living and work experience in the Maghreb, Michael Willis has crafted a brilliant guide to the ever-changing culture, society and politics of this critical part of the world. It is the best book on the subject by far, and confirms Willis's reputation as the foremost authority on the comparative politics of North Africa in the English-speaking world.' — Eugene Rogan, author of *The Arabs: A History*

WWW.HURSTPUBLISHERS.COM/BOOK/POLITICS-AND-POWER-IN-THE-MAGHREB

41 GREAT RUSSELL ST, LONDON WC1B 3PL
WWW.HURSTPUBLISHERS.COM
WWW.FBOOK.COM/HURSTPUBLISHERS
020 7255 2201

INVISIBLE INTERZONE

Julia Melcher

The lives of the exiles in Tangier pointed up the world as it exists as absurd: exile is perhaps a distorting mirror held up to reality.

Iain Finlayson, Scottish writer and biographer, and author of

Tangier: city of the dream (1992)

Tangier: a city of many legends, myths and dreams. A gate between different worlds: real and unreal, seen and unseen, magic and sometimes even tragic. In the middle of the twentieth century, the International Zone of Tangier, located at the Strait of Gibraltar, not only guarded the passage to Europe and the Mediterranean Sea but also embodied a sanctuary for outcasts, for people living on the margins, for adventurers and fugitives from Western societies. Artists, criminals, lost souls and sensation seekers found a home in a city they never really belonged to. Some of them sought freedom from American puritan morals and laws, some sought inspiration in the exotic and oriental environment of Morocco, some longed for sexual adventures, while others just fled from legal prosecution or financial ruin. 'On all sides you see men washed up here in hopeless, dead-end situations, waiting for job offers, acceptance checks, visas, permits that will never come. All their lives they have drifted with an unlucky current, always taking the wrong turn. Here they are. This is it. Last stop: the Socco Chico of Tangier,' wrote William S. Burroughs in his short story collection called *Interzone*, the short form of International Zone which he used to refer to his fictional version of Tangier. In this short scene, Burroughs describes the atmosphere of the Medina as well as the status of many of the expatriates who were stranded there. They all found refuge in a place that belonged to Western powers in name only, where they were tolerated by the natives, safe from their past deeds, lulling themselves into the timeless workings of an unreal city, a political non-zone, an Interzone where the boundaries between reality and dream constantly blurred. Due to the sheer unlimited possibilities of intoxication and sexual mergence, enshrouded in mists of *kif*, and due to the hidden but solid line that Tanjawis drew between their native place and the foreigners who invaded and inhabited it, Tangier hosted many invisible creatures with invisible desires and goals.

What is the origin of the dropout utopia of Interzone, where these invisible creatures dwelled? Tangier was declared an International Zone in 1923, while the rest of Morocco had been divided between Spain and France since 1912. The International Zone was established to neutralise the colonial competition over the city by European powers who, under the pressure of American intervention, declared the city a free port that was administered by an assembly of eight nations and representatives of the two most important religious groups in Tangier, Islam and Judaism. However, the American government under President Roosevelt intervened in the negotiations mainly out of interests that primarily focused on a dominant position within the North African trade economy and not so much on a mutual agreement with the other European states that formed the assembly. Thus, the US not only refused to join the city council but also insisted that US citizens living in Tangier were not subject to Moroccan law and taxes until 1956, when Morocco finally regained its independence. The political solution of establishing the International Zone at this important economic hub additionally served as a means of concealing imperial interests. A treacherous form of colonialism indeed – as the freedom such a place promised only came into existence by means of colonial suppression and by taking away freedom from others. The dodgy expatriate freedom of the city only existed within the framework of a legal vacuum. But still, freedom was the flagship of Tangier, the utopian honeypot round which the various outlaws hummed like bees.

Amongst those honey-seekers were prominent literary figures, such as Paul and Jane Bowles, William S. Burroughs, Alfred Chester, Tennessee Williams, Djuna Barnes, Brion Gysin, Jack Kerouac and Allen Ginsberg. Yet their cosmopolitan attitudes and hunger for adventure were not able to conceal their blindness towards a culture which they visited but never fully understood.

In 1954 William S. Burroughs, inspired by Bowles's *The Sheltering Sky* and *Let It Come Down,* fled the United States towards Tangier after a series of inconvenient incidents. Apart from his habitual abuse of morphine and associated criminal record, the accidental shooting of his wife Joan in Mexico

City caused him to seek friendlier climes across the Atlantic. Additionally, Burroughs's quest through the South American Amazon for the mythical drug Yage had proved rather anticlimactic and Burroughs, equipped with 'an insatiable appetite for the extreme and sensational, for the morbid, slimy and unwholesome', yearned for more.

Wherever he went, William Lee (Burroughs's literary and autobiographical alter ego) took his own personal junkie hell with him. This also applied to the first three years of his residence in Tangier, where he mostly spent his days in a shabby hotel room, lying on his bed feeling sick for the next shot, celebrating the vicious routines of an addict. At home in the US, his amorous advances had been rejected by Allen Ginsberg, his literary fellow, and Burroughs suffered badly from the feeling of being unwanted. He sought physical and intellectual closeness with Ginsberg but only found that his overwhelming desire for proximity was too much for the younger man. In order to flee from his legal and moral responsibilities and also from his lovelornness, Burroughs drained the very last supplies of Eukodol, a morphine-based synthetic painkiller that was, by that time, illegal everywhere else but in Tangier, from the city's pharmacies. At Dutch Tony's, a shabby little hot-sheet hotel that also rented out rooms to permanent lodgers, he settled down to numb his emotional pain in ever increasing doses. There he also regularly met his Spanish lover Kiki, who came at around eight o'clock every day. Kiki offered Burroughs's tormented soul a brief span of pleasure, and the older man used to enjoy the boy's regular company. Unlike many other homosexual expats, Burroughs did not indulge in the habit of frequently engaging the services of hustlers for sexual adventure. He was once introduced into the boys' scene of Tangier by a man he refers to as Don Cotton. According to Burroughs, Cotton paid only sixty cents for two boys to satisfy his voyeurism, and on Burroughs's asking why they were so cheap, he simply said: 'They are hungry.' Burroughs, disgusted by the whole scene, stated that he felt like 'sort of a dirty old man'. He later knitted the experience into the sequential fabric of *The Naked Lunch*, his seminal novel mostly set in an imaginary Tangier, in which political parties and drug dealers fight over power and control. In fact, he used many of the images of sexual and colonial exploitation that he encountered in North Africa into the novel, but transferred it to the fictional Interzone. Burroughs's aim was never really to criticise Western practices and acts of colonialism in his novel, as he was more concerned with deconstructing the Western system of morals and state control. His literary vision partly approximates the paranoid sexual and violent fantasies of the desperate and misanthropic junkie he actually was, but also reveals a political vision that, in later years, was considered to have 'social value' and thus saved the book from banishment.

Nevertheless, for the first three years in Tangier, Burroughs's excessive drug abuse was causing him a severe writer's block, or perhaps vice versa, which he blamed instead on his regular encounters with Kiki: 'God damn it, every time I get ideas for writing, I am occupied with a boy. Or maybe it's the other way around … hmm.' He only began writing in 1957, after he finally rid himself of Eukodol. Still, his writing habits turned out to be much more chaotic than his junkie habits. His fragmentary thoughts were written down on scattered sheets of paper that used to lie around on his hotel room floor, and he needed the help of his friends Allen Ginsberg and Jack Kerouac to put his vision into readable order. The apparent mess Burroughs created was part of the literary cut-up technique that he had developed with the painter Brion Gysin, who had initially invented the method for his paintings and photo collages, but also used it in his own writings.

Jack Kerouac, who came to Tangier in February 1957, catalogued the loose sheets of paper and arranged them in proper order. But he did not stay for long as he found it difficult to adapt to the Moroccan climate and cuisine. Thus, after a couple of weeks of indigestion, he returned to the States and passed the burden on to Allen Ginsberg. Ginsberg spent some weeks there with his new lover Peter Orlovski, which eventually caused jealous tantrums on Burroughs's part, or at best his complete ignoring of the third man. Aptly observed, Ginsberg later wrote about his friend's exile: 'The most loathsome types produced by the land of the free are represented in the American Colony of Tangier.'

During his years in Tangier Burroughs was named 'El Hombre Invisible' by the natives, because he had made it his habit to notice other people long before they noticed him and to silently disappear around the nearest corner. In this manner, he was able to vanish whenever it suited him. He paid specific attention to the Arab population of the city who, as he thought, usually took advantage of inexperienced and wealthy travellers. Many of them were luring visitors into guided city tours and various other kinds of trade, demanding a fare for the invasion of the Interzone. Burroughs, familiar with their local business, avoided them whenever possible. In fact, he avoided Arabs in general, and made his attitude towards them quite clear: 'What's all this old Muslim culture shit? One thing I have learned. I know what Arabs do all day and all night. They sit around smoking cut weed and playing some silly card game. And don't ever fall for this inscrutable oriental shit like Bowles puts down. They are just a gabby, gossipy, simple minded lazy crew of citizens.'

Burroughs's dislike for Arabs and Arabic culture turned into hostile behaviour. When he showed Kerouac through the city, passing a group of Tanjawis, he muttered: 'Just push 'em aside like little pricks.' Like many travellers from Europe and America, he shared Orientalist views on the nature of Arabs, and most of Burroughs's biographers note that he did not seem to show much interest in Moroccan culture and language at all, or at least, that he did not show the same enthusiasm and curiosity that Paul Bowles addressed towards the native culture of Morocco. Arabs, it seems, become invisible subjects in Burroughs' narratives just as they did in his everyday life. He did not want to be seen by them and equally, he did not want to see or acknowledge them, particularly not in his literary experiments. His focus lay on the unreal nature of Tangier, on the possibilities of a city that gave him the opportunity to escape the state control and bigotry of the US, a place where he could express his homosexuality. Burroughs only made some distant observations about Arab culture and recorded them in some of his autobiographical notes and short stories. Those observations capture the Orientalist spirit of the foreign settlers, who on the one hand longed for the exotic utopia of Morocco but on the other very much despised Maghrebi culture: 'I talked with an American psychoanalyst who is practicing in Casablanca. He says you can never complete analysis with an Arab. Their superego structure is basically different. Perhaps you can't complete analysis with an Arab because he has no sense of time. He never completes anything. It is interesting that the drug of Islam is hashish, which affects the sense of time so that events, instead of appearing in an orderly structure of past, present and future, take on a simultaneous quality, the past and future contained in the present moment.'

Although Burroughs made use of this blurring of time structure in his narratives, as did Gysin in his paintings, he didn't analyse this American analyst's statement, taking for granted that Arabs are different, inferior, underdeveloped in comparison to western Nazarenes.

Paul Bowles came to Tangier to escape the homophobic climate of the United States in the 1940s. He was also curious about Oriental cultures and found a good deal of inspiration for his novel *The Sheltering Sky* and short stories like *Tea on the Mountain* or *The Time of Friendship* in the remoteness and silence of his exile in the Moroccan desert. Even though Bowles strove to build up friendships with Moroccans and fostered artistic exchange with writers and painters such as Ahmed Yacoubi, Mohamed Mrabet and Mohamed Choukri, he never fully crossed the invisible boundary between himself and his Maghrebi friends. Bowles wrote about a 'self-imposed non-being' in his essays. According to Allen Hibbard, who wrote Bowles's biography, the writer preferred to hide his real intentions and to remain uninvolved in the lives of others. Like Burroughs, he often sought to remain unseen, invisible. However, the contrary was the case; not only was he an object of invisibility, but the very culture he claimed to study and write about remained opaque to him. All his life, in fact, Bowles lived on the intellectual margins of the subjects and themes he so vividly depicted, as a silent observer, emotionally remote and definitely not free from Orientalist thought and perception. Ralph Coury compares Bowles's attitude and social performance to that of an 'intellectualised non-being', a term that refers to many of his fictional characters as well, who often fail to acknowledge their own imperial worldviews and the impossibility of reconciling West and East under those cognitive and intellectual premises. Many of them die a violent death in the desert or experience some other form of existential loss. Bowles repeatedly expressed the dilemma of the impossibility of communicating and translating culture in many of his narratives; however, he never solved the problem for himself as long as he lived in Tangier. And even though he has been widely praised as a cultural mediator and critic of colonial practice, he is now also seen as an enforcer and circulator of Orientalist discourse. In some of his interviews he stated his personal views of the Moroccans quite openly, views that contradict the image of the author that has been established so far: 'I don't think we are likely to get to know the Moslems very well, and I suspect that if we should we would find them less sympathetic than we do at present. And I think the same applies to their getting to know us. At the moment, they admire us for technique. I don't think they could find more than that compatible. Their culture is essentially barbarous, their mentality that of a purely predatory people.'

This does not sound like the curious and benevolent Bowles hailed as a mediator between cultures by European, American and Moroccan critics alike. Neither does it sound like the Bowles who admired Moroccan art and tried to imitate the magical and timeless structure of Arabic folk tales in his short stories. The tone of Bowles's critics has changed, therefore, as becomes evident in Abdallah Laroui's harsh comment on the writer in his role as a translator of Moroccan literature and music: 'All folklore entails a centre and periphery. Paul Bowles makes a Moroccan speak into a tape recorder and believes that he is capturing a most authentic way of life that a Moroccan lives, but what he is capturing is nothing but his own fantasy. The empty time, the zero degree of existence that he imagines he detects in his subject, are in reality his own.' And here, Bowles falls prey to the Orientalist illusion of discovering an entirely different culture and translating it into Western context. Maybe there is nothing that has to be translated, because it can be just taken and left as it is, but maybe it also depends on the perspective of the translator and his vision of the object of translation.

What did Bowles see, and what remained unseen in his vision of Morocco and Moroccans, of Tangier and the Tanjawis? Did his desire to become invisible, like Burroughs's ability to vanish, simply grow out of the wish to remain distant from a culture that he regarded as savage and disorderly, worth examining with a hunger for sensation and exotic adventure but not worth understanding in all its differences and ambiguities? He was close to Moroccan culture, but his biased eye and his understanding eye did not look in the same direction, and so he writes: 'The sky trembles and the earth is afraid, and the two eyes are not brothers.'

While Paul Bowles and William Burroughs were actively endeavouring to gain invisibility, Jane Bowles involuntarily slowly faded away. Even though she had chosen her life as an expat at her husband's side, she struggled with her inability to feel at home in Tangier. Additionally, she suffered from a disease known by many Western women who tried to step outside the trodden paths of the accepted models of femininity and who were badly prepared for doing so by the dominant system of education. She tried to ease the pains of her disease, known as depression combined with anxiety disorder, with alcohol and drugs, which only made the condition worse. While Paul cut his own path through the silence and seclusion of the Moroccan desert, Jane fled into neurosis in order to counteract the feeling of panic the very same silence and seclusion caused her. Paul, mostly self-reliant and satisfied with his life in Tangier, sometimes failed to notice how his wife struggled with her ambiguous feelings towards the place that somehow antagonised her loyalty towards him. She desperately tried to feel at home in Tangier, but found it difficult to find friends and love amongst either expats or natives.

Jane was a creative woman, one who did not conform to the expectations of her own society. Like many women, she had been brought up to believe that there was something entirely wrong with her because of that. Feelings of insecurity were natural reactions to this form of socialisation. These feelings did not leave her when she met her husband Paul, a kindred spirit, and did not leave her when she followed him into the exotic exile where Western mores did not seem to count so much. Where Paul found himself as a writer, she lost herself. This deterred her from following her own creative path, and ended in a never-ending writer's block. She constantly hid her own talent behind the fear that she might not be as good as Paul. She kept herself submissive, dependent and demanding in response to the love she so desperately needed but could not find, neither with Paul nor with her lesbian girlfriends. For a while, she kept herself busy in an unhappy relationship with a Moroccan woman named Cherifa, to whom she gave all her money and her house, and whom Paul suspected of being a witch who had cast a spell on his unreasonable wife. Especially when Jane suffered her first stroke, Paul saw this theory confirmed and accused Cherifa of poisoning his wife. The stroke was more likely caused by Jane's heavy drinking habit in combination with the medication against high blood pressure she used to take in irregular doses. Jane's disappointments in human relationships, her struggle with loneliness and the inability of the men that surrounded her to become emotionally available, are frequently mirrored in her work. Her female characters usually end up in dissatisfying romances, undecided where they should go or what they should do next. Maybe Jane Bowles's characters obfuscate their reference to real-life counterparts more than those of Paul or Burroughs, as Jane's stories were not set in Morocco. However, the parallels to the events in the author's real life are quite apparent.

Paradoxically, even if Jane was desperately struggling with writing, it remained her only means of expressing the very anger, frustration and anxieties that so often kept her from writing. Paul, unable to see her troubles, demanded that she pull herself together. The woman he had decided to marry had been an aspiring writer, his intellectual counterpart, but ironically the longer she stayed at his side, the more she dwindled. Thus his well-meant advice did not yield fruit for a woman that felt utterly lost in this expat world of men.

Jane did not identify with concepts of femininity on either side of the Atlantic, as on both sides, a woman's realm was still the marital home. Unlike Burroughs, she was not equipped with an indestructible desire for life and experience. Where Paul kept himself distant from experience and Burroughs sought 'the morbid slimy and unwholesome' on purpose, she haphazardly slid into turbulent, sometimes unpleasant situations and relationships, only to confirm the very expectation that she was not worth loving. Jane became invisible, she made herself invisible, by slowly starving the strong and creative woman she once was until finally she spent the last years of her life blind. The literary vision she could have produced fell prey to the adverse conditions of patriarchal societies, where men could be odd but women not.

Tangier was finally given back to the Moroccans under the reign of King Mohammed V, and many of the expatriates started to leave. After the International Zone was dissolved, the place seemed to lose its attraction. The artists, writers, gamblers, hustlers and occasional criminals moved on and took a part of the myth of Tangier with them. Only Paul Bowles stayed there until the end of his life in 1999, because after all, he seemed to like the place and maybe also the people there. He kept moving into the desert, recording the Master Musicians of Jajouka, translating Choukri and Mrabet, sharing his memoirs with the rest of the world, and caring for his ill wife until she passed away. Slowly the expatriate scene of Tangier crumbled and made way for those who reclaimed the city as their native place.

But how did those natives, the Tanjawis, perceive the invaders of their city? What are their accounts of the whole story? Do their voices remain unheard and their faces invisible in the discourse and representation of their colonisers, or do they finally claim their own ground in the narrow streets and shadows of the dreamlike city? Cunningham Graham once summed it up in a rather trenchant observation: 'They were objects of wonder to the Moroccans, who looked on them with awe, mixed with amusement, and regarded them as amiable madmen who, for some purpose of his own that he had not disclosed, Allah had endowed with the command of fleets and armies, and with mighty engines of destruction, so that it behoved the faithful to walk warily in their dealings with them.' Whether this is true or not, Graham convincingly shifts the perspective. It's not the colonised Arabs who were the objects of wonder or madmen of odd cultural background in this whole narrative of Moroccan colonialism. On the contrary, the Westerners who lived there themselves often exposed a good deal of their own sometimes dysfunctional culture and way of living, bringing their various neuroses and addictions, longing to escape the morals, norms and state control of their home countries. However, Bowles writes in *Let it Come Down*: 'Europeans in Tangier were more prudent than passionate; their fears were stronger than their desires. Most of them had no real desire, apart from that to make money, which after all is merely a habit. But once they had the money they never seemed to use it for a specific object or purpose.' Thus, the white madmen and madwomen may come and go, declare international zones and free ports as they wish, but in the end they return home having learned nothing, blinded by Orientalist prejudice and the illusions of white supremacy. They vanished, leaving behind ambiguous traces of their erratic lives, merely invisible footprints, taking some cultural artefacts and souvenirs with them to pose with, presenting the works of native artists as an achievement of discovery. The invisible cultural boundaries remained solid, even if some writers dared to sporadically cross them and put down some notes on their love-hate relationship with the place and its people.

In contrast, the Moroccan writer, Tahar ben Jelloun, so poetically and vividly declares his love for the city in *Leaving Tangier*: 'Tangier! Even swollen and stretched by all extremities, you continue to astonish me. I like to leave you for the joy of returning. I love to betray you, the better to compare you with other faces I know, now that a town is a story one never ceases to tell and which will remain ever unfinished, closed on a mystery and an enigma.'

BERBER SPRINGS

Hicham Yezza

The wave of popular uprisings that has shaken the Middle East and North Africa is popularly seen as an 'Arab Spring'. A number of alternative terms, deemed more appropriate, or less misleading, have also been proposed, including the 'Arab Awakenings', the 'Arab Intifadas', the 'Arab Revolutions' or the 'Arab Rebellions'. What seems incontrovertible is that these were 'Arab' phenomena. But this obstructs an important reality, particularly in the Maghreb region: many of those involved in organising or participating in the pro-democracy movement in the Maghreb did not identify themselves as 'Arabs'. Moreover, important segments of these protest movements were explicitly framed as representing the demands and aspirations of the Maghreb's Berber populations.

As Libyans, Moroccans and Algerians descended into the streets to join the widening protest movement across the region, most international coverage and commentary on the protests portrayed the demonstrations as being, in essence, a further iteration of the 'Arab Spring' protest phenomenon – echoing those in Tunisia, Egypt and elsewhere. While the protests in the Maghreb were broadly framed around calls for social justice, individual liberties and human rights, they contained a strong and unmistakable element of Berber rights campaigning, something that was almost entirely overlooked in the international media coverage. The Amazigh awakening had been obscured behind the catch-all term of the 'Arab Spring'. In fact, even in instances where coverage did allude to issues of cultural identity rights, this was mostly in the intra-Arab context of disenfranchised religious or sectarian groups such as the Copts in Egypt or the Sunnis in Syria. This framing, while valid enough in the *Mashreq*, struck a dissonant note for many in the *Maghreb* who saw their quest for the recognition of their Amazigh heritage and culture elbowed out of the mainstream narrative even as it was being written.

Indeed, one of the lesser known impacts of the 'Arab Spring' in the Maghreb has been the significant resurgence of Berber activism across the region, both as a constituent element within the broader pro-democracy movement, and as a separate and self-contained movement in its own right. In fact, the movement for Berber rights has been at the forefront of the fight for democratic emancipation in the Maghreb for more than five decades, and understanding its role in shaping the pro-democracy struggle in the region and beyond – and the cultural specificities of such struggles in countries like Morocco, Algeria and Libya – is crucial to a better assessment of what lies ahead for the people of the Maghreb.

Berbers and Berberists

The Berber people, or the Imazighen, are the original and earliest known inhabitants of North Africa. Their ranks comprise a vast and varied plethora of tribes and communities, including the Kabyles, Chawis and Mozabites in Algeria, the Ifoghas Touaregs in Mali and Niger, the Chleuhs and Rifians of Morocco, the Zenagas in Mauritania, and the Infusen in Libya. While debates around the precise ethnic and anthropological roots of the Amazighs in North Africa continue to this day, there is solid consensus on a few elements of the story. The Amazigh presence in North Africa is at least 3,500 years old, with the oldest Berber kingdoms occupying modern day Algeria and Eastern Morocco. The geographical frontiers of the Amazigh sphere extend from the Canary Islands to the Siwa Oasis in Egypt, and from the Mediterranean coastline to sub-Saharan enclaves in Chad, Niger and Burkina Faso.

However, contemporary population estimates are harder to come by, with official statistics often produced in the context of post-independent policies that perceived Amazigh demographic weight as a serious threat to the 'One Nation' narrative that was at the heart of the post-colonial self-image for most Maghreb nations. The most reliable estimates currently place the worldwide total number of Berberophones at 45 million native speakers, most of whom reside in Morocco and Algeria, though pockets of Tamazight-speaking communities continue to persist in Tunisia, Libya and elsewhere. In Morocco, official statistics estimate the Berberophone component of the population at 30 per cent; a contested figure, which some insists is actually is nearer to 60 to 70 per cent. Census statistics issued by the Moroccan ministry of population in 2004 estimate the number of Moroccans who use Tamazight in their daily life at 28 per cent. A similar story is found next door in Algeria, where most estimates of native Berber speakers range between 25 and 50 per cent.

The Berber language, commonly known by its speakers as Tamazight, is the Mediterranean's oldest surviving language, having outlived the ancient variants of Hebrew, Egyptian and Greek. Although most of the Maghreb has been Arabised over the past ten centuries, Berber-speaking regions persist, particularly in the mountains of Kabylie and the Aurès in Algeria as well as the Moroccan Atlas. In Morocco, there are three dialects: Tarifit in the Rif region, Tamazight in the Atlas plateaus, and Tachelhit in the Souss. In Algeria, we find the Kabyle in the Kabilye region, the Chawouia in the eastern Saharan Atlas range, the Mozabites in the region of Ghardaia at the gates of the Sahara as well as the Tuaregs across the great Sahara and Sahel regions. A distinction must be noted here between a Berber, that is someone of Amazigh ethnic ancestry, and a Berberophone, who is someone who speaks the language, generally as a mother tongue. To put it at its simplest, almost all Berberophones are Berbers while the reverse isn't quite the case.

The history of the Amazigh people has been of unremitting struggle for more than three millennia, some of it against extreme climate and terrain, as well as a centuries-long succession of foreign invaders. Since the advent of Islam in the eighth century, the region has been largely Arabised under a succession of dynastic rulers, notably the Almoravides (1073–1147), the Almohades (1137–1269) and the Ottomans (1570–1830.) The French invasion of Algeria in 1830 led to 132 years of colonial rule, during which the access to education of the indigenous population was virtually non-existent. By the turn of the twentieth century, the Maghreb was under one form of colonial rule or another – principally French but also Spanish and Italian.

The origins of the movement for Berber rights can be traced back to the early days of the independence struggle. From the 1920s onwards, there were significant waves of immigration from the Maghreb, predominantly from Berber-speaking regions, to France. Many of these immigrants, often employed in the burgeoning automotive industry, witnessed the emergence of the trade union movement, broadly allied with the Third International, across a number of French cities. They saw North African independence as the only possible solution to a century of colonial subjugation and repression. The Maghrebi identity emerged within this context; and was shaped, as the

Algerian sociologist Mohamed Ghalem argues, by the ebb and flow of two ideologies. On the one hand, the French colonial ideology, steeped in *'Mission Civilisatrice'* myths, asserted a strict dichotomy between the Arab and Berber populations, both in its rhetoric and administrative realities, thus negating the existence of a fully-realised sense of nationhood among the indigenous populations. Unsurprisingly, such a vision absolved the colonial enterprise of its violating character. The French or Spanish presence, the thinking went, could not be seen as that of a *coloniser* if there was no compelling evidence of a coherent, identifiable *colonised*. Against this colonial ideology, Ghalem notes, emerged a nationalist one built on asserting a 'mythical continuity of Maghrebi people throughout the ages'. This vision seemed to demand the discarding of cultural and linguistic diversities for the sake of asserting the reality of the colonised nation and people. Alas, this gradually led to the consolidation of a mythical notion of the 'Arab Maghreb' as an indistinguishable and homogenous extension of the wider Arab-Islamic sphere, which seemed to relegate the region's Berber cultural and linguistic realities to the status of historical footnote.

This was, of course, a serious concern for the Berbers. Just like the Arabs, the Berbers too wished to affirm and promote their identity, along with their language, norms and culture. Those who belonged to the Berberist movement, largely a movement of ideas, sought to promote the Berber language and culture and saw themselves as acting largely in the cultural sphere. However, as Hugh Roberts notes, 'To view the Berberist movement as an essentially apolitical movement of ideas evolving mainly if not entirely in the cultural sphere is to overlook the fact that the cultural sphere and the political sphere have not been truly distinct, let alone separate, in Algeria since the French conquest in 1830.'

After the invasion of 1830, French colonial policy in Algeria was consistently based on two types of segregation: the first between the indigenous population and the European settlers, and the second between indigenous Arabs and Berbers. This manifested itself in policies that denied the indigenes the most basic civil rights, not to mention access to education, as well as systemic attempts to promote an official narrative, sustained by a pliant Orientalist academic and artistic production, pitting native Berbers against invading Arabs.

The policies produced little traction; the inexorable rise of the movement for North African independence, which first gained prominence and momentum in the 1920s, could not be stopped. As the possibility for genuine reform – notably the elusive demand by assimilationists to see French citizenship granted to non-European inhabitants of Algeria – grew more remote, Maghrebi activists started to focus their energies on building a national movement aimed at securing the right to self-determination for the Maghreb's indigenous populations.

This, however, does not mean that there were no tensions between the two communities. The 1920s and 1930s saw the launch and rise to prominence of the Muslim Reformist Movement in Algeria, in the shape of the Association of Muslim Ulamas (Scholars) led by the charismatic Sheikh Abdulhamid Ibn Badis. The association's foundational self-assigned remit, as Ibn Badis and others insisted, was to revive, protect and promote Algeria's Muslim and Arab character. This was partly an attempt to counter what many perceived to be France's attempt to de-Islamise the Maghreb. However, while many of the pioneering leaders of the Algerian nationalist movement were Berbers, the suggestion that the struggle for independence would be conducted along ethnic lines – with Berbers and Arabs presenting parallel but separate cases for autonomy – was virtually absent. The emergence of a cross-ethnic movement for independence in the Maghreb is particularly remarkable in the context of a century of colonial policies explicitly treating the two groups, Arabs and Berbers, as distinct and often deploying policies favouring one group at the expense of the other in an attempt to sharpen and solidify this demarcation.

In Algeria, during the half century of nationalist activism leading to the launch of the war of independence in 1954, and despite a number of minor skirmishes between partisans of a European future for the Maghreb and those defending the country's Muslim and Arab heritage, there was only a single moment where the Berber-Arab fault line was thrown into sharp relief. The episode, generally known as 'The Berberist Crisis' of 1949, involved the expulsion of Berber militants from the ranks of the Movement for the Triumph of Democratic Liberties (MTLD), Algeria's main pro-independence nationalist party of the time, and the latest incarnation of its dissolved precursors, the North African Star (ENA) and the Party of the Algerian People (PPA), amidst accusations that they had been promoting a distinctly Berber-centric, and thus anti-nationalist, agenda. While the historical context of the crisis is too nebulous to be explored here, it is important to note that the episode did constitute a reference point that was to be resurrected in the debate over the country's identity after independence. For many Algerian Pan-Arabists, the crisis epitomised the shaky attachment of some 'Berberists' to the national project. Similarly, to some Berber activists, the episode was merely yet another milestone in their historic victimisation as a 'suspect community' whose loyalty to the nation was forever questioned and doubted. Nevertheless, throughout the Algerian war of independence, from 1954 to 1962, the cooperation and sense of common national purpose across regions remained unshakable, despite continued and intense colonial efforts to leverage ethnic and cultural divisions to break the solidifying status of the National Liberation Front (FLN) as the sole true representative of the Algerian popular will.

Berber Rights Movements

In July 1962, six years after Morocco and Tunisia had secured independence, Algeria joined their ranks. However, in all three nations, and in the midst of post-independence euphoria, early markers were set for the emerging official narrative around nationhood and identity, with constitutions presenting an unequivocal portrait of the Maghreb as exclusively Arab and Muslim. The Moroccan constitution of 1962, for example, presented the triptych of the monarchy, Islam and Arabism as the foundational components of Moroccan national identity. In Algeria, the constitution of 1963 similarly insisted on the country's exclusively Arab-Muslim character. Post-independence Arabisation policies, notably in Algeria, as well as the general official opprobrium and stigma attached to public use of Tamazight (even prohibition, as was the case in Libya under Gaddafi and in Tunisia under Bourguiba) further intensified this institutional drive towards total Arabisation.

Over the past half century there have been various attempts to understand the reasons why the Maghreb nations opted so dramatically, and so uniformly, to deliberately ignore such a central and incontrovertible component of their ethnic and linguistic reality. The celebrated Moroccan author Tahar Benjelloun spoke of an '*hantise unitaire*', a nation haunted by the spectre of division and its assertion of a mythical sense of unity to ward off any challenge, internal and external, to the nascent national settlement. This obsession was often explicitly articulated in the shape of vituperative official attacks on 'Hizb Franca' (The party of France) or 'La Main Etrangere' (the foreign/external hand), both meant to conjure up an external enemy and its internal conduits. The insistence on cultural homogeneity was thus intended as a means of inoculating the national consensus against any challenges. Unsurprisingly, early calls for recognising Tamazight were often met with vigorous repression accompanied by accusations of counter-revolutionary or even treasonous tendencies.

While the spectre of the 'Berber Question' was never far away from Algeria's political post-independence reality, there was relatively little progress on that front for the first two decades after 1962. The post-revolutionary fervour and optimism offered little encouragement to any project that could be perceived as a challenge to the imagined nation united in toil and blood.

But this changed following a defining post-independence episode for the Berber rights movement: the 'Berber Spring'. On 10 March 1980, Mouloud Mammeri, one of Algeria's most renowned writers and a vocal champion of Amazigh culture, was scheduled to deliver a conference address on ancient Kabyle poetry at the University of Tizi Ouzou. The conference was cancelled at the last minute by the university authorities. The cancellation was interpreted as a deliberate political act of censorship and provocation by the central government, and it caused widespread outrage among the university and local populations. Over the course of the following month, a series of protests and general strikes were repeatedly met with heavy-handed police repression, including the arrest of twenty-four student and activist leaders. The unrest culminated in an assault on the University of Tizi Ouzou's premises on 20 April, a day commemorated ever since.

This 'Berber Spring' produced in its wake a new generation of politicised Berber rights activists, many of whom, like Said Sadi, the author of *Askuti*, generally considered as the first Berber novel, went on to found political parties based on secular republican ideals after the introduction of the multi-party system in 1989. In 1995, a new stand-off between the Kabylie activists and the government over the recognition of Tamazight as an official language led to much of the education system in the region going on strike for a year.

The 'Berber Spring' was followed by the 'Black Spring' (*Le Printemps Noir*). On 18 April 2001, Massinissa Guermah, an eighteen-year-old high-school student from Béni Douala, in the Kabylie region, was arrested by local gendarmes. Later that day, he was shot inside the National Guard station, and died two days later. Some claimed the killing was a deliberate provocation orchestrated by President Abdelaziz Bouteflika's enemies. It led to two months of rioting, protests and mass unrest, leaving 127 dead and 6,000 injured.

The wave of indignation was marked with a huge march in Algiers on 14 June 2001, during which a fifteen-item manifesto of demands, 'The Platform of El Kseur', was made public. What is most striking about this document is the fact that it included not only the expected demand for Tamazight to be unconditionally granted official and national status, but also a series of demands on the political and economic front. For instance, item number 9 of the platform called for 'a state that guarantees socioeconomic rights and democratic freedoms', while another demand was for 'all executive bodies, including the security apparatus, to be put under the direct control of elected legislatures'. Moreover, the platform featured calls for an urgent economic programme for the Kabylie region, as well as a wider shift in public economic policy away from 'the politics of under-development and pauperisation.' Finally, the document repeatedly referenced the need for a return to the rule of law, and an end to the abusive practices and injustices against citizens by agents of the State.

The Platform of El-Kseur merely articulated in a concise and clear format the long-standing demands and aspirations of the Berber rights movement across the Maghreb. As such, its tone and ambition have found remarkable echoes in the numerous calls issued across the Arab world in the wake of the uprisings in Tunisia and Egypt. Indeed, parallels between the genesis of the Tunisian uprising, with the death of a street vendor, Mohammed Bouazizi, following his victimisation by an agent of the state, and the death a decade earlier of Massinissa Guermah in official custody is hard to ignore.

The Black Spring of 2001 represented a turning point for Berber activists, with many leaving the mainstream parties to join more radical initiatives such as the Movement for the Independence of the Kabylie (MAK), founded by Ferhat Mhenni, a veteran of the original Berber Spring of 1980. Although the MAK remains relatively insignificant in terms of political weight, it is gaining in numbers at a brisk pace, bolstered by the aggressive and uncompromising approach of the authorities. This was brought into sharp focus on 20 April 2013, when Tizi Ouzou, a city in north central Algeria, saw the first official presence by the MAK in the traditional commemorative march marking the original Berber Spring of 1980. Meanwhile, the autonomist rhetoric continues to harden, with Mhenni recently declaring that Algeria's independence did not bring an end to the colonial state but merely to 'its recycling in a new form'.

The legacy of the Black Spring has been a complex and long-lasting one. The immediate political fallout, notably the weeks of unrest and popular anger, was also accompanied by a moral one. On more than one occasion, I heard the same remark emanate from Berber activist friends, archly noting that while Kabylie convulsed in anger, there were no expressions of outrage or solidarity anywhere else in the country. For many, the sense of a dislocated nation, estranged from itself, was more resonant than ever.

In 2002, it made the first serious inroads towards recognising Tamazight by declaring it a 'national' language. This fell short of the demand for it to be constitutionally enshrined as an 'official' language. Moreover, cynics dismissed the move as an empty gesture intended to deflate the protest movement. Many veterans of the Berber rights movement have repeatedly warned against the drift from a search for an authentic 'Berbérité' to one concerned with celebrating a folkloric 'Amazighité'. Indeed, over the subsequent decade, the fight for Berber rights in Algeria turned into a meandering and convoluted process, riddled with infighting and confusion. Some hope emerged from the eruption of the 'Arab Spring', which was seen by many as the necessary jolt to breathe new life into the movement, not just in Algeria, but across the Maghreb. By the time of the Tunisian uprising, the Berber rights movement had seemed out of breath.

The 'Arab Spring' has had surprisingly little impact on Algeria. Attempts to explain this have been numerous and varied, but they seem to pivot around the recognition that Algerians, having just emerged from more than a decade of murderous civil war, which claimed more than 200,000 victims as well as untold suffering and tragedy for millions more, simply had little appetite for what many considered to be a renewed leap into the unknown. However, there have been attempts to ignite the sparks of an Algerian Spring. Throughout January 2011, as Tunisians were jubilantly celebrating the departure of Ben Ali and Egyptians clamoured in unprecedented numbers for Mubarak to follow suit, Algiers saw a number of Saturday marches demanding democratic reforms and cultural openness. These took place over a period of weeks before fizzling out by March as popular momentum failed to materialise. This setback was largely ascribed to two related but distinct factors. First, unlike uprisings in Egypt and Tunisia, the Algiers protests were officially called and organised by a political party, the *Rassemblement pour La Culture et La Democratie* or RCD, one of the country's two parties whose traditional powerbase is in the Kabylie region. As such, the protests never managed to transcend the partisan tag and were easily dismissed by official critics as a narrow and unrepresentative initiative with no popular support to speak of. The second factor, which ensued from the first, was the successful attempt by official and semi-official propaganda circles to brand the protests as primarily 'Kabyle' in nature. Indeed, the regime played the anti-Kabyle card with extreme efficiency to neutralise the movement by keeping it confined along both partisan and ethnic lines. Significantly, and predictably enough, the Saturday protests of January and February 2011 routinely descended into exchanges of hostile chants along Arab-Berber lines between the protesters and their opponents.

Berber activism in Morocco emerged in the 1960s but only attained critical momentum in terms of influence and reach at the turn of the twenty-first century. In the past decade, a number of pioneering organisations, including Tamaynut, the Amazigh Citizens Network (Azetta) and the International Amazigh Congress (CMA), have emerged, combining local outreach efforts with national and international strategies.

When Mohammed VI ascended to the throne in 1999, hopes were raised that he would usher in a new era in the country's handling of the Berber question. Early signs were promising, notably his visit to the predominantly-Berber Rif region, the first by a monarch in decades. Like Algeria, the Moroccan authorities' initial response to this increased growth in amplitude and politicisation of the Berber rights movement was a series of actions intended to contain and neutralise its most radical tendencies. Most notably, the Moroccan king announced the creation of a Royal Institute of Amazigh Culture, the introduction of Amazigh language provision in schools, as well as a Berber-speaking TV channel. But these steps did not quell the demands for Berber rights.

The Arab Spring triggered a series of demonstrations across Morocco. They started on 20 February 2011 and continued till the spring of 2012; the organising group, consisting largely of students, took its name from the date when they began – the 20 February Youth Group. The country waited with belated breath for the official response to the Berber rights demand. In a speech delivered on 9 March 2011, Mohammed VI reiterated the 'plurality of Moroccan identity, united but rich in its diversity, at the heart of which lies Amazighity, the communal heritage of all Moroccans', and he surprised many by announcing the creation of a commission for constitutional reform, headed by Abdelatif Mennouni, President of the Moroccan Association of Constitutional Law. Mennouni was instructed to deliver a new draft to be put to a popular referendum. Mennouni's report, delivered in June, recommended granting official status to Tamazight and further acknowledged that Morocco's 'cultural and linguistic diversity was a source of richness that needed preserving in a pluralistic society.'

Morocco's historical – and somehow unexpected – granting of official status to Tamazight was described by many as a seismic shift. In the subsequent days, observers in Algeria nervously awaited the official reaction from their own regime, noting that Morocco's precedent would surely provide a compelling rebuttal to standard warnings that making Tamazight an official language would trigger widespread popular unrest. After an initial period of cautious silence, Algeria's president broke the deadlock with his own speech on the 15 April, in which he announced a constitutional reform process to be launched in the lead-up to the 2014 presidential elections. Although it isn't yet clear if the Berber question will be a key feature of the reform process, the signs aren't promising. Bouteflika's speech ominously insisted that, while the consultations would cover all themes, this excluded 'the national constants'. For many, this was an explicit confirmation that official recognition was off the menu. Yet others insist this isn't the case.

Calls for Algeria to emulate Morocco's pioneering move have since grown louder and more confident. As the debate continues to evolve, Louisa Hanoune, the leader of the Workers' Party, and the first woman presidential candidate in the Arab world, became the latest high-profile Algerian politician to add her voice. The momentum is predicted to grow further. As Djaffar Tamani put it in an editorial in *El Watan*, Algeria's independent French language newspaper, Morocco's recognition of Tamazight as an official language 'showed this represented nothing dramatic or perilous for the country's stability'. He noted the irony of the Moroccan breakthrough considering 'it was in our own country that the fight for Amazigh identity has been the most active'. Tamani predicted the region would be moving away from being a 'club for heads of states' to a true 'Maghreb of the people'.

However, many Berber activists view Tamazight success as a merely partial victory, with some going so far as to describe it as an attempt on the part of the Moroccan royal establishment (the 'Makhzen') to sabotage the larger rights agenda through tactical concessions aimed at neutralising the most radical demands of the movement. *L'Observatoire Amazigh des Droits et des Libertés* (OADL) and others pointed out that Arabic and Tamazight are mentioned in separate, differently phrased, lines in the new constitution. Whereas Arabic is granted elevated status and legal protection, with its promotion a duty upon the state, this is not the case with Tamazight. Many see this as an indication that the constitutional concession was a deliberate attempt to co-opt and neutralise the movement with a view to stifling its more radical ambitions and demands. In particular, it has been pointed out that Tamazight teaching only reaches 15 per cent of Moroccan children.

Moreover, there are concerns about the attempt to dissociate the cultural dimensions of the Berber rights movement from the political and economic demands of the pro-democracy movement as a whole. After all, many Berber rights campaigners point out, linguistic and cultural emancipation cannot take place without a corollary of economic and social openings to address the vast and decades-long inequities that Berber-speaking regions have been subjected to. In Morocco, this quest has manifested itself in calls for increased regional autonomy for Berber regions and a fairer distribution of state resources and infrastructure spending. The 20 February protests confirmed that the call for Berber rights was an integral and key part of the wider movement for democratic change and social justice. This link was later made explicit in the 'Tinmouzgha Call for Democracy', released on 20 April 2011, which declared Berber cultural rights an inseparable component of the quest for a democratic and open society. Such expressions of unity and solidarity did not pass without friction, however. In early March 2011, Moroccan Berber rights activists refused to join marches or sit-ins after their request to display Amazigh flags was rejected by the other groups.

In Libya, the Berber population is concentrated in a number of enclaves, mostly in the west of the country, in Zwera, Tataouine and Djebel Nefoussa, as well as the Infusen, the mountain range in the south-west of Tripoli. It is estimated to be around 10 per cent of the total population. While cultural expressions in Berber were largely tolerated in Algeria and Morocco, Libyan Berbers were prohibited from using their mother tongue in public under Gaddafi's forty-year-long rule. Unsurprisingly, the first stirrings of the 17 February 2011 revolution were received with enthusiasm in the Libyan Berber community. Indeed, long marginalised and forced to accept a second-class status, their desire to overturn decades of neglect and repression was a key factor in the instrumental role played by Berber groups in the military insurrection that eventually led to Gaddafi's downfall.

Within weeks of the uprising's start, the Libyan TV station was broadcasting in Tamazight alongside Arabic, and three Tamazight teaching centres had opened in both Tripoli and Nefoussa. In the two years since, numerous gains have been secured, including the lifting of numerous prohibitions on public expressions of Berber culture. Berber radio stations and newspapers have been launched, cultural centres and museums opened, and Tamazight lessons introduced; there has also been a resurgence of traditional Berber folk singing.

However, two years into the post-Gaddafi era, tensions are growing. Many in the Berber community are angry that despite their early engagement in the uprising, the expected recognition of Tamazight as an official language in the new constitution has failed to materialise. Instead, the issue is the subject of heated divisions in the new parliament. 'They're not ready to recognise our rights, our culture' is the common cry of Libyan Berbers.

Decades of mistrust and hostility between Libyan Berbers and the central government continue to cast their shadow on the present. If the community does not obtain what it feels is its rightful place in the new Libya, the prospects for its unity will grow even more precarious. Indeed, as the security situation continues to deteriorate, ethnic Berber militias have refused to take a back seat in the quest for domination and control that has marred post-Gaddafi Libya. On 15 August 2013, Berber militias stormed the Libyan Parliament building in Tripoli to register their dissatisfaction with the central government's policies, occupying the premises for days.

The Tunisians too were prevented from publicly using Tamazight. A vigorous Arabisation policy pursued under the country's first post-independence president, Habib Bourguiba, and continued under his successor, Zine Al-Abedine Ben Ali, resulted in the shrinking of the Tamazight-speaking population to an estimated 150,000. Most of them are concentrated in a number of enclaves such as the southern city of Matmata and Douiret, and the touristic island of Djerba. Following the fall of Ben Ali, calls for a re-examination of the status of Tamazight have so far met with general silence from the country's new political class. However, Berber rights activism continues to grow, particularly in the cultural sphere. In April 2011 the first ever National Congress was held in Matmata. Three months later, 30 July saw the creation of the Tunisian Association for Amazigh Culture. At the World Social Forum, held in Tunis between 26 and 30 of March, 2013, workshops on Berber culture and rights were noticeably prominent.

In April 2013, in direct homage to Algeria's Berber Spring anniversary, Tunisian activists organised a march demanding the recognition of Tamazight, the 'country's first language', with hundreds of men and women draped in Berber flags and chanting slogans. Echoing similar demands across the Maghreb, the protesters reiterated their call for the introduction of Tamazight teaching in schools as well as a higher profile, and larger space, for Berber cultural expressions.

What's in a Name?

The exclusionary plight of the Berber community in the post-independence Maghreb has been economic, social, cultural and artistic. It's hard to find a more eloquent indication of this wounding experience than the politicised official taboo on Berber names. Indeed, half a century after independence, parents across the Maghreb still continue to have their choices of names for their new born rejected because of their etymological roots. Established Berber names, such as Massinisa, Jugurtha and Koceila – of famous Berber kings and leaders – are often rejected as unacceptable by municipal authorities. Official initiatives to address this absurd state of affairs have been slow and paved with the complicating absurdities of zealous bureaucracies.

In July 2013, the Algerian interior ministry published a list of 300 Berber names (150 for each gender) that were deemed 'acceptable'. The move prompted much derision and outrage, not least because a thirty-year-old law already existed for that very purpose. Instead, the news further highlighted the arbitrary and unreasonable basis of the censorship process itself, and thus its political dimension. In any case, dozens of cases continue to surface each week, with recent press reports estimating 300 cases of babies that have been left without legal names in the Kabylie town of Tizi Ouzou alone. When raising the subject with an activist friend of mine, he pointed out that such policies, rather than protecting national cohesion, were merely exacerbating the resentment of citizens and further strengthening proponents of the autonomist agenda within the Berber rights movement.

In Morocco, similar cases have also been reported, under a 1996 law instituted by Hassan II, which instructed administrative agents not to accept names that were not 'Moroccan.' This law was duly understood, and applied, as a prohibition against Berber names (the law claimed the measures were needed to safeguard the country's 'national security' and 'cultural integrity', no less). Thus, a Moroccan can call his daughter Shams (the Sun, in Arabic) but not Tafoukt (The Sun, in Tamazight). Such absurd injustices have left many parents unable to register their children, depriving them of a legal identity, for weeks, sometimes years.

In 2009, the parents of five children lodged an official appeal, presented under the auspices of Human Rights Watch (HRW), to the Moroccan Interior minister, against the overruling of their choices for the names of their babies. The resulting publicity and embarrassment were undoubtedly crucial in securing victory in all five cases. In April 2010, under the combined pressure of international NGOs and local activists, the Moroccan interior ministry released a directive acknowledging that, indeed, some Berber names were 'Moroccan' in character, urging officials to show less haste before rejecting names.

Such small victories have led some Berber activists, across the Maghreb, to herald the dawn of a 'Golden Age' for Berber rights. In Algeria, the post-Arab Spring shake-up has already yielded remarkable openings, including a growing number of cultural and scientific festivals, a booming film industry and an increasingly robust expansion across the cultural space. However, despite the undeniable gains of the Berber rights movement, both before and since the Arab Spring, the situation of Berber communities and regions remains precarious.

In Algeria, against official rhetoric and concessions, Tamazight continues to be taught in only five of the country's forty-eight districts, while further practical hurdles continue to hamper its expansion. Tamazight teachers are often paid late, assigned to prohibitively distant schools and have to work with extremely limited budgets. Berber-language media remain tightly controlled by the state, with Berber political folk music, a hugely influential art form, often the subject of censorship and harassment. Meanwhile, the Kabylie region continues to be a major frontline in a number of key battles shaping the future of the nation. Security remains precarious as Islamist groups, as well as criminal gangs, continue to find refuge in the region's notoriously inaccessible and protective terrain. This has further fuelled popular local resentment against the central government, accused of deliberately evading its duties and using the Islamist threat as a means to further unsettle the region, the better to keep it under control.

Ironically, while the 'Moroccan Spring' managed to shift – albeit in an reluctant and stuttering fashion – the country's official stance on Tamazight, it also led to the ascent of the Islamist Justice and Development Party (PJD) which has allied itself with the pro-monarchy Arab nationalist Istiqlal party in opposing further openings for the expansion of Berber identity, seeing in them a threat to its own Pan-Arabist and Pan-Islamist narrative. Indeed, subsequent to the PJD's victory at the legislative elections of the 25 November 2011, the Amazigh Observatory of Rights and Freedoms issued a statement denouncing the PJD-Istiqlal alliance as an obstacle to the true implementation of the recommendations enshrined in the new constitution.

Meanwhile, the MAK has attempted to deploy Arab Spring rhetoric to argue for the creation of a federalist system with the Kabylie region enjoying autonomy from the central government, with many MAK activists pointing to Catalan autonomy in Spain as a reference. Similarly, the 'Tinmouzgha call for democracy' of 20 April, includes a call for Morocco's exit from the Arab League.

Indeed, many observers view the on-going convulsions of the Arab Spring as signalling the end, rather than the much-heralded revival, of Pan-Arabism. In this regard, the ultimate irony, one might argue, is that the Arab Spring could prove to be the long-awaited springboard for a Berber political and cultural resurgence in the Maghreb. A resurgence that, many predict, could take place at the expense of the region's civilisational ties to the rest of the Arab world. The prominent Berber linguist, Salem Chaker, puts is simply if starkly: 'The Arab Maghreb is over.'

THE JEWS OF THE MAGHREB

Louis Proyect

Zionist historians have an ideological mission. They must look back into history and draw essentialist conclusions about the 'enemies' of the Jews no matter the countervailing evidence. As long as there have been gentiles determined to persecute and even exterminate the chosen people, there will be a need for an Israel armed to the teeth with jet fighters, advanced missile systems, and nuclear weapons.

Benzion Netanyahu, the father of Israel's prime minister, published a book on the Spanish Inquisition that traced what he called 'Jew hatred' to ancient Egypt, long before Christianity. Naturally that would give his son the license to create an apartheid-like system in the West Bank. Despite nineteenth-century Germany's vanguard role in forging an Enlightenment that would give Jews full equality, Daniel Goldhagen wrote a book that depicted the German race as essentially bent on the destruction of the Jews from time immemorial.

But pre-Zionist Islam constitutes the biggest challenge for the ideologically-driven historian. Against the preponderant evidence that Jews flourished for the most part under early Muslim rule, there is also some evidence that they were persecuted. This evidence is generally subsumed under the category of *dhimmitude*, a neologism based on the Arab word *dhimmi* that is applied to non-Islamic peoples like the Jews and the Christians who were supposedly second-class citizens. The *dhimmitude* front received a boost from Paul B. Fenton and David G. Littman's *L' Exil au Maghreb: la condition juive sous l'Islam 1148-1912*, published in 2010 but never translated into English, but the book's tendentious findings have been picked up by Muslim-bashing bloggers. Littman's Islamophobia is of a long-standing character. In 2005 he contributed several articles to the collection edited by the well-known Islam-basher Robert Spencer titled *The Myth of Islamic Tolerance: How Islamic Law Treats Non-Muslims*.

Over on the aptly named jihadwatch.com, there's a review of Fenton and Littman by one Ibn Warraq, who despite his Arab lineage is an Islamophobic stalwart. His best-known book is *Why I am not a Muslim*. Warraq states that the book offers 'proof of the abject condition of the Jews in the Maghreb in the nineteenth century, destroying along the way a number of myths that were current up to that time.' Of course, it is understandable why attention is paid to the nineteenth century rather than the period most scholars deem as a golden age for Jews under Islam. As should be obvious, any attempt to describe relations between Muslims and Jews across continents and across millennia is a fool's errand and one that obviously recommends itself to the Zionist historian.

You can get a sense of what is in *L' Exil au Maghreb* from the introduction to *Jews under Muslim Rule in the late Nineteenth Century*, an earlier Littman title that is available in English:

Till the last decades of the nineteenth century and even into the twentieth, the Jews in many parts of the Maghreb – as in most other Muslim lands – were still obliged to live in isolated groups amidst the general population. They resided in special quarters and were constrained to wear distinctive clothing, the carrying of arms was forbidden to them and their sworn testimony was not accepted in any Muslim Court of Law. Their discriminatory status remained that of *ahl al dhimma*: a 'protected' people, i.e. people enjoying the protection of Islam and the Koran, while at the same time subject to the disabilities and humiliations laid down in specific regulations known as the Pact of Omar (634 – 644 C. E.), which degraded both the individual and the community.

For Littman, the wearing of 'distinctive clothing' was identified with the Nazi policy of making Jews wear a Star of David. There is little interest in showing what Jewish life was like in the Maghreb apart from identifying policies that would not be permitted in today's enlightened European landscape that allows skinheads to beat up or kill Arab or North African immigrants with impunity. Littman, who died in May 2012, was a lightning rod for student protests against Islamophobe appearances on campus. Wikipedia reports that when he submitted a proposed speech to be given at Georgetown University in October 2002 on the 'Ideology of Jihad, Dhimmitude and Human Rights' to student organisers, a Jewish student requested that he not deliver his lecture. He, like Muslim students, felt that charges of sexual abuse against Muhammad were better suited for the website of Pam Geller, the notorious campaigner against the 'creeping sharia' in America, rather than a major academic institution. Littman attributed the objections of Jewish and Christian students to a *dhimmi* mentality.

All that being said, it is necessary to draw a balance sheet on the experience of Jews in the Maghreb. If Jews were forced to wear special clothing and were not permitted to carry arms (or ride horses for that matter), what does that really say about what life was like for them in its totality in Algeria, Morocco, Tunisia, and Libya – the four countries that make up the Maghreb?

To get a better understanding of Jewish life in what some scholars regard as a golden age, there's no better place to start than with Shelomo Dov Goitein's five-volume *Mediterranean Society*. This monumental work attempts to recreate the daily lives of Jews through the examination of the Cairo Geniza documents, a collection of 300,000 manuscript fragments from the storeroom (*geniza*) of the Ben Ezra Synagogue in Cairo. There were both religious and secular documents ranging from 870 AD to as late as 1880. These were largely of a quotidian nature sought by historians trying to write 'history from below'. They were preserved only because they were written in Hebrew, God's language, and as such could not be destroyed. In other words, the *geniza* was a glorified trash bin.

While reading the full *Mediterranean Society* is a task relegated to the specialist, I can recommend the 263-page 'Jews and Arabs: a Concise History of Their Social and Cultural Relations' to the non-specialist. In fact I would consider it required reading for those trying to combat Islamophobia on their campus or in their various social movements.

While acknowledging the decline of Jewish economic conditions in the nineteenth century, a period that Littman and Fenton dwell on (and which requires further analysis), Goitein describes the golden age under Fatimid rule as one with the 'absence of oppressive discriminatory economic legislation' that 'can be judged from the great variety of professions and crafts followed by the Jews in Islamic countries as opposed to the few trades available to them in Medieval Europe'. The Fatimid Caliphate was a Berber Shi'a ruled dynasty that originated in modern day Tunisia in the tenth century and that eventually made Egypt its centre. It derived its name from the belief that they were descended from Fatima, Mohammad's daughter. It extended across the entirety of the Maghreb and through the Middle East and was marked by tolerance toward non-Muslims. Chapter six of Goitein's book, which deals with the 'economic transformation ... of the Jewish people in Islamic times' concludes that Fatimid rule was salutary for the Jews at least on economic grounds:

> Our survey of the economic conditions and social institutions of the Jews during the first, creative, five centuries of Islam, has shown that there were many agents which worked toward a revival and a gradual unification of the Jewish people inside the Muslim world: the economic rise and entrance of the Jews into the class of business and professional people; commercial and family relations connecting Jews from many Muslim countries; the new institution of the 'Representative of the Merchants'; the allegiance to ecumenical and regional central authorities; travel for 'the seeking of wisdom' and for pilgrimage to holy places; the application of the same law to all Jews wherever they lived; and, finally, Jewish charity which, like its Muslim counterpart, was not limited by political boundaries. The new economic and social conditions did not fail to exercise a marked influence also on the cultural life of the Jews inside Islam.

Goitein's analysis of the status of Jews in early Islamic history was echoed in Richard Hull's *Jews and Judaism in African History*. He emphasises the network of trade that allowed the Fatimids to function as a vast *entrepôt* linking the far western reaches of the Maghreb with India and China. Key to its success were the Jewish traders of North Africa who became so instrumental that Ali Kilis – a Jew despite his name – became the first vizier of the Fatimid Empire. Hull writes:

> Jewish life flourished under the Fatimids, and as we've already discovered, by the eleventh century the city of Kairwan in modern Tunisia had become a major centre of Jewish learning and economic activity. Jewish scholars travelling between Europe and the Middle East rested, studied, and taught in Kairwan. Robert Seltzer tells us that 'academies were established by important talmudists and prosperous Jewish merchant families supported Jewish scientists and philosophers' (Seltzer 1980: 345). Egyptian and Maghrebian Jewry flourished, and Jews from the old Abba-sid territories began to migrate to Africa.

However, as a reminder of the need to avoid romanticising this period, Hull points out that in Fez, a Moroccan city that had a high concentration of Jews, there was a brutal pogrom in 1033 that left thousands of men killed and their wives, sisters, and daughters sold into slavery. But despite this tragedy, Jews remained in Fez and rebuilt it as a major economic and cultural centre.

Neither does Goitein romanticise the period. He refers to 'ridiculous laws' that required Jewish women to wear shoes of different colours, one white and one black, as well as the code that prevented Jews from riding horses – a law that he likened to Nazis preventing them from owning a car. While undoubtedly there were similarities between the codes of medieval Morocco and twentieth century Germany, as Littman was so determined to point out, there was never an 'existential threat' to Jews in early times on the scale of Nazi Germany. That only manifested itself in Europe and particularly in countries that regarded the economic success of the Jews as a threat to Christian interests. When capitalism began to take root in fifteenth century France, Spain and Britain, the older Jewish trading and financial networks were seen as rivals and worthy of *total* elimination with the Spanish Inquisition setting the pace.

Probably nothing militates more against facile attempts to make an amalgam of Maghreb Jewish-Islamic relations with Nazi Germany than the phenomenon of *mellahs* of Morocco, the Jewish quarters that bore a superficial relationship to fascist-imposed ghettos. In 1438 the Sultan created a *mellah* near the palace after a number of Jews were killed in the aftermath of a rumour that they had placed wine in the mosques of Fez, a city with a large Jewish population. On first blush, they 'made the Jewish communities appear as outcasts, isolated from the wider society', in the words of Daniel J. Schroeter.

But in fact the Jewish quarters were quite porous. Jews were able to move in and out of the *mellah* and even settle in other cities where there were none. Schroeter writes:

Finally, and most important, the walls of the mellahs of Morocco hardly constituted impregnable barriers to outside influence. The mellah indeed constituted 'Jewish space' but not an isolated part of the city. It was a locale from which the Jewish community interacted with the city as a whole, and with the wider world. Finally, it should be pointed out that the term 'mellah,' which became the generic term for the Jewish quarter in Morocco, eventually implied not only the physical space of residence but also the Jewry of a given locale, which was the case throughout the small communities in the Moroccan countryside, especially in the south of the country where often no distinctly physically separated residential Jewish quarter existed.

In other words, they were not that different from the orthodox Jewish enclaves of Brooklyn, N.Y. today.

Moving closer to the present day, there are factors that come into play that partially explain growing tensions between Jew and Muslim in the Maghreb. In the nineteenth century anti-colonial movements took root that drew upon both nationalist and Islamist themes perceived as inimical to the interests of the urban Jew who tended to identify with France, the mother country of Tunisia and Morocco, or Italy as is the case for Libya.

Mark A. Tessler and Linda L. Hawkins point out that France exploited the existing differences between Jew and Muslim, using the time-dishonoured technique of divide and conquer. In Algeria, France offered citizenship en masse to its Jewish population. Elsewhere, Jews received preferential treatment, including easy access to French schools – a measure that almost guaranteed assimilation into the dominant culture. Tessler and Hawkins write:

> Jewish assimilation of French culture was enhanced by the Alliance Israelite Universelle, an independent international educational foundation that operated in North Africa with support from the colonial establishment. Through its extensive network of primary and secondary schools, the AIU spread the French language and culture far more broadly than did elite and settler-oriented French schools. In a few instances, as in Djerba in southern Tunisia, traditionalist elements successfully resisted the incursions of the AIU. In general, however, Jews welcomed the AIU and viewed it as an agent of progress. Together, the AIU and the colonial mission narrowed the cleavage between indigenous Jews and those of European origin and taught many Jews to accept France as their spiritual home. Thus, they greatly increased the cultural distance between Jews and Arabs. They also produced among many Arabs a view of the Jew as collaborator. Jews were seen as profiting by, and indeed becoming a part of, a political force that most Arabs considered oppressive and humiliating.

In Algeria, where colonial oppression was most extreme, most of the French-oriented Jewish population fled the country after the National Liberation Front (FLN) took power. But not every Jew identified with the imperialists. Henri Alleg, a member of the Communist Party and still living at the age of 92, became a partisan of the FLN and endured torture for his activism. Despite Alleg, some Jews became members of the French military-fascist group, *Organisation de L'Armée Secrète* (OAS). This prompted the FLN to issue an appeal to Algerian Jews in 1962:

Some among you have perhaps forgotten that era in order to knowingly involve yourselves in the crimes of the colonialists under the pretext of counter-terrorism in Constantine and Algiers. Recently, in Oran, demonstrations provoked by young hotheads in the Israelite neighbourhood took place, followed by fires set in stores belonging to Muslims. These acts are the clearest illustration of how some of you attempt to thoughtlessly align yourselves with the racial policies of the ultras. Will you today make yourselves the accomplices of the backwards colonialists by rising up against your Algerian brothers of Muslim origin? We refuse to believe this, because you know the anti-Semitism of the activists and seditionists of Algeria.

Libya endured the same unfortunate clash between native Muslim aspirations for independence and Jewish identification with the mother country. Maurice Roumani, a Libyan Jew, is the author of *The Jews of Libya*. In a chapter titled 'Mussolini, Fascism and Libyan Jews', he describes the 'warm welcome' the Jewish community in Libya provided to the occupying powers. It includes this startling description of the relationship of Italian Jews to Italian fascism, one that was shared by their brethren in Libya:

When Mussolini first established the nucleus of his Fascist Party *Facci di combattimento* on March 23, 1919, Jews already made up a significant portion of his support base. In fact, for over one hundred years, Jews stood staunchly behind the Italian Nationalist movement because they traditionally belonged to the bourgeoisie and anti-socialist movements.

If the contradictions between the Jews of the Maghreb and the less privileged Arab colonial subjects sharpened over such matters, they finally came to a head with the creation of the state of Israel. Like the Mizrahim – the Arab Jews of Syria, Iraq, and Egypt – the Maghrebi Jews poured into Israel out of a sense that conditions would worsen for them through no fault of their own. Despite being thoroughly integrated into their communities in places like Fez that had known a Jewish presence for a thousand years, they left businesses, jobs and friends behind in order to enjoy the 'safety' of the heavily armed Israeli state.

The Ashkenazi (European Jews) powers that ruled Israel regarded the newcomers as barely distinguishable from the Palestinians they had just expelled. As Israeli journalist Arye Gelbaum declared:

This is the immigration of a race we have not yet known in the country. We are dealing with people whose primitivism is at a peak, whose level of knowledge is one of virtually absolute ignorance and, worse, who have little talent for understanding anything intellectual. Generally, they are only slightly better than the general level of the Arabs, Negroes, and Berbers in the same regions. In any case, they are at an even lower level than what we know with regard to the former Arabs of Israel. These Jews also lack roots in Judaism, as they are totally subordinated to savage and primitive instincts. As with Africans you will find among them gambling, drunkenness, and prostitution ... chronic laziness and hatred for work; there is nothing safe about this asocial element. [Even] the kibbutzim will not hear of their absorption.

Eventually the Maghrebi Jews were assimilated into Israel like their Mizrahim relatives and now constitute the backbone of the ultra-Zionist Shas Party.

In looking back at the tortured relationship between the Jews of the Maghreb and their Muslim brothers and sisters, you are left with the conclusion that 'progress' is not necessarily tied to the quintessential product of the modern age – the national state. The development of state powers in North Africa and the Middle East have tended to create ethnic tensions that were far less pronounced in the Middle Ages when a Fatimid Caliphate had no problem elevating a Jew to one of its most powerful posts.

The spiritual and moral exhaustion of the Zionist state as well as the Baathist dictatorships that exemplified Arab nationalism invite us to consider alternatives that leave the narrow considerations of ethnic and religious exclusivism behind. While the Fatimid Caliphate is obviously no model for our modern world, the twenty-first century will surely have to evolve in the direction of a polity that evaluates people without regard for their confessional roots. Sectarianism has been a dead-end for most of the twentieth century and certainly deserves to be interred for good as we make our way fitfully into the twenty-first.

REVOLUTION IN MAGHREBI CINEMA

Jamal Bahmad

Mainstream narratives of the Arab Spring have been both simplistic and influential. The coverage of the uprisings in the Maghreb and the Middle East has been dominated by the notion that the events were as unforeseeable as they were sudden. But for the observer of social change and cultural production in North Africa, the 2011 uprisings were anything but surprising. In fact, from Egypt to Morocco, filmmakers have been predicting and projecting the growing wrath of youthful populations coming under increasing pressure from economic globalisation and have been projecting for decades. The attentive viewer will have glimpsed in these films the indigenous voices of disaffected youth and ordinary people. Contemporary North African filmmakers have painted remarkably subtle portraits of their changing societies.

In the early 1980s, the countries of North Africa began to implement the International Monetary Fund's Structural Adjustment Programmes. What was initially perceived as a short-term strategy to tackle recession-induced public deficit and soaring international debt transpired to be a decades-long era of privatisations, austerity, high unemployment and low human development rates. Rapid neo-liberalisation engendered deep social and political transformations. Market forces consolidated the regimes' hold on power while poverty levels soared, public education and healthcare deteriorated, and loss and uncertainty characterised the everyday lives of the people of the Maghreb. This is the world that has formed the region's new generation; and this is the world that is depicted on the screen.

In the face of the rapid social change, political repression and economic hardship of the neoliberal era, North African filmmakers have resorted to realist representations of globalisation from the standpoint of its victims. With the exception of Egypt, which enjoyed a large film industry in the first half of the twentieth century, indigenous cinema in other countries of the region is largely a post-colonial affair. Upon the independence of their countries in the 1950s and early 1960s, indigenous filmmakers sought a cinema capable of articulating the postcolonial condition. In a seminal essay, Tunisian director Nouri Bouzid contends that the defeat of the Arab armies in the 1967 war with Israel brought home to North African filmmakers the need for a new realism in the representations of their societies. As Egyptian director Youssef Chahine puts it:

Confrontation — there must be confrontation; confrontation with the self... Where has all this started? How have we come to this? How have we been deceived and put in the wrong? How and where have we erred? Only then can we begin to settle the account with ourselves, so that we could possibly begin to accept ourselves, a necessary precondition for others to accept us.

Influential films by Egyptians Chahine (*The Sparrow*, 1973) and Shadi Abdel Salam (*The Mummy*, 1969), and by the Syrian Mohamed Malas (*Dreams of the City*, 1983), for example, found resonant echoes in the Maghreb. Bouzid places his own film *Rih Essed* (*Man of Ashes*, 1986) within the genre of New Realism that swept across North African cinema after the debacle of the 1967 Arab-Israeli War. He coins the phrase 'the cinema of defeat' to describe this new wave of realism

To post-colonial filmmakers across North Africa, 1967 brought home not only a sense of defeat but also, to use Bouzid's own term, an awareness of the 'decadence' of their civilisation. Therefore, they perceived cinema as 'a social necessity' and 'a vehicle for the spreading of awareness and a tool or forum for analysis and debate'. The new cinema's politics are succinctly outlined by Bouzid: 'Admitting defeat, the new realism proceeds to expose it and make the awareness of its causes and roots a point of departure.' The filmmakers turned their lenses away from master narratives to the everyday life of ordinary individuals. It was a time of transition from the cinema of the collective hero, which prevailed particularly in the Algerian cinema of the 1960s and early 1970s, to a preoccupation with the embattled individual in Maghrebi society. Besides the 1967 disaster, rampant poverty, despotism, illiteracy and gender segregation were among the reasons behind what Hélé Béji calls 'national disenchantment' that led to a loss of faith in the meta-narratives of liberation and nationalism. In the film world, disenchantment turned into an uncompromising realism, and cinema became more conscious of defeat.

Bouzid's debut feature film, *Man of Ashes,* won multiple accolades on the festival circuit and broke box office records at home. It is also widely credited with sparking Tunisian cinema's golden decade (1986-1995), marked by internationally acclaimed films, which Bouzid often co-scripted, like Férid Boughedir's *Halfaouine: Child of the Terraces* (1990) and Moufida Tlatli's *The Silences of the Palace* (1994). However, *Man of Ashes* is less known and discussed in the Western academy than Boughedir and Tlatli's feted films. Whether in compliance with the European co-producers' dictates or out of a desire to break into the world cinema market, many North African filmmakers accommodate the common Western viewer's preconceptions. Bouzid, in contrast, addresses local audiences first and foremost through a social psychology of pain.

Despite their undeserved obscurity at home and overseas, pre-1990s films like *Man of Ashes* hold clues to understanding post-colonial Maghrebi societies in the twenty-first century. Their social realism is replete with insights into the dynamics of social and cultural change. For example, looking at the origins and aftermaths of the 2011 uprisings in North Africa, key elements seem to flow straight out of *Man of Ashes*. North African youth's struggle for emancipation in 2011 bears affinities to that of Hachemi and his double, Farfat, in Bouzid's film, set in the provincial town of Sfax. For this visionary dimension alone, *Man of Ashes* ought not to remain unknown beyond small circles of film lovers in Tunisia.

Bouzid was born in Sfax in 1945, and attended the Institut National des Arts du Spectacle et Techniques de Diffusion (INSAS) in Brussels. Upon graduation in 1972, he worked for Tunisian state television and became active in radical politics. He was jailed from 1973 to 1979 for his political convictions, an experience revisited in the semi-autobiographical film *Golden Horseshoes* (1989). With eight feature films to his credit, Bouzid is one of the most prolific and original filmmakers of his generation. Based on his own screenplay and produced near the end of President Bourguiba's autocratic rule (1957-1987), *Man of Ashes* opens on the eve of Hachemi's arranged marriage. In lieu of the joy which customarily accompanies this rite of passage in North African society, the young woodcarver is unsettled by an outburst of gossip and the enigmatic appearance of the graffito

'FARFAT IS NOT A MAN' on the small town's walls. Meanwhile Farfat, Hachemi's boyhood friend, is banished from his parents' home. The scandalous incidents drown Hachemi in acute doubt about his own manhood. When they were ten-year-old apprentices in Mr Levy's carpentry workshop, he and Farfat were raped by the master carpenter Ameur. Hell breaks loose as painful memories of rape flash back into the present. Hachemi, notes Bouzid, 'is the baffled "hero" who can neither accept his ordained lot – to perpetuate the practices of his forebears – nor truly resist and reject it by any effective means'. In contrast, Farfat defies his society's patriarchal homophobia. By Bouzid's own admission, Farfat is Hachemi's double. Hachemi wears a wounded gaze whilst revisiting his traumatic childhood, seeking help to account for it from his three fathers: the uncomprehending biological father lashes him with a leather belt for soiling the patriarch's honour in refusing to consummate the hetero-normative marriage; the second father is none other than the paedophilic carpenter; his last resort is old Levy who, seeing Hachemi's distress, sings him a song from the latter's childhood. The task is helped by a bottle of Boukha, the fig brandy dear to North African Jews and Muslims. However, Mr Levy succumbs to sleep just as Hachemi begins to relate his traumatic story. Jacko, Levy's grandson, was Hachemi's best childhood friend and his departure alongside most Tunisian Jews after independence is as castrating as the rape at the carpentry workshop. This intertwined story of individual and collective traumas is instructive. Levy dies alone the next day. His demise is met with the indifference of his Muslim neighbours, who have increasingly harboured antagonism towards their Jewish countrymen with the spread of Nasserite Arabism.

The closer the marriage night comes, the more severe Hachemi's agony becomes. His childhood friends, Touil the blacksmith and Azaiez the baker, suggest a bachelor party in Ms Sejra's brothel. Hachemi proves his virility with Amina, a prostitute dressed as a bride for the night, and Farfat does likewise with her companion. When the jealous Azaiez reminds Farfat that 'everyone knows' (of his and Hachemi's rape by Ameur), Farfat dashes into his molester's house. Ameur emerges from behind the crowd of neighbours gathering in the alley. With Hachemi's complicity, Farfat fatally stabs Ameur in the groin, and takes flight. The next sequence is of police chasing an ecstatic Farfat. He makes an enigmatic exit from the scene by either jumping on a train or being run down by it. Probably a reference to the immortality of freedom rather than to Farfat's physical survival, the next scene is of him shirtless in his usual blue dungarees running and jumping across the city's rooftops ('Farfat' means butterfly). In acknowledgement of his newfound masculinity and in defiance of patriarchal society, Hachemi seeks asylum in Sejra's whorehouse, where he has found happiness with Amina. His request is refused. Anis, Farfat's young companion, proceeds to erase the stigmatising graffito as the final credits appear.

Before taking his last breath, Ameur uncannily tells Hachemi and Farfat: 'You'll always be my apprentices. I taught you everything'. Besides suggesting that the past lives on in the present, we can also read the master carpenter's words in the context of contemporary Tunisia's history. The mentor is an allegory of Habib Bourguiba, the autocratic moderniser in power from 1957 to 1987. In a perfect example of 'the state is me' syndrome in the post-colonial polity, Bourguiba uttered these words in a lecture to university students in the early 1970s: 'I hope you will know the history of our country better by listening to he who made it'. Under his rule, however, Tunisia benefited considerably from a range of progressive social and economic policies in sharp contrast to other countries in the region. When Bourguiba died in 2000, Bouzid mourned him in a way which echoes Hachemi's feelings about Ameur: 'I was arrested and imprisoned from 1973 to 1979. But the day of Bourguiba's death, I felt as if I had lost my father and I wept. The man handed down positive and interesting changes, such as the Personal Status Code. He hurt me, but at the same time, I respected him'. This filial relationship is vital for an understanding of Bouzid's semi-autobiographical film. Tunisian academic, Nouri Gana, author of *Signifying Loss: Towards a Poetics of Narrative Mourning*, contends that the paradoxical modernity of Bourguiba's rule, which combined secular discourse and autocratic patriarchy, has informed 'the psychodynamics of manhood in postcolonial Tunisia'. Bouzid himself confesses that the 'attitude that the father is sacred and the difficulty of ridding oneself of him is present in all the films I've made'. Hachemi's crisis of manhood evokes the embattled situation of contemporary Tunisia torn between secular reforms and authoritarian fathers.

Bouzid's film is representative of New Realism's investment in the North African individual's defeat and solitary struggle for emancipation from societal, economic and political regimes of oppression. The issues addressed by *Man of Ashes* – youth, patriarchy, homosexuality and repression – are still prevalent and relevant today. It is thus hardly surprising that the post-2011 transition in Tunisia thrust a sixty-six-year-old Bouzid to the forefront of public attention. In April 2011, he appeared on national television with a bloodied gash above his left ear. He had been stabbed by a young fanatic. The attack did not seem to surprise this film director who had set out 'to subvert norms, refuse prohibitions and unveil sensitive areas such as religion, sex, the authorities, the "father figure"'. Scholarly interest in Bouzid's lost film classic can therefore yield nuanced interpretations of the ongoing evolution of Tunisia and other postcolonial societies. The plight of Hachemi in *Man of Ashes* charts a complex genealogy of postcolonial youth's disaffection, which culminated in Bouazizi's self-sacrifice and Tunisia's Jasmine Revolution.

Social and political change in North Africa in the wake of structural adjustment policies implemented in the 1980s was accompanied by the rise of a neo-neorealist cinema in the following decades focused on ordinary people's daily struggle for survival. The protagonists are often youth in search of agency and meaningful subjectivities in rapidly changing societies and an interconnected world. Of all Maghrebi cinemas since the 1990s, it is the Moroccan one which has been thriving most, thanks to sustained state funding and a young generation of diaspora filmmakers coming home to shoot the new social realities of globalisation. Moroccan cinema has been tremendously popular at home by virtue of its defining focus on ordinary people and everyday life as a counter-archive to discourses of power, on the one hand, and a critical examination of postcolonial subjectivities and the everyday potential for historical change, on the other . The latter is configured on-screen not just as a space of routines, rituals and uncritical everydayness, but also strategically as what French Jesuit scholar, Michel de Certeau, qualifies as an 'inexhaustible', and 'constantly unfinished realm of historical possibility'. Moroccan films mine the everyday's critical potential in projecting the lived experience of ordinary Moroccans and thereby uncovering spaces of resistance to sundry forms of oppression. Everyday life on screen is, to borrow the words of cultural theorist Ben Highmore, 'inherently resistant' and 'framed by bodies that are at variance to the machines they operate'. Postcolonial subjectivity or the becomings of the postcolonial subject take shape in the mundane spaces of everyday life on the screen.

A central theme in Maghrebi cinema since the early 1990s is the struggle for control over urban space. The city is a site of conflict because it is shot through with society's power relations. Different interest groups are embroiled in a constant struggle for spatial control and, by extension, power distribution in society. In neoliberal Casablanca, for example, the cityscape is ostensibly under control by an urbanism that panders to the interests of the upper classes and banishes the poor and disproportionately young multi-million population to the margins. However, this account would be remiss if it were to write out the practices of everyday resistance among marginalised youth and ordinary people in urban space. In his theory of everyday life, de Certeau distinguishes between the strategies of power and the tactics of resistance. Unconscious and repetitive, everyday life in the city is a battleground for the 'clever tricks of the "weak" within the order established by the "strong", an art of putting one over on the adversary on his own turf, hunter's tricks, manoeuvrable, polymorph mobilities, jubilant, poetic and warlike discoveries'. This critical framework of power and popular resistance can account for the strategies invented by youth in their quest to reclaim the city as postcolonial subjects living under globalisation. Subversion is as omnipresent and multipolar a force as is domination in the North African city on the screen. The city is a space of memory, calculations, manipulations, signals and codes.

For an example of how Maghrebi cinema has been cognitively mapping an unevenly globalising society, look no further than Abdelkader Lagtaâ's groundbreaking *Hub Fi Dar el-Beida* (*A Love Affair in Casablanca*, 1991). The protagonist Salwa is an eighteen-year old girl in search of liberation in a sprawling metropolis. Heartbroken after her decision to end their love affair, the middle-aged Jalil arranges a meeting of reconciliation in the last sequence of the film. He disarmingly tells her, in words which ironically echo the Tunisian president Zine El Abidine Ben Ali's desperate speech in colloquial Tunisian rather than his customary Modern Standard Arabic on 14 January 2011: '*Ana fehmtkom*' ('I have understood you'). Salwa laughs him off before deserting the scene. This fateful encounter takes place in a downtown park, a strategic site prefiguring public space in the neoliberal city as the battlefield of generational clash and youth's revolt in twenty-first-century Maghreb. Salwa rebels against the tyranny of the father figure as would millions of youth in 2011. Shocked upon discovering his father's relationship with Salwa and hence the reason he was prevented from having a relationship with her, Jalil's son Najib runs home and seizes a knife in his fury. He symbolically kills his absent father in the bedroom before taking his own life in the bathroom. Looking back at this dramatic ending from the vantage point of the youth-led 2011 uprisings reveals Lagtaâ and cinema's perceptive cognitive maps of North African society's evolution and fraught social and political landscapes. Like Najib in Casablanca two decades earlier, stifling oppression pushed the street vendor, Mohamed Bouazizi, to take his own life by setting himself on fire – the seminal trigger event of the Arab Spring – in Tunisia, where Lagtaâ's film was released to wide acclaim in 1992. The final credits of *Love Affair* roll up against a freeze shot of Najib in his bloodbath. Salwa blames Najib's suicide on Jalil. The viewer can hear them fiercely fighting off-frame with Salwa, knife in hand, threatening to kill the father. The film closes on this suspenseful moment with Najib's frozen frame still filling the screen. In this sense, the 2011 events had somehow already taken place, and centre stage on North Africa's film screens.

When the mass protests of 2011 erupted across the region, Maghrebi cinema was again at the rendezvous with history. Hicham Lasri's feature film *They Are the Dogs* (2013) opens in the main square of Casablanca, where a large crowd of young protesters are shouting slogans against corruption and calling for the fall of the regime. A TV crew is also in the public square desperately looking for an interesting news story. An emaciated man stands out in the crowd. He looks not only lost but out of time altogether, like an alien from outer space. As we learn later, he has just been released from jail after thirty years. When all the surviving detainees from his cohort were released in 2001, he was not, because his existence was forgotten even by his jailers. He was imprisoned during the Bread Riots which engulfed Casablanca in June 1981 when thousands of young and unemployed people took to the streets after the government's decision to lift subsidies on essential foodstuffs. Hundreds were killed and thousands jailed, dumped in nondescript burial grounds or 'disappeared' by the regime. Our freshly released Unknown or 404, who remembers his matriculation number but not his name anymore, was arbitrarily arrested after he went out to buy stabilising wheels for his kid's bike and flowers for his wife. Upon his release in 2011, he gradually discovers how much the world and Casablanca have changed. Hungry for a sensational story, the TV crew accompany him around the city in search of his wife and children. In one scene, 404 visits his grave in the cemetery, where he was buried after the authorities informed his family of his death in the Bread Riots. Most of his friends have died and the surviving few have metamorphosed from ardent socialists in the last century to plain mouthpieces for the neo-colonial regime in the twenty-first. 404 ultimately finds his wife and children, but they refuse to accept him back. For them he is dead and should have never returned. In leaving the house, he runs into his grandson, who has just been released from the police station, where he was detained and tortured for taking part in the 2011 protests. Perhaps 404's detention was not in vain after all, and the flames of resistance will be kept alight by a new generation of disaffected youth.

In Lasri's low-budget film, the handheld camera of the TV crew with its extreme close-ups and shaky frames makes the journey in urban space intensive, intimate and full of violent suspense. The *cinéma vérité* footage captures the everyday effects of uncertainty and arbitrary violence which characterised the 2011 protests in Morocco and around the region. In the film, radio and TV coverage of the revolts acts as the soundtrack for 404's search for his bearings. The speed-fire movements of Lasri's guerrilla camera render the urgency of the historical moment. It maps out Casablanca as a totality of stark socio-economic disparities and rampant psychological violence, which erupts or threatens to do so at any moment. The camera also runs (often literally) into the ordinary man on the street. The Unknown, who was left on the margins of history for 30 years, suddenly finds himself at the centre of history repeating itself. Thirty years have gone by, but the same symptoms of poverty, anger and desperation are visible in Casablanca. The world has changed, Casablanca has experienced three decades of physical and social transformations, but the roots of oppression and its victims are still the same. In the course of two days, 404 rises back from the ashes to put these transformations to the test. After exposing the violence and resilient structures of oppression in his own city and country, the ghost of history goes back whence it came. The film ends here and now, but history continues its course. By bracketing the story of an ordinary Casablancan unknown subject between two pivotal moments in the history of contemporary Morocco (1981-2011), Lasri's film and Maghrebi cinema continues to chronicle Moroccan societies. Over the last few decades, this cinema has offered a realist critique of the neoliberal present and a critical repertory of ordinary subjects' small acts of resistance against daily regimes of oppression. Cinema is thus one of the contemporary Maghreb's compelling postcolonial archives and, in decades to come, a source of social history and perhaps lessons and seeds for change at the hands of a people yet to come.

INSIDE MAURITANIA

Anita Hunt

Mauritania is undoubtedly the most overlooked country in the Maghreb. The largely desert Islamic Republic, with an Arab and Berber population in the north and black Africans in the south, is seldom in the news – unless it has something to do with al-Qaida. As Mauritanian social network activist Nasser Weddady explains:

Mauritanians are very conscious that they and their country are a footnote in the world, and more so in the Arab world itself. We are almost never talked about, very few people can even locate us on the map. Most Arabs don't even know that we share with them a common language and in the case of some, common ancestry. Furthermore, when fellow Arabs talk about us, the clichés and stereotypes veer quickly into the realm of the exotic.

Mauritania covers more than a million square kilometres of the Saharan desert, its two main population centres punctuating the 800-kilometre Atlantic coastline. Stretching east into the Sahel from these two pins on the map, the angular northern borders wedge against Morocco, Algeria and Mali, while the Senegal River valley softens the outline along the southern edge. The immense desert contains a wealth of natural resources such as copper, gold, gypsum and iron, but the extractive industries offer few employment opportunities for unskilled labour. Meanwhile, persistent drought, desertification and poverty in the interior gradually push tens of thousands of Mauritanians to abandon a life of humble self-sufficiency as nomadic livestock herders or smallholders in rural village communities. They arrive seeking new means of survival in Nouakchott and Nouadhibou. But they find that high unemployment means few work opportunities, even for trained workers or university graduates, let alone semi-nomadic herdsmen or farmers with only a rudimentary education. The inevitable result is a sprawling mess of urban slums, many of which are routinely bulldozed by the authorities, the inhabitants forced to beg for charity. The towns were not built to cope with such dramatic population shifts, and meagre efforts to create or improve essential infrastructure are failing to keep pace.

The bustling economic capital of Nouadhibou huddles beneath Western Sahara, to the north, maintaining a vantage point from which to survey the nation's massive fishing grounds, its cubist landscape of squat terracotta buildings and rickety shacks scoured by desert sand and sea salt. Beyond the jumble of boat yards, warehouses and dry docks, massive foreign trawlers and container vessels jostle alongside smaller fishing boats and supply ships. While the sea holds the promise of a sustainable fortune in fish, very little finds its way to Mauritanian tables: most is processed at sea in huge factory ships and shipped directly to distant lands. The local and artisanal fishing sector is dominated by immigrant workers from nearby Senegal with stronger sea-legs. Nouakchott lies to the south, a little over halfway to Senegal, on a site first established by colonial invaders, and was selected as the national capital in 1960 when Mauritania gained independence from France. It boasts the presidential residence, known locally as the 'grey palace', a few embassies or diplomatic missions, and a handful of multi-storey buildings. Expanding under the relentless influx of new residents, Nouakchott oozes out from the centre, retreating from the ocean into the unforgiving desert, the buildings growing progressively smaller and shabbier towards the margins, finally dissolving into salvaged scraps of wood and flapping tarpaulin. The rather drab and dreary aspect of the twin capitals allows them to serve as an unobtrusive backdrop to their vastly more interesting and ethnically diverse inhabitants, comprising Moors of both Arab and African descent, Berbers, and West African ethnic groups such as Fulani, Songhai and Wolof.

The richness of Mauritanian cultural diversity reveals itself through a vibrant social tapestry of customs and traditions, rooted in pre-colonial history yet often embroidered by the experience and impact of French rule. The official language is Arabic, although French is widely used, and there is a strong tradition of speaking the local Hassaniya dialect, which now features in conversations between the growing networks of social media users. Facebook is the dominant social network, with Twitter trailing behind in the popularity stakes, and there is a small but dedicated, and very vocal, blogging community. Less than 5 per cent of the country has reliable internet access, although the telecoms operators promise that this is set to change, with the recent installation of a new high-capacity undersea cable connection to Europe. True connectivity depends on the rest of the country being able to connect, and judging by the lack of progress on infrastructure projects in general, it could take several years to reach even partial penetration.

Through their various online interactions, Mauritanians have tentatively begun to record their history and tell their stories, but the majority of their efforts are completely overshadowed by Western media narratives, which tend to focus on isolated and often sensationalist topics, such as slavery, terror threats, or the practice of force-feeding known as gavage. Mauritanians also write about these issues, and discuss them quite candidly online, but serious research requires patience and stamina, and should include both Arabic and French language sources. It is not unusual to see Arabic, the Hassaniya dialect and French being used in the same online conversation, even in posts from the same user. It is not uncommon to meet multilingual speakers who move seamlessly between different dialects and languages, which makes holding a normal conversation an incredibly challenging exercise, although it could be a very rewarding experience. There is a fairly strong sense of national identity in Mauritania, at one level, but this is overlaid with a patchwork of social and political ideas and beliefs, ranging from candid Arab nationalism to outright racism against anyone of sub-Saharan or West African descent with several shades in between. Language – especially the choice between languages, and how that is played out – both feeds into, and springs from, this sense of cultural identity mingled with fear and prejudice.

The enduring oral tradition of Mauritania has several unique facets, including traditional Mauritanian singing, performed by both men and women, to the accompaniment of Moorish hand drums and stringed instruments and the enthusiastic, rhythmic, clapping of the audience. Far smaller, but popular among urban youth, is a more Western-influenced interest in popular music, notably rap and female solo vocalists. The annual Assalamalekoum Festival draws talent and support from Africa and Europe to Nouakchott for a cultural week of music, dance, and poetry. It is the brainchild of Limam Kane aka Monza, one of a handful of Mauritanian rappers who has earned international recognition, as much for his passionate commitment to promoting a culture of tolerance through art as for his music. Other notable Mauritanian rappers include Waraba 'The Lion' Brahim Fall, and the rap trio Ewlad Leblad.

Poetry is undoubtedly the best-known and most enduring pastime, widely loved and practised in subtly different forms by young and old, causing Mauritania to be known across the Arab world as 'the country of one million poets'. So deeply ingrained is the poetic tradition that a blogger recently described prose as relatively new and uncharted territory for Mauritanian writers, explaining that poetry was, for so long, the only prevailing literary standard. He goes on to suggest that prose was the outcome of 'displacement from the open nomadic horizon into the narrow space of the city with all its impositions and inclinations', and relates that to the emergence of central government in post-colonial Mauritania during the 1960s and 70s. The discipline is actually quite male-dominated, but women can and do write poetry. There is even a special form of poetry used only by women, known as *intebra*, consisting of two highly condensed poetic phrases, and used exclusively to convey romantic meaning. The joke between one of my Mauritanian friends and I goes that Mauritanian poetesses perfected the micro-poetry format, placing them far in advance of Twitter. Whether male or female, *griot* is the name used to describe someone who combines poetry, storytelling, humour, gossip, and occasionally political commentary, as a performance art, and who quite literally embodies a living history of the country and the events that shape it.

Borrowing from the poetic tradition and the role of the *griot* in sharing news, an enterprising radio presenter working for the country's first national radio station, Mohamed Lemine ould Agatt, introduced a new programme. It was shortly after the declaration of independence in 1960, and the government was keen to tackle the challenge of fostering a sense of identity and unity among the mainly nomadic community, at that time still spread across the desert wilderness. The programme is known as 'al-Balaghat' or 'messages', taken from its full title which translates to 'the people's messages and communications', and is still broadcast every week night. The messages are delivered or relayed to the radio station's office by citizens at home or abroad, and composed by the presenter into a unique format to be read out on air in the Hassaniya dialect in an exaggerated, sing-song intonation. The result is part poem and part song that is best described as a kind of 'singing telegram'. Individual messages are known simply as *balagh* and, through the genius of ould Agatt, became the first new oral tradition to enter Mauritanian culture for centuries. As with the *intebra* feminine poetic form, each *balagh* engages the imagination of the listener, turning what would otherwise be a fairly terse missive into a more rounded communication, reminding them of their heritage and history. After more than forty years, every Mauritanian knows about the *balagh*, its formats and traditions, and it has become the stuff of legend. The story goes that the first president, Mokhtar ould Daddah, warned ould Agatt that the telegraph and postal services would feel threatened by the popularity of the programme, and would try to close it down. Ould Lagatt is said to have promised the president that the show would be aired in the evenings, to avoid competing with the other media. Decades later, mobile telecoms have dominated the sector, usurping the national landline network for domestic consumers, telegrams are reserved for formal state occasions, and the postal service is virtually non-existent, but *balagh* and Radio Mauritanie are still going strong.

The local dress is as colourful as the language. The typical robe worn by most women shrouds everything but the face, hands, and feet like a brightly-patterned mist, and is a single length of fabric, usually fine voile, about two metres wide and six metres in length. Wearing the *melehfa* is almost an art-form, and the end result is effortlessly elegant, even a little mysterious, as one is forced to ponder how the flimsy fabric is able to remain in place without coming adrift at the slightest movement. Despite being swaddled in this cloud of fabric, women do not seem to find it any impediment to physical activities like driving or working. The small group of women who have pilot's licences tend to wear more practical garb, and women who serve in the military wear regular uniform, but elsewhere, work clothes are often worn on top of the robe.

Men seldom wear the full national costume, which includes a waistcoat-style sleeveless or short-sleeved top, and loose fitting pants reaching just below the knee. The pants are fastened by a long length of leather worn as a belt, which dangles rather precariously from the waist, as if waiting to trip them. It takes very little imagination to realise that such an accessory would be extremely useful to anyone living a nomadic lifestyle, and needing to draw well water, hobble the odd camel, or pitch a tent in a sandstorm. Indeed, the main garment, the *dara'a*, can double as a tent in an emergency. A diaphanous gown, made from two man-sized sheets of heavy cotton damask joined at the shoulders and the hem, the *dara'a* sports a large shield-shaped front pocket, positioned slightly to the left below a deep asymmetrical 'V' neckline. Many are embellished with geometric shapes, of which diamonds are prevalent, in shades of light umber or gold, like the sands of the Sahara. The gowns themselves are only ever seen in white or blue, although there are many shades used, from the pale of a winter morning to the deep azure of the ocean. The wide shoulder seams drop from the neck to the wrist to form loose open sleeves, and are usually folded into broad pleats which rest on the shoulders. To complete the ensemble, men veil themselves with a strip of cloth worn turban-style. It is called a *hawli* and can be tied using one of several methods, leaving the eyes uncovered, sometimes also showing the nose or the chin as well. The various methods of wrapping the *hawli* can sometimes indicate membership of specific cultural groups, but most often it's just an optional mode of dress, and many men go bareheaded. More colours are used for the *hawli* than for the *dara'a*, but certain colours have special significance. Black, for example, is worn for weddings by the groom and his entourage, to match the bridal robe, which is all black. The bride herself remains out of sight during most of the wedding celebration, and is sometimes hidden by her bridesmaids and female relatives, to force the groom to search for her and also to prevent the guests from staging a fake kidnapping, which is another part of the wedding tradition.

Weddings are extremely popular in Mauritania, and part of the excitement they bring is from knowing that, despite the severe economic hardship, the groom has managed to gather enough money to cover the cost of the wedding and to support himself and his bride in their new life. A change in financial circumstances, however, can signal the end of the relationship. Although polygamy is legal it is not that popular, and with two out of every five marriages ending in divorce, second or third marriages are common. Women can divorce and remarry as often as they wish without attracting any social stigma. In fact, it is not unusual for women to celebrate their divorce with a big family gathering. There is a recent, somewhat disturbing, trend of women insisting on marrying men who have not been previously married, yet retaining their right to divorce and remarry. An increase in this behaviour could create a quite devastating social imbalance. The level of inequality such attitudes generate has already opened wounds, to the extent that one man founded an NGO to defend the rights of Mauritanian men. Compared to most Arab countries, women in Mauritania are considered to be extremely emancipated, something that is surprising for a conservative Muslim society with a legal system based partly on Islamic principles and partly borrowed from France. This perception of gender equality sits uncomfortably alongside stories of female rape victims being jailed for breaking the law, female hereditary slaves being used for non-consensual sex by their masters, and girls as young as five being sent off to 'fattening farms' in the countryside to be fed large volumes of camel's milk and greasy bowls of millet porridge with added lard. Mauritanian society undeniably has many troubling issues to contend with. Hence the popularity of civil society groups, including some dedicated to women's and children's rights, and others promoting the abolition of slavery. Yet there are few tangible signs to suggest serious progress on any of these issues.

However, these issues are regularly highlighted by a burgeoning local media, with hundreds of journalists writing for newspapers or news websites. There are also several dozen political parties and many small independent charities. Mosques, sometimes with small schools attached, are another major feature. These Qur'anic schools, or *Mahdaras*, are vitally important, especially in rural and regional communities, often representing the only source of education for marginalised local children living in poverty. Sustained and widespread access to religious education and places of worship, supported by over 8,000 mosques, has created a society in which Islam is as natural as breathing. Formal education opportunities are patchy at best, with a mixture of state, military, and private schools, including some French academies. The country has only one university, in Nouakchott, and two Islamic education institutes, with demand for places outstripping supply many times over. There are hundreds of highly committed teachers across the entire education sector, but they are almost all rendered powerless by an inefficient government administration and lack of funding. Many state schools struggle because of a severe lack of basic supplies, including desks, chairs, chalk, and textbooks. Qur'anic schools face even more hardships since they rely almost entirely on student contributions and charitable donations, in a country where more than 42 per cent live below the poverty line.

In July 2013, at the end of the school year, the education ministry published lists of examination results for secondary school students preparing to enter high school, and also for high school students who had taken the Baccalaureate, many of them hoping to enter university. The Baccalaureate results were disappointing for two reasons. First, because the pass rate was less than ten per cent, and second, because an analysis of the spreadsheet indicated that the results had been tampered with. While the implications of this twin tragedy were still sinking, the high school student results were released, a little later than promised, but the report was incomplete. There was no official explanation. So I decided to take a look myself and got hold of a copy of the file. One feature stood out on a casual inspection of the high school entrance examination results. That partial list, containing many thousands of names, recorded an identical date of birth for every child, most of whom were born in the past ten or twelve years, but surely not all on 31st December. No one knows the actual size of the Mauritanian population; one can only speculate why the government does not bother to undertake a census. But the prevailing theory is that the ruling class, dominated by Moorish Arab elites, is afraid to reveal that they are outnumbered by an oppressed majority of black Africans. For a state to impose a situation on its citizens where they are casually assigned the same date of birth on the only official records indicates a level of callous neglect beyond most people's comprehension. It also brings to mind the chilling effects of entrenched poverty and illiteracy, where entire villages might not have access to even a basic calendar, and would struggle to read one even if they did. Villages where the nearest health clinic is more than a hundred kilometres away along unmade roads, where the registrar of births and deaths is even further away, where the only means of transport are walking or riding a donkey.

Mauritania is not only steeped in history, it is also trapped in it. For the marginalised majority of Mauritanians, time is almost at a standstill. This New Year's Eve, if you toast the coming year, remember that you are also celebrating the state-imposed birthday of countless uncounted Mauritanians.

AN AMERICAN IN MOROCCO

John Liechty

When my Moroccan wife of a year needed a visa to enter the United States it seemed simple enough – a trip to the American Consulate in Rabat, then on to visit friends and family. There were a number of good reasons to expect the procedure to go smoothly. For one thing, Fouzia had been to the States half a dozen times and had attained half a dozen visas in the recent past. The woman was, furthermore, an example of the respectable professional types who so baffled the unprofessional likes of my colleague Wendell and me, who'd slid into teaching as haphazardly as balls finding their slots on a roulette wheel. Fouzia regarded the teaching of English as a serious profession, and had once served as president of the Moroccan Association of Teachers of English. Her visits to the States had all been white-bread. She had led groups of Moroccan high school students and had spent two years in the States as a student herself. She had broken none of the Great Satan's laws. She had no incendiary political views. She was not destitute. She had a job in Morocco she had worked hard to get and was working hard to keep. Jumping ship was far from her mind.

In short, as my wife and I walked into the US Consulate we had little reason to expect that Fouzia's application for a tourist visa would be anything but routine. The year was 1989. The consulate had just undergone a facelift, moving from the easygoing, friendly, rather unassuming place it had been to the defensive, ill-at-ease, rather forbidding stockade it was becoming. Security measures had been taken – an indicator, it seemed to me, of insecurity. The Greatest Nation in History was aware of its waning status as world friend, world leader. A dozen new 'flowerpots' squatted along the pavement separating the street from the consulate wall. These massive blocks of concrete were to deter anyone piloting a vehicle full of explosives. That the blocks held enough dirt to support a few geraniums or Norfolk pine could not disguise their purpose, or the fact that they were ugly as warts. The facelift featured higher, reinforced walls topped with concertina wire, a new, more sophisticated barrier gate and screening point, a roof bristling with surveillance equipment, and closed circuit cameras in every direction.

Advocates of such changes would argue their necessity, observing that we live in a dangerous world. Maybe. The Rabat Consulate facelift had come in direct response to the Iranian Revolution. In 1979, security at the US embassy in Tehran had been spectacularly compromised and hostages had been taken. The history of America's myopic meddling in Iran was familiar enough. While many individuals within the US government were aware that it had to some degree brought the deluge down upon itself, the official response was typical: pretend the revolution came out of nowhere, feign ignorance or innocence concerning American partnership, and attempt to avert future embarrassments by implementing cosmetic defensive gestures. Hence the 'flowerpots' appearing along US embassies and consulates from Karachi to Rabat. I considered them a waste of money and time, a misapplication of energy, a gratuitous snub.

But what did I know? Fouzia and I waited our turn, then approached the plate glass to present her application. She had to submit proof of employment, a current bank statement, rent, gas, and water receipts, and a copy of a reservation for a return ticket. These were duly collected by the vice-consul, Ted Kuntsler III, whose pseudonym may yield a hint of my feelings for the man, feelings that were undoubtedly reciprocal. Kuntsler was pink and large, reminding me of one of the pigs at the tail end of *Animal Farm* – one of those humanised pigs on two legs. Kuntsler asked us to resume our seats while he made copies and considered. He then called us back to the window, sliding Fouzia's dossier back under the bullet-proof plate.

'The application for a tourist visa is denied,' he stated. 'However, as the wife of an American citizen, Ms Sabil has the right to apply for a resident visa to the United States.'

'But she doesn't need or want a resident visa. And we're meant to be leaving in a few weeks.'

'If you want to discuss the decision further you can arrange an appointment through my secretary.'

We arranged the appointment and left, Fouzia with tears in her eyes and I with a lump in my throat. The visa rejection gave me a taste of the rage the routinely rejected feel towards America, particularly within the Muslim world. In time I became grateful for that. But for the moment I merely wanted to blow up the consulate. If there had been a hawker outside the door peddling bombs I would have bought one without hesitation and tossed it over the concertina wire in hopes of frying Kuntsler III's bacon.

The 'discussion' took place a few days later. It did not go well. Asked to explain his decision, Kuntsler referred to inadequate proof that Fouzia would ever return to Morocco. What about the other times she had been to the States and returned? Not a guarantee, Kuntsler said. What of her job? Someone with Fouzia's qualifications, Kuntsler noted, could easily find a better one in the Land of Opportunity. What of family ties? What of a mother, what of brothers and sisters? Kuntsler seemed mildly amused. 'Each year literally hundreds of Moroccans happily leave their families for a chance to live in America,' he explained. What of Fouzia's marriage to an American? 'That is why she has the right to apply for a resident visa.' What of the fact that she didn't want a resident visa? 'There is simply no proper guarantee,' Kuntsler sidestepped, 'of return.'

'What would constitute a proper guarantee? Give us an example.'

'For instance, if you had a couple of children you were leaving behind in Morocco. That would be considered a very strong guarantee.'

'You mean like hostages,' I suggested. Kuntsler did not savour the analogy. If there had been any hope at all of his revoking the decision, it disappeared now. My words grew less guarded, more bitter. My arguments degenerated towards insinuations that the vice-consul was an asshole. At some point Kuntsler observed that he didn't need people like me telling people like him how to do their jobs. He said it was a very difficult job and that half the time even persons equipped with superior discernment and the best intentions found it overwhelming. In that case, I suggested, might as well hand a monkey a set of dice and let him be vice-consul.

I am largely passive, slow on the draw, easily cowed and intimidated. The comment about the dice-throwing monkey rates as one of very few made over the course of my life that might be called courageous. Yet Kuntsler III, pinkening, refused to acknowledge its appeal. As we had wasted half an hour of his time, he suggested that the best thing for us now would be to leave.

I went home and wrote a letter, feeling powerless, voiceless, inadequate, and a liability to my wife. For all I knew, Kuntsler may have given Fouzia her visa had she not been married to me. To this day I do not understand the motives, but Kuntsler seems to have suspected us of attempting a green card marriage, a scam to get to America without going through the bureaucratic rigmarole. I addressed my letter to the 'Ambassador of the United States to Morocco', and waited for a response. Surely, I thought, the ambassador would call us in for an interview, issue a heartfelt and appalled apology, and set things to rights.

My ignorance was boundless. A response came a week later, thanking me for my concern but upholding the decision of the vice-consul. Translation? Fuck Off, signed by the ambassador. We showed the letter to Rabia, a friend of Fouzia's working at the Consulate.

'So that was you!' Rabia said. 'The ambassador didn't even read your letter. And he for sure didn't write the response. I should know. Kuntsler dictated and I typed. All the Ambassador did was sign.'

I felt like vomiting. 'You mean... The ambassador didn't read...?' I sounded like a child who's just learned his letters to the North Pole have been written in vain.

'Oh, don't take it too much to heart,' Rabia advised. 'It's how things go. One of the consul's jobs is to screen the ambassador's mail.'

'How would one go about getting a letter to the ambassador – one he was sure to read?'

Rabia graciously agreed to steer the next edition of my letter towards the Mighty One's desk. She bore no great love for Kuntsler III. So I at least had the satisfaction of knowing my letter was read at some point by the person it had been written to. I had the further satisfaction of hearing through the grapevine that Kuntsler was made to sweat for his sins. Had we not known someone personally, had we not been given an inside glimpse into the workings of the machine, even these small compensations would have been denied.

In the end, there were no larger compensations – no interview with a sheepish ambassador, not so much as a squeak of apology, and of course no visa. Americans of a certain stripe are forever asking and will forever be asking why so much of the world seems disenchanted with America, the place Madeleine Albright modestly dubbed the Indispensable Nation. 'Why do they hate us?' these innocents ask, with beetled brow. I often wish they could experience a run-in with one of the several Kuntslers working for the Indispensable Nation's government. It might assist their understanding.

In February of 1991 more than 400 Iraqi civilians were killed when two bombs were dropped on a bunker in the Amiriyah neighbourhood of Baghdad. The place had served as a civilian air raid shelter during the Iran-Iraq War. US intelligence claimed it had since been converted to a military command centre. To the 408 people incinerated underground, which of the claims or counterclaims were true hardly mattered.

I was living at the time in the Oudayas, a popular area of Rabat. The Amiriyah bombing marked the low point of a low-down war. The news made me sick to the stomach. I didn't feel like going out, didn't feel like facing the faces in the street. My friend Andrew came by in the evening to collect me to go to the *hammam*. I'd forgotten it was our bath night. The house Fouzia and I lived in was old, damp and cold. The closest thing you could get to a bath there involved heating pans of water on the stove and dumping them over your shivering carcass beside the bathroom drain.

At the *hammam*, in contrast, you could sit for hours steaming out the chill. You ducked from a side street of the medina through an ancient doorway into a room with horseshoe arches and tiled floors. The lower third of the walls was tiled with green and cream *zellaj* – the upper two thirds were sloppily daubed in whitewash. Aziz, the stoned receptionist behind the battered wooden counter, took your money. Past the counter you stepped up into a little changing room the shape of a freight car. Around the perimeter were rickety wooden benches where you sat to remove your clothes. Men were not to strip naked as I once discovered to my embarrassment. Etiquette required you to keep your shorts on. You stuffed your remaining clothes and towel into a bag and turned it over to Aziz, who gave you a couple of rubber buckets in exchange. Then in you went for your bath.

'I guess not tonight,' I sighed. Andrew was a Scot, free from a passport issued by the Hope of the Free World. 'You go on. I think I'll just stay here stewing in shame.' But Andrew didn't want to go to the bath alone. It was a wet, windy night. Hardly anybody was in the streets. And the trip would do me good.... It didn't take him long to persuade me. I've always been grateful for that because something good happened that night of the Amiriyah bombs. It could not change the news or the fact that 408 souls seeking shelter under the earth had been erased by what the Pentagon referred to as the latest in bunker-busting technology. What happened that night at the *hammam* did not make me feel any better about my country or myself or the war. But it made me feel better about the human race and its possibilities.

Andrew was right. There was next to nobody out. Sensible Moroccans were at home eating *bissara*, drinking tea, enjoying their families. They were not out patrolling the streets in the event that a guilt-ridden American citizen might be headed for the *hammam*. We had the changing room all to ourselves. I relaxed, reflecting that the accident of my nationality was more disturbing to me than it was to most Moroccans. Aziz certainly didn't mind, but then Aziz had been sucking the *sebsi*.

We handed him our clothes. He handed us our buckets. There were three vaulted chambers in the wet part of the bath. The first was unheated, a sort of decompression chamber. We didn't need it yet, and proceeded to the second vault. The walls were dripping, the air warm. A body lay sprawled on the floor. We passed to the third and final chamber, dipping buckets of water from the tank, one scalding hot, one cool. The we stationed ourselves at an end of the vault, placing our gear around us. We each had a dipper to transfer water from bucket to body. We had a bar of soap, a comb, shampoo. And we each had a bath mitt, the abrasive pad needed to remove the week's buildup of hide. After a while the heat caught up with us, we felt woozy and entombed. We collected our stuff and rose to relocate.

'*Salaam aleikum.*' My heart fell. It was our fruit-seller from the medina, a man known as Haj Brahim. Brahim was the most pleasant, most scrupulous, most all-round decent person one might chance to meet. I bought apples, grapes, melons, pomegranates, and oranges at his stall. There was never any danger that you might overpay or find green or overripe items in your shopping bag. Such was not the case with the average fruit and vegetable vendor in the medina, who thought nothing of slipping you a dud peach or selling you a kilo of potatoes that weighed 800 grams. The only reason I kept a wary eye on Brahim was because he was likely to give more than you'd paid for, and I didn't want him going broke on my account. He reminded me of my Aunt Shirley. If you weren't careful, you ended up with the shirt off her back.

Haj Brahim and Aunt Shirley shared a further similarity. They were openly, comfortably, devoutly religious, while the fact that you were not did nothing to diminish you in their eyes. Haj Brahim had one of those prayer plums in the middle of his forehead, a darkish bruise that indicated prostrations five times a day. His face had a religious shine to it – not the facile sheen that reflexively made me want to go forth and sin – but something deep that commanded respect.

So why did my heart sink when I saw Haj Brahim at the *hammam*? I simply hadn't wanted to meet anyone that night, certainly not bad people, but just as certainly not good people. I hadn't wanted to show my face or talk to anyone. A pair of American bombs had just wiped 408 souls off the face of the earth, trusting souls who'd believed they'd taken safe refuge in an air raid shelter. That was a fact. One side put it down to naked aggression. The other held that the shelter was a legitimate military target, that the civilians present there had been used as 'human shields'. The truth would never be known. Both sides were old hands at lying, both believed their own lies, their own accusations, their own pretexts. Both sides had learned to dismiss the blood of children as acceptable spillage in the pursuit of power.

Waleikum Salaam... La Bes?... Bikheir?... Al-Hamdullilah!... Barakallahufik! Andrew and I supplied our share of the singsong necessitated by familiar encounters in Morocco. Haj Brahim looked pale and pasty in his underpants, the pallor offset by a black bush of beard and sun-struck neck and forearms. He went into the third room, reappearing moments later with two buckets of water, which he set on the floor before us. Without a word he put a bath mitt on his right hand, stood over me, and began sanding my back, gently at first, then more vigorously, sloughing off rolls of last week's skin from the places I'd have found hard to reach. He next went to work on Andrew. When he was done he went back to the hot room.

Andrew and I continued what the Haj had started, scraping ourselves pink as crabs. He was gone before we had finished. The *hammam*, he noted on the way out, made him dizzy. I don't know if Brahim was conscious of what he had accomplished that night. I hadn't forgotten the war or its shame. But I'd been reminded what an honour it was to be associated with a race that counted the Haj, Aunt Shirley, Andrew, and Aziz as members. They were part of a world worth living in. I felt the way one would hope to feel on leaving a *hammam*, halfway clean.

Moroccans were not always easy people to get on with. Many were easy-going and even-tempered enough but many struck me as edgy, bristling for a fight, addicted to confrontation. No transaction was simple. The taxi driver sized you up, ascertained you were a foreigner, and snapped the meter off.

'Why did you turn the meter off?'

He would give you one of those 'What can I do? Ain't fate a bitch?' looks, and say: 'It's not working.' And then he would add a phrase I never learned to abide, *Chnou ghadi n'deer?*, meaning: 'What can I do? Ain't fate a bitch!' The confrontation came at the end of the ride when one was asked to pay a fare four times what the meter would have shown had the meter been turned on. You could pay it and feel like a chump. You could argue in hopes of bringing down the extortion rate, only to be made to feel like a petty skinflint in the process. You could throw a tantrum and threaten to call a policeman… There was just one thing you could not do. You could not win.

At such times you felt your life was not your own, that you were little more than a life-support system for a dollar. Transactions that should have been a simple pleasure, or at least simple – buying a ballpoint pen, flagging a taxi, checking into a hotel – they all became potential flashpoints, all became occasions for yet another feud or stand-off. Much of the problem had to do with me. My Arabic was weak and I was doing little to raise it to a level where I might defend myself or pull off anything close to diplomacy. The prospect of having to defend myself sickened me. I was naturally reserved, soft-spoken, unassertive. Turning the other cheek came more naturally than being forthright. Staying silent came more easily than standing up for myself. None of my qualities, inasmuch as they were qualities, was worth a Moroccan damn. I prided myself on my patience – from the start it proved a useless commodity. I was merely weak, and a foreigner on top of it – fair game for every opportunist, impromptu guide, con artist and cadger in the country.

After my wedding, my sister and her husband wanted to see something of Morocco beyond Casablanca and Rabat, so a few days later we boarded the train to Fez. Fouzia was unable to go with us, but promised to accompany us to Marrakesh and Essaouira once we were back. Fez glowed in the guidebook… atmospheric medina, sumptuous food, ancient university, historic mosque and Jewish quarter, medieval madrasa, enchanting fountains, vibrant craft industries. There was no mention of tiresome touts.

The train was not crowded. We had a compartment to ourselves. As we passed Meknes and drew closer to Fez, we debated strategy. Would we find a hotel, or dive straight into the enchantments? Would we admire the arts and crafts, share a pot of tea, pass by the Kairaouine Mosque, or simply wander through the medieval (that word kept surfacing in the guidebook) medina? There hardly seemed time to cover the things that begged doing. The compartment door opened. Hassan stepped in. It took us a few moments to get over our good fortune. Hassan was in his early twenties, a native of Fez, a lifelong disciple of the city and its charms. To top it off, he was a student who wished only to practise English. He was not, he emphasised, one of those insufferable leeches we might have heard about, one of those insufferable, unshakeable mercenary guides.

We had never heard of such parasites, but were relieved that Hassan was not of their tribe.

'What would you like to see first?' he proposed. 'I will show you the old city.'

'But...' we demurred. 'But your studies... your family...your time. 'We didn't want to impose.

'Not a problem', Hassan assured us. 'You are hungry? First we will go to a famous restaurant in the heart of the old medina.'

We considered a second, and decided we were not really that hungry.

'But you must be hungry,' Hassan countered. It sounded more like an order than a speculation. We protested, but somehow ended up in the famous restaurant in the heart of the old medina. The place didn't strike us as overly famous. It wasn't very restaurant-like. In fact it had the air of a neglected spare room in a private house. We were the only souls around (no great surprise at 4 in the afternoon) apart from a sleepy man whom Hassan declared to be among the finest chefs in Fez. So far as we could tell we were not in the heart of the old medina. We didn't really know where we were, but it felt more like the bowel or the gizzard. Hassan had led us up, down, and around.

'You want belly dancer.' It wasn't a question. 'Very cheap. Very good.'

On this point we were adamant. We had no more need for a belly dancer than for an eleventh toe or a third nostril. Hassan shrugged and looked at his watch. He had grown a lot less charismatic since the train.

'You want hasheesh?'

'Why is the food taking so long?'

Hassan shrugged anew. 'Famous place, you wait a long time. After you eat, we go to carpet shop.'

We vetoed the idea. Hassan looked at his watch again. 'So what will we do after you eat?'

'We don't know', I said. 'Maybe just walk around for awhile. Maybe find our hotel.'

'I'll take you to best hotel. Very cheap.'

'I think', my sister said, 'you probably need to go study now. We have a guidebook. We know the hotel we're going to.' This wasn't strictly true, though we had some ideas.

'Guidebooks no good', Hassan observed darkly. 'Out of date. You need a guide.'

'But you're not a guide, remember?' This seemed to throw him for a second. He shrugged, but didn't budge. 'You're a student. Really you need to go. We would like to be alone.'

'What about my tip?'

Everybody was turning sulky now. Eventually Hassan left. A little later, three salads reached the table with a flourish.

'Does salad come with the meal?' my sister asked. 'We didn't order salad.'

'Yes, yes!' said the sleepy man, who'd splashed some water across his face. 'Salad! Soup! Starter! Bread! Main Course! Dessert! Tea! Special menu. All one price!'

We were doomed and we knew it. The food wasn't bad, though nowhere as good as the food we had been getting in people's homes. When the bill came we pretended to find it rather reasonable. This was mere face-saving. The bill was preposterous. There was little consolation in making concessions for Hassan's cut.

Outside the restaurant we took our bearings, blinking like hostages who've had their blindfolds removed. We knew nothing beyond that we were somewhere in Fez. We had blown half our budget, needed to find lodging, still hadn't seen anything, were missing the enchantment. And now it was getting dark. We eventually stumbled across one of the hotels mentioned in the guide. We lay back on our beds, reluctant to admit that the only thing we really wanted to do at this point was bolt the door, curl up in a fetal position, pull the covers over our heads, and go to sleep.

We stayed barricaded in the room another hour. The guidebook proposed evening as a good time simply to enjoy a stroll round the medieval city. A stroll sounded good. Alas, we had yet to master the art of strolling in Fez. Stepping from the hotel was reminiscent of a team of horses in a B-movie stepping into a stream boiling with piranha. If we didn't want to have the flesh stripped from our bones, we would have to keep moving, which explains why a trio of gringos could be seen bolting through Fez, trailing a chain of prospective guides.

We pulled up by a stall where my sister bought 200 grams of olives simply because she could think of nothing better to do. 'Listen', one of the retinue said urgently, the way you'd speak to a man hanging over a precipice. 'Pay me 20 dirhams. That's all you have to do. All these other guides will disappear. That's why you need a guide. That's why you need me.' I may not have liked the notion, may have considered it a form of extortion, but in those few seconds it entered my skull that strolling in Fez was a privilege you paid for. I turned over 20 dirhams. Just as the young man had promised, the money brought respite.

The lad's name was Youssef. When our time was up, we arranged to meet again the following morning. Twenty dirhams for an hour's peace was starting to feel like the shrewdest bargain we were likely to make in Fez, cheaper than toothpicks at our famous restaurant in the heart of the old medina. We tried to forget the meal and Hassan. Tomorrow promised better things.

Nonetheless, it got off to a strange and disagreeable start. Up early I headed for a café down the street, where I had a cup of coffee. So far, so agreeable. Back at the hotel I stood in the sun along the wall watching a remarkable air show put on by squadrons of Alpine swifts. The birds shot down the street like schools of flying fish, squeaking with excitement, rapturous. Gnats or midges, flies or mosquitoes – whatever was on the menu, the swifts were in glory, buzzing the corridor of the street again and again.

Abruptly my attention was drawn earthward. 'Look at me when I'm talking to you', a man was saying, the same who'd just given my arm a tug. 'I said "Good morning".'

I looked at him, mute with incomprehension. He was in his early thirties, scruffy and down at heel, scowling, prickly, acting for all the world like he had just been slapped across the face. 'I said, I said "Good morning".'

'Good morning,' I complied.

'What gives you the right to stand here with your nose in the air?'

'What are you talking about?' I could feel myself bristling. I didn't know how to stroll in Fez. It seemed I didn't even know how to bloody watch birds there.

'When somebody talks to you, you talk to them. It's basic humanity. Or is that beyond you?'

'I was just watching the birds, okay?'

'You don't have to treat me like a dog.'

'I wasn't treating you like a dog.'

But that's what tourists did, the man protested. They treated people like dogs. It broke the rules of basic humanity.

'I was watching the birds,' I repeated.

'What?'

'I was watching the birds.'

'Birds are more important than people?'

'I'm going inside.' I left him cursing the cheek of foreigners, and fled back to the room. By the time we returned to the street, the swifts were gone. Youssef was right on time though, and I was right glad to see him. We visited the Jewish quarter and cemetery, the medrassa, a pottery shop, the tannery... and we strolled now and again, having paid for the privilege.

As the train neared Rabat that evening, a slim figure slipped into our compartment. His name was Karim. He sat down and asked where we were headed. He seemed pleased to hear we were going no further than Rabat because as luck would have it, he knew that city like the back of his hand, was going there himself, and hoped we might enjoy the windfall of his expertise. Not for money, he explained.

'I am a student, wishing only to practice my English. I am not one of those...' He stopped short. A darkness had fallen over the compartment. Ascertaining that this was not the moment to speak of students or guides, Karim got up and slipped out as deftly as he had entered.

We thought the trip down to Marrakesh in the company of Fouzia would be a relative breeze, but it wasn't. It proved particularly hard on Fouzia, who discovered the price one paid for hanging out with gringos. Every seventh step she seemed to become engaged in a verbal firefight with anywhere from one to four young males. These *shabab* were uniformly hostile and high-strung. Fouzia meanwhile was no pushover, no tender bud of Moroccan femininity. She charged into the fray at the slightest slight, intent on holding her own. The *shabab* perceived this refusal to yield as a personal insult, an assault on their testosterone, the least admissible of Fouzia's indiscretions. They started with accusations that she was a tout infringing on their turf. They ended with accusations that she was a shameless slut, a disgrace to the nation.

Fouzia defended herself every inch of the way, tongue blazing. She won her share of battles, but steadily lost the war. We staged a retreat from the shaded medina. In the Djemma F'naa, the great central square of Marrakesh, we bought glasses of orange juice and drank them down. We swirled with the mob under the afternoon sun. The temperature was over 100 degrees Fahrenheit. A kid tossed a snake round my brother-in-law's neck and feigned anger when no photograph was demanded, no tip was forthcoming. An old lady latched herself to my sister like a lamprey and rode her round the square until a few dirhams released the grip. An imp of an acrobat ran up, swirled the tasselled fez he was wearing, snatched the hat off his ringworm-scarred scalp, inverted it into a begging bowl, and wheedled until a coin arranged his disappearance. Poor Fouzia felt responsible for everything and everybody. She fought valiantly and lost steadily.

In time one came to accept this state of affairs whether one wanted to or not. It might be disagreeable, but in one way at least it was admirable. Moroccans simply weren't inclined to roll over for the tourist industry. It was their country, after all, and the fact that it wasn't much fun to beleaguered visitors didn't blow people's hair one way or the other. If tourists wanted to be left alone, they should have stayed home. But if they'd gone to the trouble of coming all the way to Morocco, it was Morocco they were going to get, by God, and one way or another they were going to pay for it. 'Hey!' I once heard a kid snarl to a tourist after a bitter altercation. 'You should be happy! This your vacation!' Indeed.

We maintained our drift round the Djemma F'naa, day softening as evening approached. A man with flashing eyes and long gray hair was motioning to me. He had a dignified air, and looked to be in his seventies.

He was sitting cross-legged under an umbrella on a pair of cushions. Before him on a holder lay an open Koran and alongside that a glass of water. The man again motioned with his hand, and with his eyes. It was captivating, compelling… It felt like fate. He willed me to come and I wanted to go.

'Don't do it!' Fouzia warned, battle-weary. But I was already on my way to engage destiny.

The man was well-preserved and good-looking, with a mane of silver hair. For five dirhams he offered to consult the *djinn* and wrest from them my fortune. After a day of 100-degree heat and wrangling with the *shabab*, it felt like a bargain. The seer grasped my hand and perused its palm. He consulted the Book, penned a verse on a scrap of paper, dunked the paper in the glass of water, and bade me drink the inky result. He then closed his eyes and muttered awhile with the spirits. Presently he detected hints of an interesting and exciting future. Along the far horizon he saw someone of the order of a tall dark stranger. He saw… Wait a moment… Hold on, it was something important, but the connection wasn't what it had been.

The old man opened his eyes. 'The *djinn*', he confided bluntly, 'need five more dirhams.'

Our bus to Essaouira was scheduled to leave the next morning at 9.00. We knew it would be a long, hot ride. Had we known how long and how hot, we would never have boarded that pressure cooker. But then we would never have come to Essaouira, and that would have been a great loss. The bus was packed. It left in the manner of Moroccan buses. Around 9.00 there was a great commotion, a crush of passengers, a revving of the motor, a sounding of the horn. A blind musician, a story teller, a liniment salesman filed down an aisle so packed with humanity that their passage seemed in defiance of physics — two bodies, more than two bodies, could in fact occupy the same space at the same time. In between came beggars. Urchins with pans of homemade *mille-feuille* entered the maelstrom. More came with gum, paper cornets of toasted pumpkin or sunflower seeds, penny sweets, bottles of water and pop. A man appeared with a live chameleon he seemed confident someone should want to buy. Outside, kids hawked bananas and tangerines, reaching the fruit up to their customers in plastic bags on sticks.

'*Ashara! Ashara! Ashara!*' The liniment seller talked fast and furiously. He had to as the bus seemed set to leave at any moment, and the benefits of his product seemed infinite. It was good for relatively small things – headaches, dizziness, sniffles, cramps, stomach ache, muscle aches, nosebleed, insomnia, fatigue, chilblains, blisters, ear ache, bee stings, tick bites, diarrhoea, constipation, worms, indigestion, sexual misfires, bedbugs, head lice, and sore throat. But it worked as well to combat the relatively big things such as cancer, depression, snakebite, infertility, and the evil eye. As time grew shorter and the list of attributes longer, the price of the liniment unexpectedly dipped to eight dirhams a bottle.

At 9.10 the driver threw the bus into gear and hit the gas. The thing began to rock forward, raising a cry of '*Bilati! Bilati! Bilati!*' inside and out. The driver held up his hand, fingertips together, in a gesture that suggested exasperation. He then cut the motor and disappeared into the café next door. The bus now showed no more sign of moving than a dead dog. A few passengers trickled out to tend to some last minute business, followed by a few more. From 9.30 on the temperature began to mount. A woman came through selling fans woven from palm fronds. We bought four.

Around 10.00 the bus was hot enough to bake bread, and was pitching forward again. '*Bilati!*' someone called. Someone else was banging the side. But this time we actually did take off, pausing just enough to let the last of the hawkers jump to the street. The driver barrelled along a few miles and we smiled, thinking that at this rate we would hit the coast in no time. Then the bus slowed. Then it stopped to (Could it be possible?) take on a few more passengers. We seemed to jerk along in this fashion all the way to Essaouira. The ride took seven hours.

By the time we tumbled out there wasn't much left of us or the fans. We limped for the city walls, listless as plants blasted by the sun. Yet it is miraculous how quickly the cool of evening will bring a plant around. We had only been walking ten minutes before making several observations, which if they held true, signified nothing less than deliverance. First, we had not as yet been pestered. Passersby did not offer to be our guides, or ask where we were from (*Ingleez? Alemagne? Canada? Ameriki?*), or insist we be assisted in finding a hotel, or claim to be students, or throw snakes round our necks, or charge us with tourist chauvinisms (*Why do you treat me like a dog?*), or steer us into famous restaurants in the heart of the historic medina, or wheedle us towards their uncle's carpet shop… They simply did what passersby are supposed to do. They passed by, ignoring us in the process.

Second, it was no longer insufferably hot. A breeze blew off the Atlantic that had us pawing through our bags for long sleeves. We were people who just a few minutes ago had been on a bus sweating freely as cheeses, wondering whether we would live to see another dawn or simply wilt into oblivion.

The place was quietly beautiful, and it felt like we were invited to be part of it. The beach ran for miles, ours for the walking. We stopped by a stall to look at some baskets. We were allowed to look. No one pressured us to buy. No one appeared to care. We tried a hotel and were astonished to discover a reasonable rate for a pleasant room facing the sea. We checked in, then walked at our leisure round the port and boat yard, ate at our leisure in one of the seafood stalls under an enormous pine, drank coffee at our leisure at a café built into the wall along the edge of the square, bought figs and nuts, looked out from the ramparts where Orson Welles had filmed scenes from *Othello*, returned to our hotel around midnight. We had been in Essaouira seven hours. Those first ten minutes had not been a fluke. Whatever Fez and Marrakesh had taken out of us, Essaouira was graciously restoring.

In time I developed a little rulebook on the subject of travel in Morocco:

Go to places like Fez, Marrakesh and Tangier if you must, but go forewarned – your life there might not be your own.

Try smaller quieter places where tourism is relatively dead: places like Chaouen, Zagora, Figuig, Essaouira, Midelt, El Jadida, Asilah, Taza, Sidi Ifni. Your life there may be proportionately more your own.

The Back of Beyond is the best bet of all.

A few visits to the Back of Beyond later this last rule seemed to be holding. I rode a bus over the Tizi'n'Tichka and walked twenty miles in the Djebel Sarhro, a section of the Anti-Atlas range, to a godforsaken village called Nkob. For a mile or two I had a companion, a Berber man who presently suggested he didn't have all day, wished me well, and left me behind like a Porsche distancing itself from a hobbled donkey. I saw neither man nor beast until I reached Nkob.

Another foray into the Back of Beyond led to a village called Igherm, reached after a pounding ride in the bed of a truck. For ten dirhams (less than a dollar in those days) I arranged to stay on the floor of a concrete cubicle. There was no electricity and no bed, but there was a plastic mat and I had a sleeping bag. 'Is there a toilet?' It was in retrospect a rather stupid question, but the curmudgeon who'd shown me to my room nodded, led me outside to a section of wall on which was written the ubiquitous *Mamnuaa il-boul* ('urination forbidden'), and left me to it.

A further trip landed Andrew and me in a place called Agadir Tissint, where we stayed in a little *fondouq* whose small rooms opened onto a central square blessed with a trickle of water and shade from a gnarled tree. Our room featured a lantern, a table and a bed. The walls were mud, whitewashed partway up. A *dhub*, a type of large lizard, roamed the courtyard, and a pair of hedgehogs made the rounds from room to room. The hedgehogs, our landlord advised, were to keep the scorpions down. We paid 20 dirhams for the room, and another 20 to the landlord to prepare a tagine with the potatoes and bit of scrag we had bought at the market. More wonderful than Marrakesh's Mamounia, and a sight cheaper.

I assured my wife that the best of Morocco was to be found in the backwaters, and she believed me. It sounded plausible. The further you got from Tangier, Fez or Marrakesh, the likelier you were to encounter the salt of the earth – such was the theory. I had a few days off that winter, and decided to spend them encountering the salt. I rode a bus to Taroudant, and another to Tata. The next morning I took a minibus on to Akka. I knew nothing about it save that on the map Akka seemed as far south as I could get in the time available. It was close to the border of Algeria and the disputed Western Sahara. I had no strategy for what I might do there, but I had a day or two and a sleeping bag.

My strategy was determined, as it often is for those with a sketchy hand of their own, by the hand of fate. Akka had a few buildings, a road, and a café. I went to the café, drank a coffee and looked for clues in my *Rough Guide to Morocco*. There weren't many. As there seemed to be a series of oases to the north, I decided to try my luck that way. Meanwhile, a young man approached the table and introduced himself. His name was Miloud.

'Have you come to see the *gravures rupestres*?', he asked. I didn't know what he meant, so he explained: prehistoric rock drawings of animals that no longer existed in North Africa – rhinoceros, elephant, ostrich and more. He produced a dossier – a couple of crumpled photographs, and an article written in Italian by a team of archaeologists. 'If you want', Miloud proposed, 'I can take you.'

I wanted all right. I'd had nothing beyond a vague notion of what to do once the coffee was finished. Suddenly I'd been handed a plan.

To see the *gravures rupestres*, Miloud explained, it would be necessary to walk a few kilometres, ten or thereabouts, to a village, his village, Um al-Aliq (Mother of the Leech). Once there we would spend the night at Miloud's house. His father, he said stoically, was dead, a victim of the war with the Polisario. There were no brothers or sisters left at home. Miloud stayed on for his mother's sake.

We walked to the southeast through scrub desert. Miloud made pleasant company. Neither of us had much to say, and both of us seemed to prefer it that way. The day was bright but not hot. We met a man riding sidesaddle on a donkey. I had several tins of sardines in my bag, and gave him one.

'You shouldn't have done that,' Miloud scolded once we had put some distance between us. 'These people are always taking liberties. He's got plenty.'

'Well', I observed. 'It's just a can of sardines.'

'Um al-Aliq', Miloud said at last. I couldn't see much beyond a cluster of date palms. A bit later I made out several mud structures. 'Let me talk to my mother before you go in. She's not feeling well and since my father died, she doesn't trust strangers.'

This seemed more than understandable. I waited outside a blue-painted metal door featuring a bit of decorative scrollwork, through which Miloud reappeared after a briefing with his mother. She had no problem with my using the guest room. And she had agreed to prepare a tagine for us that night. I needed to understand that she was shy around foreign men, that I might not see much of her, might not see anything of her.

'No problem,' I said. 'I'll just be staying a night or two. I need to get back to Rabat by Sunday.'

Miloud calculated. 'That doesn't give you much time. You'll have to take the Tiznit bus, and that's at 5.00 in the morning.' Thus it was determined that I would have just half a day and half a night in Um Al-Aliq.

The guest room was a narrow mud chamber at the south end of the house, with grilled windows giving out to the desert. I leaned my stuff against a wall. Miloud rounded up some bread. I provided sardines and figs. Miloud's mother made a pot of mint tea. She was wrapped Sahrawi woman fashion. I caught a glimpse of her in the doorway, but it was Miloud who brought in the tea.

'She says hello', he said. 'But like I explained, she's shy around men and not feeling very well since the operation.'

'The operation?'

'Ever since father died, she's been having fainting spells. Finally they decided to do an operation. Thank God she came through it all right. She's better now, but the medicine…' His voice tailed off. I could see he didn't care to elaborate. I was struck again by his stoic acceptance of what was.

'How long has your father been gone?'

'A couple of years now.'

'How did it happen?'

'He was shot by the Polisario. Right up against the house.' A few minutes later Miloud showed me the bullet holes in the wall. There were no tears, no self pity, nothing beyond a shrug.

Miloud drew water from the little well nearby and we washed our hands and faces. 'We'll go see the rock drawings now if you're ready. It's not far.' We took a bottle of water along.

We walked towards a flat-topped hill, what would have been designated a mesa in the American Southwest. The top was fringed with rock-lined foxholes. Here and there lay a spent cartridge, an empty tin, a battery. There had been fierce fighting over the position, Miloud said. The Moroccan soldiers had in the end been forced to surrender. They'd been shot against the same wall as his father.

The desert stretched to the southern horizon. Somewhere out there ran a berm of sand thinly guarded by Moroccan troops. The 'wall' was 2,000 miles long and several metres high. Governments seemed unable to tie their own shoelaces most of the time. Then every so often they'd find the combination of will and wherewithal needed to leave behind a 2,000 mile long ribbon of sand, or some comparable futility.

A short distance beyond the mesa a ridge of dark rock broke the sand, like dorsal fins. 'The *gravures rupestres*', Miloud said. We went to a series of tilted slabs. The representations on the burnished surfaces had been put there by a skilled artist or group of artists. They had not been made by percussion. The lines were deftly incised, pale like scar tissue on the smooth gray skin of the rock. There were gazelles and antelopes, some with oryx-like horns. There was an elephant, a giraffe, a rhinoceros, a crocodile, horses, ostriches, and some oxen or buffalo.

Miloud, who'd seen it all before, went to sit in a swathe of shade where he smoked and drowsed. It was a fine afternoon in that open-air museum. By the time we started back, a red ball of sun sat trembling on the western horizon. Then it slipped over, leaving a slow wake of stillness and stars.

We ate by candlelight on a mat on the packed-earth floor of the guest room. Miloud's mother had prepared a chicken tagine with olives and pickled lemon. The bread was hot from the oven. We finished off with mint tea. When we stepped outside Venus blazed bright as a flare. The sky was dusted with stars, some sharpened to bright points, some merged in the smoke of the Milky Way.

We turned in early, as one tends to do in places without electricity. Besides, we needed to get up before 4.00. The walk to the road would need an hour.

'How much do I owe for the meal and the night?'

Miloud shrugged it off. 'Pay what you like. Anything is okay.'

I gave 100 dirhams for the accommodation and food, and another hundred to help with his mother's medicine. I needed enough to make my way back to Rabat, or I would have given more. I added a flannel shirt and my jacket. Miloud seemed pleased with the settlement package.

At 3.30 we got up and headed out. The night was cool but not cold. Somewhere a dog started barking, but gave up early. The moon was high, sparing enough starched light that we didn't need the torch Miloud carried. Thank God he was along. We walked fast, in a beeline I could never have achieved on my own. At quarter to five we met the road and pitched ourselves on the far side. We saw the lights from the bus skittering like heat lightning well before it got there. It topped a last rise, headlamps boring holes in the night. Miloud stepped onto the road, rotating an arm like the blade of a windmill. The bus pulled over.

I couldn't find words for goodbye. We shook hands. Then I was up the steps and paying the driver. Then the bus was rolling west. I imagined Miloud watching the ruby taillights before heading back to Um Al-Aliq.

It was among the best trips I'd ever taken, maybe the best. Perhaps I should have left it there. But the following fall Fouzia and I fired up the

Renault IV and headed over the mountains, full of anticipation. Bound for Akka.... The stoical son, the father shot against a wall, the enduring mother, Um Al-Aliq, a guest room facing the desert, rock drawings beyond the mesa, the little well, the sublime silence, the sky choked with stars. Fouzia had been fully briefed.

We eventually found Um Al-Aliq, though the house lacked the patina it held in my memory. It was a relief to see the door opened by Miloud's mother, still alive, in apparent good health, younger than I'd gathered from my glimpses of her. She did not seem particularly shy this time around, nor did she remember me at first.

'I was here last winter', I explained. 'With Miloud.'

'Miloud?'

'Your son.'

Miloud's mother narrowed her eyes and processed my image a few seconds, before emitting something close to a snort. Her name was Hassania. She invited us in, instantly hitting it off with Fouzia. Over tea, we learned for starters that Miloud was not Hassania's son. She spoke of him with what might be called good-humoured contempt, proclaiming him a liar and a cheat. He brought tourists by the house after telling them any number of things. He cajoled her into cooking meals and barely compensated her labour, though he at least furnished groceries. Miloud's father was a moderately high-ranking military man, thoroughly alive. Um Al-Aliq had not been besieged by Polisario fighters, though it was true that a Moroccan unit had once hunkered down on the mesa top.

To sum up, I'd been taken for a ride in the Back of Beyond. Miloud had merely delivered what I'd come predisposed to find. That so much was made of moondust was beside the point. Fouzia and Hassania laughed a lot as they prepared dinner.

We slept well that night in the guest room. The stars, authentic to the best of my knowledge, sparkled through grilled windows. The next morning I showed Fouzia the pockmarks in the wall where Miloud's father had no longer been shot. They looked merely like pockmarks now, no different from the thousand others peppered across the wall. Then we headed for the mesa.

SOUK SHOPPING IN TANGIER

Barnaby Rogerson

It was shopping that first inclined me towards an interest in Islam, though it must be said that the lupine line of hassling touts that in the old days awaited the visitor immediately outside the old Tangier dock gates did their best to keep the secret well-springs of their faith well hidden. Indeed one could be forgiven for imagining that they were waging some small personal war against each and every one of the foreign visitors, determined to avenge the slights afflicted by the crusaders and colonists of the past. Their weaponry included a formidable range of languages and the imagination to make the best use of them, by provoking some response, be it laughter, irritation, guilt or mere exasperated anger. But they knew any crack could be opened into some sort of relationship. And above all they had persistence, those hassling, touting guides. For time they had aplenty, while the foreign tourists had all the other advantages – the freedom to travel, the passports, the visas and the money. And there was no such thing as a poor traveller coming from the north, however unwashed their skin and distressed their clothes might look, for even the dole translated into a very enviable number of dirhams. They made their money in the time-honoured way of all financial dealings, using their wit to act as a broker on a sliding scale of commissions.

I, however, seldom suffered from their multilingual offensive, for I was too young to be looking to buy either hashish or carpets, and had no backpack or suitcase that indicated the pressing need for either a hotel, taxi or train station. I was also often burdened with panniers for buying fruit (the buying of which earned no one any commission) and knew my way towards the food markets of this supposedly wicked and definitely run-down old town. But most crucial of all, I tended to use the dawn boat, and Tangier being renowned as the city of smugglers, clubbers and night-time fishermen, was unique in Morocco in that no one ever got up early. The beach strip which had once been fringed with hotels was no longer a stretch reaching out into a romantic wilderness of dunes. Surrounded by a vast new suburb, it had become filthy with wind-blown plastic bags, while the river that ran through the fine length of sand was grey with sewage, but that did at least mean that the beach had been returned from the hotels to the people. In the evening it came alive with dozens of fiercely fought football matches scented by barrows grilling sardines.

I was also not a once-in-a-lifetime visitor to Tangier in search of exoticism within the first half hour of landing in Africa. I was a neighbour, for my father was serving in the Royal Naval base at Gibraltar, which was then connected to Tangier by a charming but battered old ferry, the *Mons Calpe*. It did a dawn run once a week that allowed you an enormous cooked breakfast in the galleys, arriving in Tangier's harbour just as it was getting light. My mission was to buy fruit, in exchange for being given the ferry fare and some loose change for meals by my mother. It was a bizarre errand, most especially as at the bottom of our street in Gibraltar there was an itinerant Moroccan fruit seller who would literally try to press free fruit on my mother. She had intervened in his domestic life in a decisive way, encouraging my father (who had a position of respect) to write a letter encouraging the immigration department to allow the Moroccan fruit vendor's wife to visit him from Tangier, on the promise of not taking up residency. It had worked, and the man beamed affection at my mother and constantly tried to give her gifts of fruit – which she would refuse. It helped enormously in their ritual duels of politeness that she could protest that she had even fresher fruit in her house, as her son had just returned from Morocco. I loved the trips to Tangier, for as my mother realised, the sporting society of colonial Gibraltar in which she excelled – a veritable demon of the tennis club and bridge table – was not a world in which her book-loving son had any chance of participating.

My shopping trips to Tangier opened up a whole new wonderful box of living history, and to unravel the mystery of this totally other culture, I immersed myself in the stacks of the garrison library of Gibraltar. A diet of Peter Mayne's *A Year in Marrakech*, Walter Harris's *Morocco That Was*, John Hay's *Western Barbary* and Gavin Maxwell's *Lords of the Atlas* filled in the many gaps with a bright, vivid, romantic, adventurous and humorous glow. From his own reading of Lady Grove's *Seventy Days Camping in Morocco*, my father taught me that it was vital for a young man to learn no Arabic swear words (unlike the British troops he had encountered in Egypt) but to fill your mouth with grace. Lady Grove claimed that you could travel the length of Morocco, camping amongst the wildest-looking mountain tribes in complete safety by just using three expressions: *Miziam Bezouf* (very beautiful), *Baraka-Lafik* (thank you very much/a blessing upon you) and *Laila Siadaa* (good night/sweet dreams). It was also my father who advised me to give the enormous, silent, shaven-headed man who stood beside the gangway steps at Tangier the gift of a 50-pence piece with my passport when I came off the boat. It was alarming the first time, watching your passport disappear into the pocket of a total stranger without so much as a glance, let alone a numbered receipt, but it worked.

So my advice to any shopper first arriving in Morocco is to start with fruit. Maybe even stick to it. But first you must equip yourself with local bags, woven from raffia and sometimes ornamented with a leather handle or twists of coloured wool. The fruit sellers post up their prices on little black boards, or re-used pieces of cardboard, and weigh everything out before your eyes. To demonstrate my complete trust in their good nature, it was also my habit to hold out a palm full of change and allow them to pick out their price; this seldom failed to enchant them, for it showed that you knew that amongst the shopkeepers of Morocco, the fruit sellers were a race apart. As is the fruit in Morocco, picked ripe and sold without refrigeration or air miles. My second tip would be to concentrate on the most characteristic flavours of Morocco: tangerines, oranges, dates, almonds and melons. The Moroccans are often proud of the apples that are grown in the orchards in the high plateau between the Middle and High Atlas mountains, but they lack the crisp bite of English fruit and are priced as a luxury item. This is even more true of their strawberries. Britain can't boast of much excellence in the fruit line except in our summer red berries. Moroccan melons, especially in summer, are completely irresistible, and sold from great pyramid mounds of green or bright yellow by the road, right beside the fields. My third tip is not to become a fusspot about hygiene, treating everything in Morocco as an object to be immersed in a bucket of potassium-permanganate solution, sprayed with germoline solution or swabbed with a sterile wipe. Instead concentrate on fruit that you can peel, and travel with a bunch of bananas, which alongside a diet of dried toast and white rice is by far the best food for those afflicted with a disturbed stomach.

Having burdened myself with two shopping bags full of fruit, I used to totter off to the Grand Hotel de Ville de France – a wonderfully decayed establishment whose large, sloping garden overlooked the charming arabesque Anglican church, a view painted by Matisse when he lodged here. In exchange for the odd pot of tea served in ancient hotel crockery on the terrace, or the cheapest dish on the lunchtime menu, a vast salad nicoise (which I would consume by the pool) I was free to make this hotel my base for the day. I think it was Norman Lewis who declared that you never meet anyone interesting in a four-star hotel, but fortunately the Grand Hotel had slipped down in the world. Mary Tripp, who had done something vital for the British Army in the war (and who was given a front row seat at all the Gibraltar military parades), could be found there, as could Alec Waugh, the novelist father of one of my fathers' best friends in the Navy, and that marionette in the perfect linen suit was the last of Paredes, the Sephardic dynasty of bankers who advanced Nelson the money to buy gunpowder before the Battle of Trafalgar (fought just north-west of Tangier) on nothing more than his word. It has been derelict for decades now but even then its gardens were vast and overgrown, but there was a path that allowed you to slip straight down into the bustle of the main market square through a secretive garden gate. With my central mission of the day accomplished, I was free to explore the dream landscape of the medina, its twisting alleyways lined with booths, its secretive squares, mansions hidden behind great iron-studded doorways, the sky framed by tapering minarets or the crumbling tinted whitewash of a dome.

This street knowledge would later be put to use as I was volunteered to accompany guests of my parents on little explorations of Morocco to break up their fortnight-long visits to Gibraltar. This ushered in a change of scene and tempo. Humble, slow dawn ferry journeys were now replaced by quick flights across the straits of Gibraltar, the hire of giant Mercedes-Benz taxis and ambitious grown-up plans funded by fatter wallets. 'We must picnic at the Roman ruins of Lixus, take our swim in the Diplomatic Forest, but leave plenty of time for shopping in Tangier before dinner. Barnaby will show us the best shops.'

And for me it was a liberation to engage with the glittering souks, which I had previously hurried by, too young and too short of cash. But armed with an uncle, a godmother, a holidaying captain or a distant cousin, our little group of well-heeled shoppers would be overwhelmed by the practised charm of the greeter at the door and by offers of mint tea. By now I had learned a lot from the museum collections and my reading, and even at a precociously early age was driven by a quest for authenticity. The bright red fez of Morocco, worn by old gentlemen on their way to the noon-day Friday prayers as well as hotel door-keepers could be acquired – but only if it was the original proper felt article, not the hideous nylon tourist bric-à-brac. The distinctive pointed Moroccan slippers were all too easy to find, for the shopkeepers were pitched together in the same region of the bazaar, so that the gorgeous colours, set off by silver and gilt, looked like a Chinese dragon-centipede. But for the men I was strict, we must search out the original product, the whole leather article without a modern rubber sole. The colours should be either grey or white, but preferably yellow, the finished thing still baring a faint whiff of the tanneries and flexible enough to bend in two, with your heel overhanging just a touch at the end.

My advice, starved of real experience, but backed up by months of quiet observation, was copious:

It will be perfect for the office but don't leave them lying around at home. Our dogs seem to adore the whiff of real Moroccan leather. If you like we can go to the booth that binds books, I am afraid it is more a matter of weeks than of hours, but he also stocks really lovely gold-stamped folders, in all the traditional colours, a warm orange, cardimine and Morocco-red. A couple of doors down there is a stall that stocks *thuja* wood boxes, perfect for holding loose change or cufflinks. We should really buy them where they are made, down south in Mogador, but that trip is for next year. Yes, the Romans adored them, such a lovely cedar-like whiff from the wood. You might pick out something without a metal hinge, which is always their weak point, though the joinery is excellent.

A teapot? What an excellent idea, no-one should leave Tangier without a Moroccan teapot. If you are after something quite quirky we could try and find something with a Cohen brothers stamp on the inside lid. Shows that it was made in Manchester, export and import? Yes, designed in the mid-nineteenth century, some described it as a brass Yemeni coffee pot mated with an English earthenware teapot but forged out of tin, though the last time we found one, the lid had come off and the price was pretty steep and to be honest the modern ones will give better use. We might try and pick up some blue and gilt decorated tea glasses to go with it, and now and then you stumble on painted wooden boxes, lined a little like an old English egg box, with which they could be carried safely on the back of a mule. That brass box? I believe it's for holding lumps of sugar, whopped off a sugar loaf with that Viking-looking axe, but I will ask to make sure. Yes, I am sure it could make a very lovely jewellery box.

No, that is not an old ice bucket for champagne, it's designed to be a sort of beach-like metal bucket for taking squishy soap to the *hammam* – not that it can't be redirected to a new use. There was an old Tangier myth that champagne turned into milk in the mouth of such a holy man as the Sherif of Wazzan. Yes, he had a rather saintly English wife. What a pity I didn't show you her grave! It's in the churchyard where we went to search out Walter Harris and Caid Mclean's tombs.

A carpet? Are you sure? It will be fun but also a bit of a full-on event, but we are sure to be offered a whole tray of mint tea whilst at least three dozen carpets are unrolled with gusto. What, you want one as well? Well then we must certainly go, but first we must visit this fantastic little scent shop, Madini's, just off the little square where we stopped for a coffee. To be honest, I think most of the carpets are pretty derivative, but now and then you find those rather wild off-white things, quite hairy and criss-crossed with brown lozenges, that come from a real indigenous Moroccan tribal tradition.

Me, gosh no, I haven't anything like the right amount of money for a carpet and we will have to spend hours getting it down to anything like the right price, which I think should be around £300. Because that's what it would cost you back home if you wondered off Regent Street into Liberty's. But if you buy something, I might be able to throw in one of those kilim cushion covers as my commission.

It is part of the tradition that I get rewarded, rather like a stockbroker or an estate agent back home. But the role of the shopper is very honourable out here. You know there is that story of how one of the earliest Muslim emigrants when he arrived at the oasis of Medina as a penniless refuge refused to accept a gift from his host. Just point out to me the way to the marketplace, for I was a merchant in my hometown of Mecca, so I am sure I will survive. True enough by the end of his first day's trading, Abder-Rahman ibn Awf returned bearing a goatskin of butter and a cheese which he was able to present to his host. While one of the first four Caliphs, it might even have been Omar, when asked how he would like to die, replied that he would like to be taken by the angel of death whilst out shopping for food for his family in the souk.

ARTS AND LETTERS

SKIRTING ON THE SURFACE

Lina Sergie Attar

I want to
I want to be someone else or I'll explode
floating upon the surface for the birds
    the birds
    the birds

When you are on a plane, trapped in the clouds, you are nowhere. Not really nowhere: you are somewhere, a moving point in space mapped by some sophisticated cartographic technology, but you are detached from everything that transforms spaces into places; in a sense you are detached from reality, it is suspended like you within an atmospheric cushion. Somewhere within this specific dot crossing the Atlantic, I sat in the forced darkness intending to mimic a natural night, while we were buckled into our leather seats, breathing the artificial air. I tried to close my eyes, to sleep like the others around me, but sleep would not come. I glanced at his sleeping profile next to me, at his translucent skin, his straight nose, his thin lips. In his sleep, he lost his fierce intensity, the stony veneer that demanded respect. In his sleep, he looked vulnerable, and I felt both protected and protective. Without turning the light on, I opened my sketchbook, flipping through the pages quickly without lingering – past sketches and charcoals, collaged pages dried stiff with primers and glue, thin wrinkled pages covered with lists of things I had to do or should have done but had forgotten to, the faint, comforting chemical smell of gesso mingled with the chilled, recycled air – until I arrived at an empty page. With the strange music playing in my ears just loud enough to cut the throbbing of the engines but not loud enough to be perceptible to anyone else, I took out the pencil and began to draw him, my hand moving blindly in the dark. My focused but quick glances transferred the details to my fingers with an understanding that was beyond vision. Lines turned into shapes and shapes into volumes, exactly as I was once taught, the traditional way, to follow the positive space. Whenever I was under stress, I reverted to old habits and learned ways of seeing. I shaded the pocket of skin under his eye, the shadow that fell across his face, and his lips so thin they looked as if they could disappear. In the dim light of the cabin, I could not make out exactly what I had drawn. The sketch was incomplete, half a sketch of half a face. It was only an impression – or even less than that, it was a mood.

The songs playing in my head continued to speak to me even as my desire to draw ended. I began a game I have played since I was a little girl. I began to write the words I heard coming through the headphones. And the words I did not understand, that I could not decipher, I made up, filling the blanks with my own lyrics. At some point, you cannot write fast enough to the pace of the rhythm and you lose the thread. When this happens, the short lines change into sentences, and the words break into a trajectory of their own. And the words began to take over the page, to occupy the negative space around the drawing, that sacred whiteness we were taught to always respect. The scribbles in the margins became the centre and the centre shifted into the margins. I could not see the letters as I transcribed the lines, but it did not matter, I continued until the song ended. And when I looked up, after long minutes that had stretched beyond measurable time, he was awake again, watching me, his lips slowly formed a half-smile, sleepy and lazy. And although he was the one waking up, I looked back at him as if I had been the one dreaming. As if he had woken me up.

I shut the sketchbook in the half darkness, my own expression invisible as I pulled off his headphones and turned towards him.

***

How come I end up where I started?
How come I end up where I went wrong?
Won't take my eyes off the ball again.
First you reel me out, and then you cut the string.

When my grandmother gathered us to tell a story, as she reigned on the blue velvet bergère while we claimed our territories on the worn antique Persian carpet that covered her cold gray marble floors, she would always begin with a soft, trembling voice, 'Once there was, and once there was not.' We knew, of course, she told these stories to imprint her moral of the day on our impressionable ears: the young must always respect their elders; the kind always win; the obedient always get the prize; 'our' culture always prevails; nevertheless we listened, as we were transported from our boring lives to magical and grotesque lands where virtuous girls were transformed to princesses and rebellious ones were doomed to have slimy frogs spewing out of their mouths forever. As she recited her carefully formed lessons disguised as stories – hybrids of French fairy tales meshed with Arabian Nights – I fixated on those first words, that contradictory opening, on the confusing duality of what was and what was not, distracted by the impossibility of something both being and not being, of a story happening and not. Did it or didn't it? Years later, you learn that some things in fact both happen and don't happen, that your life teeters on an invisible line between existence and absence. You realise that a story unfolds in infinite possibilities; that what wasn't and what didn't define your life as much as what was and what did.

The only story that exists is the one we remember, right now, in this moment. All other versions disappear and become irrelevant. It's the truth: once there was, and once there was not. Once, the past is clear, and once again, the memory is blurred.

Gather around and listen to the tale before it is erased, listen as we glorify parts of our past and selectively change others, as we shift and stretch our truth. And so we begin with, once there was, and once there was not. But there was, there was....

My story ends where it began. Waiting. How long do we wait, thinking, 'What if'? Obsessing about 'What if'? What if the choices you thought were right were not the right ones? What if you just played a part that someone else had written for you? What if you lived your life through the words of others, the rules of others, the expectations of others, the lyrics of others? What if you waited too long, just to see what if, just to see what is? How long do you wait? Years pass as you wait, and you realise our childhood dreams of what we would be do not match up to what we have become. This is the dark age of life, when we are unable to change the past, yet we are haunted by our perfect, gained-in-hindsight wisdom, and we are unable to accept the future as we now know it will unfold. So we wait, and we delay enlightenment in perpetual procrastination. We kill time, we start over, start again.

My name is Naya, from the reeds, from the *ney,* the ancient flute made from sugar canes that grew tall on the banks of the Nile. Each golden column is picked out of the marshes, its head and tail lopped off, its sweetness sucked out, and it becomes an empty vessel, depleted and useless, until someone picks it up and puts it to his lips and breathes into the dried tube a new life, a sound, a melody, creating something beautiful out of nothing. The *ney*, the instrument of the wind and the page, is older than time. It was etched onto the walls of the Pyramids, it was prized in Roman courts, it inspired countless poems of Rumi, it was sharpened and used as a pen to fill blank pages with the history of men. When the reed grew too long to play, it was used as a walking stick, propping up those who leaned onto it for support. Sometimes, when the weight of men became too heavy to bear, the reed would splinter and puncture their tightly clasping palms, their blood staining the golden surface, their flesh digging into the vertical fibres.

You don't know me, but you have read my words, you have heard my notes. I live in your headphones, whisper in the night, and lull you to sleep. I exist to inspire, to enchant, to depress, to haunt, to tell my fragmented story. I'm in the middle of your picture, hiding in the reeds. But you don't see me, you don't hear me, for I am invisible. For I am nothing but an instrument.

***

I shift my weight from one aching foot to the other. I shouldn't have worn these shoes. I wonder if I should change into the flats stashed in my purse. It's crazy; he isn't even going to see my feet, but I'm convinced the extra four inches will improve my view. With my earbuds in place, I try to focus on the music and forget the pain shooting up the backs of my legs. I pass the time watching people walking past me to join the back of the growing queues. While queuing for a band you love, you are surrounded by people who have nothing in common with you but your obsession. Queuing for a concert is as important as the concert itself. This is where you meet the die-hard fans, the ones who upload their carefully recorded videos on YouTube, grainy evidence that they were there and were willing to stand still for an entire song to freeze the memory and share it with everyone else who could not be there. In the queue, their abstract user names flesh into reality, virtual Facebook friends who finally acquire a real face. This is where you can discuss the songs and the lyrics in minute detail without sounding crazy. You can freely analyse the implications of a change of a word in a song between live and recorded versions, and exchange theories behind the intention of the changes. No judgement. After years of no one in your real life understanding this passion, here you belong, with your like-minded tribe of fundamentalists, all searching for meaning in the same place. These unwavering, intense feelings should have been a red flag telling me I had gone too far. But is it insane to find a home, a belonging, in a Radiohead concert queue? Not at all.

The guy next to me leans against the brick wall, a lanky indie-type dressed in faded jeans and a grungy, frayed t-shirt. He was trying too hard to fit in with the nonchalant, just-rolled-out-of-bed and probably stoned majority of the crowd. Not that I cared – I didn't fit in either, overdressed as I usually am when I'm nervous. He tells me he is not from New York, he drove down from Maine. He is an environmental lawyer and used funds from a corporate settlement to bid on this last-minute charity concert for ultimate Radiohead fans to raise money for Haiti. He tells me he went to the Met today to look at the Van Goghs. He describes, with obvious pride, his elaborate, complicated theory that the singer is Van Gogh reincarnated. He goes on and on, comparing songs to paintings of bedrooms and sunflowers. I listen, having heard weirder Radiohead theories. To keep him talking and stay in my half zoned-out state, I nod in agreement.

Then he looks at me and asks, 'Do you think he has a muse?' I smile, and say, 'Every artist has a muse.'

Muse, I think. Why do people always want to find out where things come from, to dissect the origin of inspiration? We have a need to explain the intention of art, an urge to take it apart and see how it works, as if we could explain it, as if it would become tangible, as if we all could tap into it like a mythical fountain of creativity and absorb it for ourselves. An instinctive need to figure it out and steal away its magic. A muse doesn't create the art, she drives it; to be a muse is to be used, analysed, objectified. To fulfil her duty, a muse must weave an invisible web of truthful lies – deep lies excavated from memory, with a glossy sheen of truth applied to the surface – at once inspiring and intoxicating.

To change the subject, I wonder aloud about what the set list will be tonight. As expected, a heated discussion concerning possible song selections and speculation about new tracks begins between the lawyer and a group of guys behind me. I leave them completely now, relieved to be finally alone with my music and my thoughts. I used to be like them but I'm not anymore. I'm just playing the part of a regular (okay, intense) fan. When I know that with just a couple of texts I could be on the other side of this brick wall. With him.

The queue begins to move forward when the doors open, and I turn and give my new friend a piece of advice. 'Stand in front of the piano. Left of stage.' I try to erase thoughts of the past as I turn the volume up. The queue inches forward.

Listen to my story, before the wait is over, before it slips away from my memory, before it shifts again, listen, while I can still remember. Slip inside my headphones. Step into the infinite tunnel between my ears and my mind, where my thoughts are triggered by a voice, a note, a word. Can you hear them?

Once there was a muse, the daughter of memory and the lover of inspiration. She held all the desires of the world within her. Once there was not.

***

transport, motor ways, and tram lines
starting and then stopping
taking off and landing
the emptiest of feelings
disappointed people
shell smashed, juices flowing
wings twitch, legs are going
don't get sentimental
it always ends up drivel

I hate queuing. Especially airport queues. I hate check-in queues, security queues, boarding queues, queues that snake in endless labyrinthian mazes, queues that make you rock from one foot to the next, twisting your neck and your back, until every minuscule movement ails your body, and still the queues doesn't move. My people hate queuing, except in prayer. When they pray, they submit to the queue that represents the belief that all men are equal in front of Allah. But that equality evaporates at the bakery, in front of the bus stop, or in an airport; anywhere else it's every man for himself, pushing and shoving to be first. But, since the fateful September morning when *everything changed forever*, we navigate a world where we are not only not equal to, but we are officially less than all others. You must not complain, you must not attract attention. You must appear normal, you must queue and try to disappear.

I watch the smug airline employee behind his station moving as slowly as possible. Was he trained to read our collective stress, boredom, and exhaustion? I wonder how he learned to move in opposite proportion to the frustration level of the passenger, to type continuously while gazing at the screen with glazed eyes, to speak in slowing syllables in a monotone voice. He must be addicted to our suffering, inhaling our fumes of distress and anxiety. I imagine he would be a sadistic torturer in another life, in another country.

You hate it but you have to go through it, like everyone else who has to get from point A to point B. And eventually, if you make enough international flights, from the Middle East to the US and back, sooner or later, you will connect through London Heathrow. This is where I am today, on 5 January 2013, waiting, in line.

Terminal 5 is drab and nondescript. The best thing about Terminal 5 is leaving it. Whenever I'm here, I wonder why they couldn't have built a better airport, one that welcomes you to England, instead of this massive, uninspiring grey block.

I know airports are hard to design because I have designed one. Not a real one, but on paper, which to an architecture student feels like the real thing. There are not many ways to create interesting spaces that meet the endless criteria and needs of gates, security, and runways. Mechanics and logistics make it difficult to insert inspiration and so the coolness that true architecture is supposed to exude dies in an airport. The airport is a building designed for maximum efficiency of movement: moving people with their overstuffed suitcases, moving everything along, up and down escalators, zipping across walkways. The airport is made for motion; once you stop, the flaws appear. All the design mistakes crystalise in the immobile moments. The still perspectives and carefully constructed 3D renderings that architects use for presentations tend to disguise the spaces as perfect snapshots, covered in appealing surfaces and filled with happy tourists. It is far from the messy reality you only experience by being there. We try our best to distract you, to make you forget where you are. We cover the walls, ceilings and floors with signs, coloured flags or whatever cultural emblem or historical artefact that signifies: you are here; you are an international traveller; you have arrived! Like the interiors of Vegas casinos that artificially place you somewhere specific, to distract you from where you really are, the flimsy facade cannot disguise the fact that you are in an airport, in isolation. You are not in a place at all, you are expected to move quickly, spend money, and lately, strictly adhere to convoluted security policies. The slickest of architectural tricks can try to make you forget that you are a passport number in a queue, but no amount of fancy sky lights, over-designed geometric columns, or in-house museums can make frustration disappear. Nothing can make you forget that you are in an airport.

While you are stuck in a queue, personal methods of distraction and defence work the best. Your cell phone, a book (though I find it hard to read while standing), and your music are essentials. I am addicted to my new, glossy iPod, both minimalist and trendy with the all-important white ear pods. Keep the volume low or even off if you want, but keep those white earbuds in place at all costs. It is your barrier against intrusive people asking for directions, asking if there is a delay, asking if you are on the same flight, asking if they are in the right queue, or worse, just to chat. As I wait, I try not to stress because I should be in Providence right now, getting ready for studio tomorrow. But of course I can't forget, I'm stranded in Terminal 5.

***

I must admit, with all its faults, Heathrow doesn't compare to the horrid excuse for an airport that is Aleppo International. The building is an iconic representation of the smokey, dusty, and cold socialist Syrian architecture of the last thirty years. Although winters in Aleppo are mild, the desert night chill leaks through the unheated interiors, the kind of cold that my mother says seeps into your bones. In these public buildings you must wrap yourself in as many layers as possible, not just for warmth but to visually bulk up and look as unattractive as possible to avert the looks of the sleazy men who hang out in dark corners watching every person who comes and leaves. Gawkers who have nothing better to do than loiter around the airport in the middle of the night, eating you with their eyes, studying your movements like hawks, listening in on your conversations and mentally taking notes. Don't look directly at anyone; your eyes must be kept down at all costs. Here, an iPod is not a distraction but a red flag of frowned upon over-westernisation; I keep it hidden away in my bag, but I mentally shut myself down and put on an impenetrable expression as cold as the stone walls.

Although I made my teary goodbyes to my family hours ago, it always feels like I'm continuously saying goodbye until I set foot in America. Until then, I cannot think of my life in Providence or my freedom. Until then all I can think of is my home, my mother and my father, and everything I left behind. I was supposed to depart on yesterday's 3am British Airway's flight from Aleppo to London on an plane coming from Damascus, but after a series of unfortunate delays, overbookings, and missed connections, I spent last night in London and was rerouted on the next evening flight to JFK, scheduled to arrive at my final destination exactly 48 hours later than expected. Delays are a standard part of Middle Eastern travel, so in reality this Heathrow queue was not too bad.

There is a word architects love – 'threshold': the border between two separate yet connected spaces. The threshold of a house separates inside from out. At an airport, security separates being in and out of transit. Because we architects are taught to insert meaning into the mundane, we use the word to describe limits, boundaries, spaces of transition. Although I don't know it yet, the queue I wait in is a 'threshold moment', a temporal boundary, between what happened before and what will happen after. These moments can only be analysed later; no one knows what exact moment will define who we are to become: an accident, a job interview, a meeting, a coincidence. Some are obvious clichés: getting married, having a baby, the death of your parents – these are expected transitions and can be prepared for in advance. Others are hidden, encoded into your DNA, they wait to emerge, to change the future and bring the past into focus. Sometimes it's called luck, fate, free will, bad choices, all the words we use to explain our lives, but this is what my father has been saying to me for years: everything is written. We are not accidents waiting to happen.

Destiny waits with me in line. Or in two lines, to be precise.

***

Open your mouth wide,
a universal sigh.
And while the ocean blooms,
it's what keeps me alive.
So why does it still hurt?
Don't blow your mind with why.

I passed the time watching people around me, particularly in the enviously short first class queue. My only consolation was that I knew I looked better than most in the business and first class queues. I was dressed mostly in black, save the fuchsia cashmere scarf that my mother wrapped around my neck as I was leaving our apartment, to shield me from the cold, she said, and to break the depressing black. My mother always wrapped a warm gesture around a criticism. Architects, like artists, like to wear black because it is the colour of the intellectual yet artsy, smart yet creative, types. Fitted black clothes, black messenger bags, and black thick-rimmed glasses, render us a blank canvas, with no distracting colours or fussy details. My scarf peeping out of my jacket was like the sliver of a metal zipper, or the slim red strip of rubber peeking from the back of your Prada shoes. Whether an ethnic detail or trademark glasses or a discreet logo, we want to be blank but also known. We also judge harshly, even though we pretend we don't. You learn to 'curate' your image early on in art school if you haven't already in your teenage angst years. From your thoughts to your voice, every detail on and within your canvas is an opportunity to display this carefully formed image. The worst thing to happen to an architecture student is to be called a slacker (for actually needing and getting over six hours of sleep) or an idiot (for wearing bright colours or sounding too American). No one wants to sound 'too American', not even the Americans. Having a slight Euro accent is extremely useful at design school. Not too thick, just a faint sound of otherness is enough. For me having the accent was no problem, I could go either way, perfectly American at the 'Stop and Shop' grocery store, to slightly 'other' in studio, creating the coveted 'European' twinge, to the point that my professors thought I knew French or at least Spanish when I didn't. Worldliness, real or feigned, is necessary to survive. I was surprised when I found this need to be slightly foreign was so important in America. In Syria the expats' kids who were dragged to visit the homeland every summer would be tormented every time they made a mistake while speaking to relatives, until they gave up on learning Arabic and reverted to the natural American drawl that we all secretly wanted for ourselves.

I entertain myself by texting back and forth with my best friend, Lamia, already in Providence. I know I am going to be screwed with charges, but I convince myself this is necessary to keep my sanity. Rocking back and forth on the balls of my black on black leather Pumas, a familiar scent mixes with the canned airport air. I glance to my left, and in an instant I wish the entire floor of the airport would break open and swallow me.

He is in the queue next to mine, supporting a tall, blonde girl leaning casually against his chest. She whispers something to him and they both laugh. I glance at them sideways, moving slightly to hide behind the guy in front of me. They look like the typical jet-setter couple, the ones you see in magazines, the ones that tell you how you are supposed to look while traveling. Casual yet fitted jackets and jeans and just enough tonal but visible logos on shoes and bags to mark themselves as different, as better. I watch as he slowly massages her shoulders with his clean-shaven face close to her golden, sleek hair. The memory of him touching my hair chokes me. I blink back my tears and try to arrest the flush that creeps unto my face. Of all the fucking British Airways' flights from London to New York, I have to be stuck on one with him. I wish I were in studio like I was supposed to be, I wish I were anywhere else but here. I keep glancing towards them and turn away a moment too late, just as he catches me watching them. He steps out of the queue and walks over.

He taps my shoulder, says, Hey.

I slip off my earbuds, pull my shoulders back and smile, secretly grateful for stretch jeans that don't lose their cling and for freshly blow-dried hair, because as image-conscious Lamia reminded me that morning, you never know who you will meet in an airport. Because I haven't spoken for hours, my voice cracks as I say, Hi Omar.

He grasps my shoulders and kisses my cheeks three times in the Lebanese style that Syrians love to imitate. His strong cologne envelopes me in a heavy cloud of past moments just like this one.

He asks me about my classes, haven't they already started?

I tell him that I've had a bit of a delay, hating him for remembering my schedule and nothing else. I look up and watch the sympathetic words fly out of his mouth, while his ill-concealed smirk tells me he doesn't feel bad at all.

I smile and tell him it actually worked out perfectly, I had a great time in London. He keeps going, that I should have texted him, that I knew he was here for the week, that we could have had dinner together, with Elise, as he points to the blonde girl who smiles and waves perkily.

I try to think of a way out of this dead end, but I am stuck in my frozen queue, hostage to his faux compassion and annoyingly effective charm. I can hear him telling me how they just met in London, and how she lives in New York, and how she works at a museum, one of the ones I love, but I am only half-listening, my eyes taking in the fragments of him which I can get away with, his jaw, his hand gesturing, the glint of silver from his watch peeking out under his white shirt sleeve. I let out a relieved sigh when he finally stops speaking.

Tilting his head towards me, he asks, Habibiti, what's wrong? The sound of his old endearment jolts me back to my senses. He's throwing around 'my love' with such carelessness, and I wonder, not for the first time, if he's ever meant it.

My eyes slant slightly as I look up into his dark eyes, and they become tender for a moment as they always used to do when he knew he'd got to me, always so easily. He asks me how long I'm going to be in New York and before I can answer his real-life Barbie calls out in a high-pitched whine, Omar, it's our turn honey, butchering his name, O-mar, mispronouncing the first letter. Non-Arabs can never pronounce it, the guttural 'ayn they make into a long O, their mouths shaped into a perfect circle. But really, it starts with a harshness in your throat, softly bypasses your mouth to slip effortlessly out of your lips. He used to make fun of people like her.

'Isn't she cute?' he says, distracted for a moment. Gotta go, I'll catch up with you at the gate. He stops and turns back and says, Change your attitude, grudges don't suit you. How long are you going to stay mad? He gives me a quick peck on the cheek and squeezes my shoulder.

Forever, I think to myself, feeling my bones under his tight grip. But again, I just smile back.

As he walks back to his queue, I try to see what was holding up mine. The culprit is a family with two kids and a screaming baby, overloaded with heavy luggage and American 'need special treatment' attitudes. Now that I am aware of them standing three feet away from me, the cool calm I was feeling before evaporates. My applied glaze of confidence shattered into pieces, I feel exposed, standing alone, next to him but not next to him. The queue becomes unbearable as each minute stretches into the next. All I can think is, we can't be moving parallel to each other.

I wave to an airline employee patrolling the cordoned edge, and tell him that I'm about to miss my flight and need to check in immediately. I use every ounce of charm I have in me. If I were in Syria, I would have bribed him with five hundred lira, but of course all I can do here is use my sweetest tone and hope I will get my way. He eyes me with suspicion, he can tell it's bullshit, but he unclips the cord and leads me to the empty first class queue. Just wait here, he says. I can feel the rolling eyes of the economy queue on my back, but I pretend I don't care. I catch Omar's eye as I walk past, and he gives me an amused look, the one he always gave me when I would manipulate a situation to my advantage. I ignore him as well. I pull out my ticket and passport and step up to the counter.

Miss, this is a first class queue, she says holding my ticket, without looking at me.

Yes, but the kind gentleman led me here since there was no one in this queue. I say this as I think, you are such a bitch.

But look behind you, there is a passenger waiting.

I turn around and see the back of a guy. In the saccharin tone I'm still using, I say, I'm sure that he doesn't mind. Look, he's on the phone.

She proceeds with extremely slowed motions, clucking her disapproval at having to serve a lowlife economy passenger. It occurs to me that as long I am here, I may as well ask for a better seat, maybe even one in business class. I take a deep breath and say in my most sophisticated voice, with my slanted accent, Is there any way I could get an upgrade? I just had the worst trip ever and…

She cuts me off briskly, I can't give you an upgrade to first class. I hope that isn't why you came to this queue.

No, no, listen, I say, lowering my voice to a whisper, Do you see that guy in the business class queue with the blonde? He is my ex-boyfriend, and I need to change my seat, just to business, not first.

She looks at my passport again, You are only twenty-four. He looks much older than you, dear.

I know, I know, as I hide the side of my face with my hair so Omar cannot see this exchange of desperation.

She stares at the computer. I can't bring myself to look behind me at the growing queue of people who paid triple what I did for their tickets.

Sorry, I can't do anything about it now. We're completely booked. Try at the gate.

It's okay, I appreciate it, I say in my normal voice, with no effort to hide my disappointment.

You're going to have a great flight, dear.

I can't convince myself to believe her cheery prediction.

***

there are front doors,
and there are revolving doors
doors on the rudders of big ships
we are revolving doors
there are doors that open by themselves
there are sliding doors and there are secret doors
there are doors that lock and doors that don't
there are doors that let you in and out but never open
but there are trap doors
that you can't come back from

The Roseland, with its seedy history, touristy location, and banal facade, is a building with an attitude. Tonight the building with nothing to prove, with no sparkle or fancy lights, has a string of people wrapped in a necklace around the city block, which begins to overlap at the seam, starting a second human strand. As I approach the entrance, there is a solemn aura mixed with anticipation hovering around the doors. The last time they played in this former ice-skating rink-turned-roller-skating rink turned disco nightclub and finally generic ballroom, was in 2000, after the release of *Kid A*. I found out much later that the tickets had sold out in minutes, that it was one of the most anticipated shows that year. Back then, I still lived in Syria, a world away from New York, and Radiohead was just another band I listened to among many others, before they occupied my playlists alone. But tonight, I have my coveted ticket in my hand, after bidding a dear price for it in the name of charity, although it may be hard to determine who really needs to be saved, the people of Haiti or me. The concert's agenda is to be an intimate affair, a performance for the most dedicated of fans, most of whom have only seen Radiohead play at festivals, watching them projected onto massive screens while they swim in a sea of tens of thousands of people. But tonight I am prepared. I've made sure I'll get a great spot inside. I paid a homeless guy yesterday to queue for me, and a few hours ago I took his place, to experience the anticipation myself.

On the floor, I am surprised at how large the space is when empty. People rush to the front but still they are scattered. I know that soon my personal space will be as small as my footprint, bound by the people who will crowd around me. And now bodies begin to press forward, heat and odours rolling off them. By the end the scent will be much stronger but less noticeable, because, by then, after seeping into our skin and hair, it will belong to all of us. I manoeuvre myself to the front, one row behind the rail, to the left, near the piano, to be as close as possible. Everyone knows being on the rail is not cool; there's too much pressure and not enough space. Everyone knows he doesn't focus on the people on the rail, the clamouring girls and guys who spend the entire concert trying to catch his eye, holding up their cameras and phones, red lights and flashes shining in his face. He looks just beyond, at the true fans who have just enough room to dance and listen without hanging on his every breath.

In the moments before it begins, everything is still perfect, after our expectation has been set and before any disappointment arrives. It's been so long since I've looked forward to anything. It feels strange. Once I looked forward to everything. I have stood exactly in this place dozens of times in dozens of cities, and I try not to think why I am so nervous this time, why I feel this time will be the last time. I shake off the negativity and immerse myself in the crowd. They lift me out of the past and into the present tense.

***

After finally checking in, as I walk outside for a last cigarette before boarding, I text my Lamia quickly. I sit on the edge of a concrete planter and light up. Within thirty seconds I receive 'asshole' back from her. I smile, twirl my finger on the white wheel, hearing the clicks in my ear as I turn up the volume and stretch out my legs. I inhale the smoke and exhale the stress. Someone sits right next to me even though there is plenty of space around. I turn my back slightly as I text 'I know' back. Thank God for earbuds, although my obnoxiously loud music makes me feel rude. When the guy taps me on the shoulder, I take my left earbud out slowly without pausing the music, slightly embarrassed by the song blasting out of the tiny white piece, but at least it is a good song. I say, Excuse me?

May I bum a smoke? His clipped British accent barely registers on my one pounding ear.

With his black skull cap and worn leather jacket, he has grunge written all over him. I classify him in a two-second glance: an artsy type, maybe high. I dig into my bag and hand him a cigarette. As I turn away again, I hear him ask softly, Lighter, dear? I sigh loudly, take the lighter out of my coat pocket, and give it to him. It is imperative to use the Arab girl rule of survival when faced with these situations: avoid eye contact at all costs.

I text Lamia: 'This creep is sitting next to me and won't leave.' And then, 'Can't even enjoy a smoke before boarding.' She replies, 'You should quit. What did Omar say?'

I start to text something back as the song ends, and in the two second gap before the next begins, he asks, 'So where are you headed?'

Now emboldened, I turn to look him directly in the face to show him this is not okay, and I freeze when I see him. My face flushes. The guy who was behind me in the queue talking on his mobile, I wouldn't have known him from the back but I now recognise his angular, boyish face, even recognise his voice as the same one floating out of my ear pods. He watches intently as I stammer, Um, New York. Hi.

He laughs and says, Hi, I'm Thom, giving me a wave.

Naya, nice to meet you. I'm a fan.

He smiles and says, I can hear that, I know it's my music but is that even good for your ears?

All I can think to myself is keep cool, keep cool, keep cool. My phone beeps, it's Lamia's text 'Tell me more.' I slip the buzzing phone, unattended, into my pocket.

He has already turned away, towards the gray airport hardscape as his right leg shakes. He stares at his cigarette, rotating it, studying it, not really smoking. I flick mine and the ashes drop to the pavement. The silence is awkward, but I'm not about to risk breaking it.

He finally says, You didn't look too happy in there, is everything okay?

I answer, Yeah, just tired. I needed to get out of there.

I could see that. So what's so upsetting? His t's disappear completely.

I hesitate, not knowing quite what to answer, not knowing quite what he'd like to hear, and say, Well, I've had the flight from hell to get here and my ex is on my flight with his new girlfriend. So I haven't had the greatest morning. With my fingers I air-quote 'girlfriend'.

That sucks. His eyes crinkle as he suppresses a smile. His voice is low, lower than I imagined it to be. His words come out as mumbles and, along with the accent, I need to lean a bit towards him to capture the sounds coming out of his mouth. He doesn't speak directly towards me but around me, almost to the point that I don't know for sure if he is really speaking to me, or speaking to the air, or the ground, or the white-gray swirls of smoke that dance out of his cigarette.

I know, thanks for your pity. My day is getting a bit better though. I point to his ticket, New York as well?

Yeah, some meetings and stuff. He coughs again while facing the ground.

You don't smoke do you?

Is it that obvious?

Yeah. It is.

Well, not cigarettes at least, I haven't for a long time. They're bad for you! We both laugh.

I wouldn't know about smoking anything else. Sorry I cut the line. Or queue, as you say. I feel my insides cringe. If Lamia was with me, she would have known how to make an impression. I try to conjure up her aloof nature, wishing she could text me through this.

No worries, no worries. He accentuates the r's, rolling them a bit harder, faking an American accent. I enjoyed the wait, it was entertaining.

Really?

I don't usually see a girl who looks like you, blasting Radiohead into her head, trying to talk her way to a free upgrade.

I wasn't aware there was a specific Radiohead stereotype, I respond quickly, trying to hide that I'm flattered he's noticed me. Then I realise I probably haven't been an impressive sight, so I defend myself, I wasn't trying to scam the system, I was just trying to get back at my boyfriend. Make him uncomfortable by sitting nearby.

By stalking him, right?

Like pretending to smoke so you can talk to a girl?

He laughs. His leg is shaking just slightly now. He's on the extreme side of thin, like the goth guys in my class, the ones who make your thighs look huge no matter how thin you are. I try to discreetly suck myself in to make my body smaller.

We sit side by side, in silence, smoking. The wind begins to blow harder and I zip up my jacket higher.

Wind is my favourite weather, he says, looking straight ahead, speaking more to the atmosphere than me.

Wind is not a weather.

Really? Then what is it?

It's the air swirling around, I say slowly. The expression of weather. Really, it's beyond weather.

He turns to face me and I am able to see his eyes, which are much bluer in person. I know he has a lazy eye, but looking at him directly, I can't tell which one it is. He seems to contemplate what I just said, or maybe he wants to get the hell out of an awkward situation. He leans back, breaking the gaze. He grinds the cigarette on the side of the concrete ashtray.

Feeling like I've definitely blown it, I'm mentally preparing to say goodbye when he turns to me and asks, Are you still interested in making your flight? Or do you just want to hang out here and think about the weather? Or non-weather, as you put it? He stands and extends his arm to me.

I look up at him first to make sure he is not being sarcastic. He holds the pose, so I stand and place my arm in his, and ask, Do you do this with all your fans? I can't believe you have such a bad reputation.

Rumours, dear, all rumours.

Well, you are quite the gentleman. I shiver a little.

Are you okay?

Yes, just cold and nervous. Flying makes me nervous, especially now. You know, taking off and landing, passing through security.

He winks at me: Nice, sounds familiar. Let's get you inside then.

He leads me to the entrance and I hide a smile behind my scarf. For the first time in thirty-six hours I'm happy I'm wearing it. And although I'm engulfed in gray concrete and clouds, shrouded in black fabric, I feel a lightness that I haven't felt in months.

The double doors slide open like a sharp breath and clip closed behind us. Doors that swallow you whole.

(Extract from *Accidents Waiting to Happen,* a novel in progress)

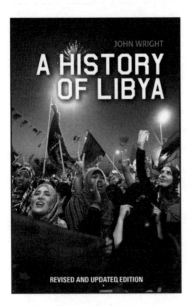

REVISED AND UPDATED EDITION

ISBN: 9781849042277
£12.99 / Paperback / 288pp

A History of Libya

JOHN WRIGHT

John Wright's concise history of Libya begins in the prehistoric Sahara and concludes with the bloody overthrow of the Gadafi regime and the emergence of a 'new' Libya in 2011. After surveying the story of the central Sahara's early hunter-gatherers and its Garamantian civilization, Wright briskly recounts the land's succession of foreign invaders, followed by the semi-independent Karamanli regime in 1711 and the return of the Turks in 1835. He discusses the workings of the historic trans-Saharan slave trade to Tripoli, Benghazi and other ports for local sale or export to the Eastern Mediterranean, and highlights Tripoli's nine-teenth-century role as a base for European penetration of the Sahara and the lands beyond it. Wright's modern history assesses the controversial Italian era (1911-43), describing in detail the long, harsh conquest while giving due credit to the material achievements of the colonial regime. This fair and comprehen-sive overview provides a clearer understanding of Libya's subsequent history, covered in four final chapters. These start with the World War Two campaigns that ended Italian rule; the fairly easy ride to an early UN-supervised independence under the Sanussi monarchy in 1951; the discovery and exploi-tation of oil in the 1950s and 1960; and Moammar Gadafi's 1969 coup bringing to power a bizarre revolutionary regime that was to last for forty-two years. Wright's final chapter summarises the main events of 2011 – the successful popular uprising; the NATO air intervention; the end of Gadafi and his regime; and the emergence of a 'new' and perhaps rather different Libya.

'John Wright's original study of Libya was a unique and masterly survey of the country's history. This updated edition possesses all the virtues of the original, together with an acute and perceptive analysis of both the Libyan Jamahiriyah of Colonel Gadafi and its humiliating end in 2011, to provide us with the most complete study of Libya's complex history to date. It is the essential companion for any scholar, journalist or interested reader anxious to understand this unusual and important Mediterranean state.' — George Joffe, University of Cambridge

WWW.HURSTPUBLISHERS.COM/BOOK/A-HISTORY-OF-LIBYA

41 GREAT RUSSELL ST, LONDON WC1B 3PL
WWW.HURSTPUBLISHERS.COM
WWW.FBOOK.COM/HURSTPUBLISHERS
020 7255 2201

LIBYA AFTER THE REVOLUTION

Naziha Arebi

My father is Libyan, my mother English, and I grew up in Britain. I guess I grew up half Libyan but never really knew what that meant. The country was always the imaginary place my dad spoke of only in hushed tones, this surreal beautiful desert by the sea, full of crazy characters and tales. So when the revolution began and I found myself at protests rubbing shoulders with other young Libyans, I thought it was time to go and discover both my heritage and my family.

The first thing I noticed on arriving in Libya was the energy of the youth and activists. It was – is – simply amazing. I wanted to help, I thought I could help, this new country, a country I knew like an estranged relative. I felt as if a natural force was pulling me towards Libya, even in this time of turbulence. I wanted to open up a visual dialogue, make an impact using visuals as my tool, to show a different face, many faces, of this country of which the world knows so little.

I won't lie. It's difficult to balance my quest to capture life in post-Gadhafi Libya with the security situation. There is a sense of paranoia left over from the regime that makes people suspicious and fearful of the camera. But that's exactly why it is so important to work on relationships with characters to gain their trust, especially if one is making a film. The country is still in transition, we are going through a difficult stage of development. Sometimes it's paralysing. It is not easy to move around. But I think this is natural: there is always chaos after a revolution.

After the fall of the regime there was a sense that people could suddenly breathe – they could talk, they could have an opinion. 'Freedom' became a wild scream. A country once silenced is now a place where everyone is talking at once, and talking very loudly. The security situation has deteriorated recently. The lack of a viable state or constitution, the increase in crime, have made the transitional phase even more acute. Everyday life has become a chore; and the lack of running water, electricity and fuel in a rich country like Libya has disenchanted many people. But this does not mean they are not hopeful for the future. It's just a wake-up call, beckoning us to work harder to create a future we want for our children.

My cousin was brought up in Libya. She too had a Libyan father, though he took her away from her English mother when we were nine years old. We had very different lives and whenever we meet I am reminded that this could have been my reality. But different doesn't mean that one is better than the other. She is married with three children, living in Misrata, and is very happy. All I know is that if I had grown up under the regime, I would not have been able to pursue a career as a film and visual artist. I would not have gone to Central Saint Martin's College of Art, where I gained a Masters in Screen, nor would I have been able to work in the theatre. I would not have had the creative freedom that growing up in the UK gave me. Being both British and Libyan allows me to see the country from the inside, but with the curiosity of someone from outside, always seeking to adjust to this duality.

Libyan men have great respect for women in their family and in the home, but on the street this respect evaporates. Some can be quite disrespectful. And when a camera is involved the situation can get a bit tense. Some men react strongly when a woman is taking their picture. I don't want to embarrass anyone but sometimes the men feel objectified, which is a new experience for them. When I am filming I spend a long time building a relationship with characters, so this generally doesn't happen. But when I am taking pictures on the streets it's interesting to play around with these gender roles, subverting the theory of the 'male gaze'. I find it fascinating to see how different people respond to the lens. The camera is never neutral, it always alters the reality, and this says something of each individual situation, whether it involves men or women.

My work is not explicitly political or religious, but these elements often resonate in the background of what I do. Our everyday reality is inescapably political. We are seeing a rise in literalist understandings of Islam sweeping the Middle East and the Maghreb in the wake of the 'Arab Spring'. The literalists are a very small minority and do not represent the masses, but it's these literalists we often see in the Western media when we talk of the region and Islam. I want to show an alternative reality. Of course, the fundamentalists exist, and one cannot ignore them, but I am worried by the drift into extremism away from the spiritual, though that is not my focus. My interest is in non-elitist forms of visual language that can spark change and help navigate towards universal human stories that challenge media stereotypes of the 'Other'. And my hope is that Libya will prosper soon; and become the bride of the Mediterranean once again.

My cousin, in traditional dress, about to go on the customary trip to see family
and friends for the Eid festival.

Boxing, banned under Gadhafi for being too brutal, has now become popular as a
way of channelling energy and frustrations.

'Weapons are supposed to protect the people not scare them' reads the placard of a young boy at a protest in Tripoli.

Every home has a firearm in Libya, and many children who witnessed the revolution are growing up to see violence and gun culture as the norm.

Voting in the first national elections, July 2012, a very special day.

My grandma's joy at voting.

At a demonstration against power cuts.

The words Baba Muamer, referring to Gadhafi as the patriarchal leader of the
Libyan people, have been erased from a street wall in Tripoli.

MAIA AND THE SWAN

Aamer Hussein

1.

I once knew a woman who loved a swan. She loved all swans, and geese and ducks and water hens too, but most of all she loved a swan she called Satin. On Sundays we went to the park to feed the birds that nested among the rushes beside the lake. They'd come running after us and pluck at our calves with their beaks. Satin would wait until she'd fed the rest, and then glide up to her with his mate. She would feed him pellets of bread she'd moistened in her mouth, and often he'd follow her like a pet, as his mate hopped along behind.

Maia – that was her name – and I lived on different sides of the park: she by the western gate, and I by the south. In summer the park was full of teenagers cavorting, boating, diving into the lake. Elderly couples strolled in the rose garden, the men with their bellies hanging out of their open shirts over their baggy shorts, their wives in thin shifts with their bare arms freckling and their faces flushed. There was a brass band, and a bandstand, and chairs for hire and people selling icecream.

Sometimes the boys on their roller skates would bully the birds. They'd tempt them with scraps of food; when the birds came over the boys would chase them with sticks and stones. Then the birds would show how strong they were. There was an urban legend about a goose that had attacked a boy with beak and claw and nearly plucked his eye out. But the swans kept to the water, their nests and their own company. Only Satin ever left the lake.

2.

Maia's parents were both from countries occupied by the Soviet Union. Her father survived the mayhem of World War II, but some years after Maia was born he defected from Stalingrad with his wife and his two children. They moved to London via Paris, as refugees. Maia didn't remember her early childhood behind the Iron Curtain. But she remembered that on one of her train journeys her mother had taught her some prayers of protection which she'd later discovered were in Arabic, and. she knew that at least one of her grandparents was a Muslim from Baku.

She wasn't terribly good at school, but she had a flair for languages, music and dance. She was very pretty, too, with long black hair and almond eyes that changed colour from brown to green depending on the light. When she was fourteen her mother put her in a stage academy. At seventeen she joined a troupe of dancers. She played some minor roles on television, and even a bit part in a Bond movie. She wasn't suited to that life, she said. 'Too many foul old men with sweaty hands.' At eighteen she met an actor and moved in with him. Often out of work, he'd clean flats for a living. He was violent and possessive. She thought he was seeing other women. One night she ran away and went back home to her parents.

I'd moved to live near the park early in '78, before my twenty-third birthday. I'd met Maia a few times; a year or two ago she had slept on my sister Sasha's sofa for a week, in Sasha's riverside flat. But we'd become friends one afternoon when I was walking by the lake and thinking about my life. 'Umayr!' She called out my name from behind – she remembered it, though she pronounced it oddly, with a 't' at the end like a Turk.

We sat down on a bench in the sick February sunshine to talk. She'd moved to a garden flat a minute's walk away from the park. Her life, she said, was going better: she'd got a job as a buyer in a fashion company, and was designing clothes as well. I worked in a bank and hated my job. It all poured out as we spoke.

We exchanged numbers and started to meet. On Saturday afternoons we walked by the lake and fed the swans. Often in the evenings we'd stroll down the High Street and eat a burger and chips as we walked along.

Then spring came and she went to Milan for a show. I was alone and had almost no friends in London. Just after my twenty-third birthday in April, I decided to leave the bank and apply to go back to my abandoned studies.

For some months I felt Maia was avoiding me. But then, that summer before I went back to university, she started to call again and we met often. I would tell her about the girl I was seeing; she'd talk about the man she'd fallen in love with. He was about ten years older – an exiled count, she said, from somewhere in Central Europe

'He walked into the store one day and my manager told me to help him', she said. 'He bought the most expensive dresses in the store – for his sister, he said – and the day after I received, gift-wrapped, the one I liked the best, with a bunch of roses and an invitation for a glass of champagne.'

She'd been apprehensive at first – she'd met many, many men who only wanted a brief fling – but he dropped her home and asked to see her again later in the week.

And then they'd seen each other again, and again

'He wants to marry me.' She showed me her ruby ring. 'Pre-engagement. He's very rich.' She pulled a sour face. 'My mother approves. She says I won't find another man who'll look after me the way he will.'

That's what had been happening to her while I was leaving my job.

We spent long days in the park that summer – Saturdays, Sundays – feeding the birds, walking, climbing trees, singing to each other, or just lying silently on the grass, sharing cigarettes. In October I was back at university, studying languages. I was singing again, too, with an acoustic folk group I'd found at college.

In the autumn evenings, if we met after a day's work, we'd either eat something together at a restaurant – a pizza or a plate of pasta – or go back to her flat for something exquisitely simple she'd cooked.

But often we'd leave each other on a twilit street corner, and be off to our other pursuits: she to her nightclubs and five-star restaurants, and I with my new acquaintances to their student haunts. Just as often I'd go to a concert or a film on my own, or home to an evening alone with a book.

3.

Maia soon found out that Maximilian, her lover, was married and waiting for a divorce.

'I'm not making any commitments till his decree is final', she said. It was November, and we had our overcoats on. We were striding rather than strolling. She'd tried to break up with him after one of their champagne-fuelled nights, and he'd gone away, but he'd rung her bell later, quite drunk. ('He's very fond of a drink.')

'He swears he'll kill himself if I leave him', she told me as we sat down on a bench by the lake and lit cigarettes.

So the fairy tale ending wasn't about to be staged yet.

'Another bloody freak', I said. 'Why do you always attract freaks?'

(I was retaliating to a comment she'd made when she met a friend of mine: 'Is she an *au pair*?' And when I said the girl was studying philosophy, she said, 'Why do you always date such *common* girls?')

'Max is not violent'. she said. 'Never ever!'

4.

In winter the park was almost empty after midday. But Maia liked to go there in all seasons. I hadn't seen her for some weeks when she dragged me out on a Saturday afternoon in early January. It had snowed so hard that the lake had frozen over. She was looking for Satin, but couldn't find him.

'He's probably flown to sunnier shores', I said. But she knew he'd be there.

And he was. He was on the island in the lake, where he had his nest, but when she called out to him he wouldn't come over.

'He's wounded', she said. 'I know. He's hurt his wing. Or a foot.'

(Was he afraid of the ice? If so, why couldn't he fly? Had his wings been clipped?)

Maia threw off her mink coat, flung it on the frost-spangled grass, and set off across the glittering ice floor

(I'd heard since I was very young that swans never parted from their mates. So where had Satin's mate gone, leaving him stranded?)

'Satin, O Satin, come on boy, come to Maia ….'

She slipped as soon as she stepped on the ice. I grabbed her before she fell. She sat down on a bench, pulled off her boots and her stockings, and set off again, barefoot, to cross the water. I saw Satin flap his wings. Maia shrieked when her bare foot touched its frozen surface.

'You'll fall', I said. 'The ice will crack.'

She said: 'There were kids skating on the lake earlier. The ice won't give way.'

I don't remember the ice cracking or her falling or whether she ever got to the island. But often I'd dream that she'd fallen into the lake, that she was calling out for help, calling out my name and waving, and then she was neck-deep in water, and I was standing there on the icy bank, with my feet frozen, dumb and unable to move, watching her drown. And the dream would overlay what really happened. But I do remember her characteristically rambling story about wardens and vets and yes, a swan hospital in Richmond, and three men struggling to get poor Satin on a boat and then into their van to get him there. He'd broken a foot and would have to be off the lake for quite a while.

5.

I wasn't serious about anyone I'd met. I'd had flings, too, but I'd never get involved with anyone who was seeing someone else. Mostly I was happy enough to study and listen to music when I was on my own. And I had Maia. Max only visited for short periods – he'd stay in a smart boutique hotel in Kensington where he seemed to have a permanent reservation, see her for dinner or drop in at her flat, and always bring her gifts: jewels, furs, gowns. Much of the time Maia was alone and we spent our best times together. More than once I got the feeling she didn't really care when Max failed to turn up. Once the first tide of joy subsided, the old pain came back – her first lover had left her with scars of betrayal that would never heal.

Over the spring, as we became closer, I felt she enjoyed talking about love, or dreaming of it, more than she enjoyed living it. (Both of us liked to be liked, but once we'd got the object of our affection we were less interested and often longed to escape the possessiveness of our lovers.) Like all dreamers, she was very unpunctual, as she sat for hours in front of the mirror, though I don't think it was herself she was looking at.

She loved eating and cooking (and like most of us who do, she often complained of indigestion and stomach ailments). Once when she was cooking for me at her place – a chicken with aromatic herbs, and a dish of pilaff with nuts and raisins – Max rang and said he'd join us for dinner, because a meeting of his had been cancelled. He was a dark-haired man of medium height, with a long nose and very black eyes. He had a slow, hoarse voice and affected mannerisms and didn't seem to be enjoying his food very much. I was waiting to make my getaway when he suggested we should all go to a nightclub near Green Park called Tokyo Joe. I watched while they danced away the night. It was the first time I'd seen him; I hoped it would be the last.

For a woman who loved birds so much and couldn't bear to see a stray dog or cat on a street corner in some southern city, Maia was unconcerned about hunting and shooting animals. So she'd put a stuffed tiger in her sitting room to shock all her eco-conscious friends. She took a photograph of me embracing the tiger and giggled because it actually wasn't stuffed at all; it was a fake. She loved taking photographs and she loved her Polaroid camera. She took pictures of me: singing, dancing, and posing in every angle one evening when the rain was coming down hard outside. Then she disappeared into her bedroom, and emerged dressed up as some long-gone Hollywood diva: Ava Gardner, perhaps, her favourite. She handed over her Polaroid to me and I took pictures of her too, some out of focus, some quite good, especially one in which she looked like a captive beauty from one of those old ballads I loved to sing, with her arms around her furry black and golden beast, looking out with yearning eyes, dreaming that he'd be transformed into a prince.

Maia loved dancing. Once, after a glass or two of champagne, she draped a few scarves round her brassiere and tucked one into her panties, put on a record of Arabic instrumental music really loud and undulated like an Egyptian, twisting her belly and swinging her hips, and clashing the cymbals attached to her fingertips, while I lay back on the sofa and lazily kept time with my hands and my feet. Then she dragged me up to dance with her and we wriggled face to face, but we rarely let our bodies touch. She was affectionate, but she said she didn't like being touched and I was afraid of what the touch of her perspiring skin might unleash in me.

We both spoke Italian and when I was a child I'd picked up a lot of Italian big-band melodies like *Volare* and *Come Prima, Piu di Prima*. I went off and learned the lyrics of those songs to entertain her; I belted them out to her in her kitchen while she baked a cheese and spinach pie, and kept on singing in the doorway of her bathroom as she soaked in her bubble bath before we sat down to supper.

There was a song by Donovan I loved but I'd never managed to learn, because its key changes were awkward for my low tenor. 'She fell in love with a swan, her eyes were full of feathers.' 'Shut up, you're out of tune,' she'd say. She thought the folksongs I loved were monotonous and girlish. At the end of the song the girl takes off her dress, lets down her hair, and then two swans fly off into the starry night. 'You're making fun of me', Maia would say when I chanted the verse to her. 'I didn't fall into the water that day in the park.'

We both worked all day; unless we met in the park just before it closed, we didn't have time to meet before dark. Since Satin hadn't come back to the lake, Maia seemed to want to walk in the park much less often. Once or twice she called out when we did go in search of him: 'Look! Satin!' But the swan we saw hadn't approached her, and she decided that it wasn't Satin after all.

We met when we could, though something or someone often came between us now: her travels, my assignments, her family or mine, but mostly Max. I told myself I didn't mind when Max turned up. I had other friends, now. The best of these was Farhad. We'd met on the way home from a university social; he'd called me several times when I'd been busy with her. Then one the day we met by the French Institute where we were waiting to find out about winter classes, and sat down together to have a cup of coffee and a cigarette. We both liked French films, Jacques Brel, and Jean-Paul Sartre.

We soon realised that, at least to foreign eyes, we were quite alike to look at. He was a little smaller and perhaps heavier, and his hair was straight and mine was wavy, but we were both quite tall and dark and we both wore glasses. Farhad was ebullient, though, while I was quiet; he was a scientist and I was a student of humanities.

Maia, who met him one afternoon when – unusually – she dropped by to see me at the campus (she hated the common room), didn't see any resemblance. And Farhad said, 'Your girlfriend isn't Azeri or Russian. She looks Armenian to me.'

'She never said she was Azeri and she isn't my girlfriend.'

Farhad left it there; he believed there was safety in numbers. He didn't bother to change girlfriends, he just waited till one or the other of them got tired of his feckless, faithless ways and dropped him, before another one appeared in his life. Anyhow, he was engaged to his second cousin in Teheran; he thought of his promiscuity as a kind of expedient fidelity. He liked going out and having a drink or two and staying out all night. It was hard to drag me to a crowded, dark place with loud music playing, except on the occasional Saturday, because I knew what it felt like to be left alone while Maia was in Rio de Janeiro and the rest of the world was drinking and dancing.

6.

Fall, leaves, please fall! I'd say to the trees when autumn approached. I was afraid of bare branches and wished the leaves would rain down now so I could get used to the naked trees. By the time the leaves had begun to squelch beneath our feet in red and yellow piles, I was too busy to think much about the park or Satin and the swans on the lake. Apart from my classes and homework, there was the work I did in an office a couple of times a week; my few leisure hours were spent with Farhad, or with my musical friends, practising for our performances in clubs and college halls.

Maia was on and off planes every few weeks. I was never very clear about what sort of business took her away – she said she was attending fashion shows and buying new designs. She had travel fever and would never turn down a chance to fly. Sometimes she was away for three weeks and I wouldn't even hear from her. Or she'd call on a bad line and wake me up at dawn because she was in Hong Kong or Buenos Aires and had forgotten the time difference.

When she was in town, we'd meet just as we always had. But our relationship was enclosed in a glass bubble now. She liked to meet in West End hotel bars, and looked around her a lot as if she were afraid of spies. She'd started to bring gifts for me: shirts, ties, a watch, a lighter. I'd wear the shirts, but put everything else away: I didn't like wearing ties, hated flashy watches with gold straps, and preferred books of matches to lighters. She seemed restless; I felt her loneliness. Max had stopped talking about divorcing his wife, who seemed to have all the money; Maia was completely opposed to the idea of being the 'mistress', as she put it, of a married man. Now other names were appearing on her list of suitors. An ageing MP. A Saudi princeling. But all of them seemed to be spoken for. She was smoking far too much and complaining of her bad appetite and recurrent stomach cramps.

Once at the Students' Union cafeteria, when I got there late after seeing her, Farhad, who'd been waiting nearly an hour for me, was sitting with three polystyrene cups in front of him. Flicking ash into one of them, he said:

'When that woman turns up and just crooks a little finger, you dump the lot us, and off you run. What's with you, man?'

And I realised that things really had changed between all of us. Though Farhad said he wasn't very political and had never really liked the Shah, I knew he was not looking forward to going back to Teheran, where all the fun, he said, had been driven underground. As if to compensate for that distant lack, he seemed to party every night. As it got colder and darker, I was falling into a lot of his ways, carousing till two in the morning even on weekdays, then stumbling red-eyed out of bed to attend my classes. I'd pretend to Maia, when she remarked on the purple shadows under my eyes, that I'd been studying till late, but she knew me too well to believe that for more than a minute. 'You're burning your candle at both ends, darling….' She'd laugh, but there was a brittle tinge to her words and to her laughter, as if I, her reliable friend, was turning into someone she could no longer lean on.

Twice in autumn I'd taken off on a whim, without telling anyone, to spend long weekends in Barcelona and Paris, and been scolded for missing lectures. The truth was that I liked it when she rang and couldn't find me. And when I came back to find that she hadn't called during those days and there was only Farhad to explain my mysterious movements to, I'd be annoyed, because telling her later that I'd been away all the time that she had just didn't have the same impact as her ringing to find me gone.

I felt guilty as I spoke to Farhad now, as if I were betraying her, but I wanted clarity, and I spoke to him as I'd never done before.

'I'm sick of it all', I said. 'I miss her when she leaves. Then just as I get used to her being away, she turns up, and if I can't see her, she sounds offended. She regularly breaks promises she makes. Let's go here or there on Sunday, she'll say, then on Sunday she'll be off to Timbuktu or Ulan Bator. Let's go to the sea, she'll say, but the only waters we've ever seen ourselves in together are in the park…'

Farhad's mind seemed to wander as he looked into the depths of his coffee. And then he said, furrowing his brow:

'Who – or what – do you think pays for those gifts she gives you? What does she ask for, in return? You're not even sleeping with her, are you? You need to find a girlfriend. What are you, like, weird?'

He passed me a Gitane.

'You know what we say in Iran? You should only die for someone who's at least ready to faint for you.'

I lit my cigarette and wondered whether he'd just made up the folksy proverb.

'I'm not going home this winter', he said. 'Fancy coming to Rome? I've never been.'

He knew it was my favourite city. I smiled and didn't answer.

7.

I saw her in the dark Hilton bar. She was just back from Milan.

'Remember those days? How we spent day after day in the park? And how we rescued Satin….' Her gestures, her words were wistful.

It was Happy Hour. She was sipping the sort of sweet slushy drink with lots of ice and a silly name she favoured when she wasn't drinking champagne.

'But that wasn't even a year ago. You make it sound like ten years….'

'We were so happy then. It's just that we were so happy….'

'I'm not at all unhappy now, Maia. Are you?'

'No, no, I'm always happy when I see you.'

But you haven't been happy for a while, I thought. Yes, you're happy for a moment when you see me and then you're off somewhere, away in some place I can't reach.

Maia's way of seeing happiness as if it was always something that had happened yesterday suddenly made me anxious for a tomorrow round the corner. I wanted to live in the present. Other people's nostalgia made me sad. Then I'd be reminded that though she listened cheerfully to the stories I told her, and asked who I flirted with or even went to bed with, our friendship was – always had been – based on her stories. And my responses to those stories. Her travels. Her troubles. And now, along with stories, there were hopes. A home. Babies. A world that was remote from me and anything I wanted.

I'd never spoken to Maia about tomorrows. But sometimes she'd say: 'We're going to be together forever. Never let me go.'

    Come prima, piu di prima, t'amero....

8.

A December Sunday. I was tired of studying and reading and even of singing. I went off by a coach to spend a day with my sister Sasha, who'd moved to Oxford with her husband the year before.

We went for a walk in the university grounds among the deer. She asked about Maia, who'd once been a friend of sorts.

'Farhad thinks I give her too much time. He doesn't believe in platonic friendships.'

'Farhad's right. This friendship's going nowhere, hmmm? Maia's involved with someone else. You'll be twenty-five in spring; you haven't even finished your studies. And weren't you going back to Karachi with Daddy next year? Aren't you planning to go on with postgrad work? And these expensive gifts she brings you...have you ever given her anything in return? You don't have a job or a decent income. You study, you sing, you live the life of Riley. Maybe it's because of you that Maia's not been able to make up her mind about her Max. Now it's up to you to think about the future....'

We turned a corner and sat down in a walled garden where Sasha told me roses grew in summer. We didn't talk for a while.

Later, as we strolled on the banks of the river, I saw a single swan glide by, and after a long, long time I thought of Satin.

9.

'I'm going to be twenty-nine on the 26th', she said. 'I thought I'd have a party here....just you and me and a few friends.'

We'd finished eating our lobster; she was drinking her sixth glass of wine.

'But you said you were going to see the Nile in winter with Max...'

'Changed my mind. That bastard hasn't done a thing about his divorce.... and you know what I found out? He isn't a count, or even Hungarian. He was born in Istanbul. His real surname is Levi and I think his family made their money selling oriental carpets in Milan.'

'Maia, I'm not going to be here. I'm going to Rome for Christmas. I'll be gone before the rush begins.'

I'd only decided as we spoke that I'd be going there, with or without Farhad. For a minute I thought she was going to cry. Then she looked up and said, 'But you'll come back for the New Year, won't you?'

It was going to be the start of a new decade.

'Yes,' I said. 'I'll be back to spend it with you, Maia.'

I knew that by the time I returned things would have changed again.

She smiled. Her eyes in the candlelight were amber.

'I've been meaning to tell you. Satin's back on the lake. I saw him.'

A few months ago I'd have told her that she'd dreamed it all: that she'd seen some other hungry swan and decided it was her old pet who'd escaped from the traps, the wicked boys, and the swan doctors; that I didn't know a thing about the comings and goings of swans or their seasonal habits and even if I'd ever had a clue I no longer cared. But tonight I thought I'd leave her with her fancies of a big white bird preening his feathers and spreading his wings on a frozen winter lake.

I leaned over the debris of dinner to kiss her cheek, but it was her mouth that met mine.

'Coffee?' I asked. 'Then I should walk you home.'

TWO POEMS

George Szirtes

Maghreb

Look, there are pearls of rain that hang and drip
in the grey light. There's the high wall with its fists
of flint, and the leaves with their green palms
open to the sky, till a gust exposes their delicate wrists

and they shudder and lift and the grey light remains.
And this is what's strange, this being anywhere
with a familiar incomprehensibility, the birds
familiar to the sky, relaxed in its homely air,

yet mad and otherwise, strange even to themselves.
You sit at your table, friend, at home with the curious
paraphernalia of your body as I am with mine.
I feel our peculiar, polyvalent, unutterably various

languages shifting underfoot. To me the names
I pass between my lips - Algiers, Tunis, Rabat -
are as fresh clothes in which my body is renewed.
May your fresh clothes be mine. May the desert

at your feet burn mine.

Spleen

After Baudelaire

I'm like the king of a rainy country, rich
but wobbly-weak, both cub and toothless bitch.
I'm through with books,and poems and string quartets:
I've sold the horses, shot the household pets.
Cheer up? Not likely, board games are a bore
and as for 'the people' dying by my door,
fuck them, and fuck that guitar-wielding clown,
who's worse than useless when I'm feeling down.
Here I'm the king stuck in his regal bed,
the girls can put on sex shows, give him head,
go girl on girl, no point, it just won't work,
nothing will jump-start this junky royal jerk.
The quack who brings me pills and knows a trick
to harden flaccid aristocratic dick,
may as well bring blood and the Roman Baths
the kind that suited those old psychopaths.
No good, once dead in muscle, nerve, and brain.
It's all green Lethe and that bloody rain.

VOYAGES

Sarra Hennigan

Voyage Atlas

Chefchaouen at dusk
Africa pink solitude, lavender like Paris in the snow
does he remember his birth high in the Atlas with silver bracelets
but no chains? the centre of freedom
being bevelled

Voyage in Vein

The village café is closed today so I stay in
a bag of candy and nails, band-aids, healing hands
I am too tired to read the ceiling and my father's voice sounds
like where I will be – admiring my weakness
there is no such thing but one day
I will know this is ending in
good blood

Voyages with the Master (for J.K.)

The devil does not play with me (I do not drink vodka) (didn't you have
too much once?)
covering my hands in black (the devil is afraid of me) (he should be) (I will
break all bottles of fear) (I will read books of doubt backward until they
are unwritten) The letters that make up your name are unfamiliar (my
love is great but I die for no man) I am becoming illiterate s-u--n-f-l-o-w-

e-r (words are my master) I cover what I can touch with my face that is violet ἰοειδής stained with laughter. I am also blind (too late to learn braille? never too late!) what I want to feel I feel (I can still hear purple music) what I feel covered in gold, my hands can reach around your neck leave a mark (very small Chinese characters metallic ringing, tao te ching singing) love prints vibrate greenish blue bruises (atomic Arabic calligraphy right to left, right to left, Jerusalem ascensions) all the forgotten jewels, more colours than exist in this world, only me garnet, where are you ruby? onde está você agora? (How far is Japan from here?) you say you feel 'strange'

(more words that do not make any sense) I try to forget one language to learn another (Pashto vs Portuguese vs Farsi vs Finnish) I try to forget all languages (you are on holiday in Vienna or Rio, either way it's drinking coffee memories) also (heaven is here) How I knew you (the devil knows us all) or did not know you (willingly with angelic amnesia)

I try to be a little younger (I am no fool) then when I was young (I am not fooling anyone) a little less than what I wanted to be (not much) a little more free (high hopes) (so much) proof (a growing garden) not there yet (I swim in earth's soil) light on your skin (you are a seventh heaven Persian poetry beauty) erased marks (I used to be beautiful before we were born) a secret sound (the ocean!) no words at all (we are all fit for paradise, here) a bouquet of wildflowers (who brought these?) air (God) aloe vera on all our burns. Love. Nothing to prove (nothing to prove).

Nothing and nothing to love. To prove love, simply love.

Voyage to the Netherlands

Juliana Queen of the Netherlands dreamed
I drowned in the Wad Den Zee
she failed to realize I was born in a Barbary state of art
formed swimming, stealing breath, warmth for my limbs, soul
gold hidden accounts for my bread
I can steal what I need…
escape
warnings

I reached the shore
ran from Marathon to Athens
to sing melismatically
with all the transgressions against me, I still sing sweetly 'I am alive'
the Greeks defeated the Persians
yet I prefer Zoroaster to Aristotle, I like jumping over fire!
Juliana fled to New Amsterdam to die part of the land
dust and petrified wood transmigrating…

I dreamt she danced an impersonation of all that is real in a woman drums,
yaki deer songs
while I continued to do laps from continent
freestyle to new borders and limits broken ships of passage
I thought I would rather dance
dance, dance Samba
shake, shake. Let it shake softly to love
I will not judge, feel anger
What is 'The Last Judgement' but the latest judgement of a man who thinks
he knows me…

I NEVER pursued the depraved
but perhaps the 'promiscuity' of my thoughts
made them *feel* like they had the right to imprison me
within perfection
without
PERFECTION
I lay down with old Finnish poets using trochaic verse
Kalevala in the land of heroes, women who use knowledge of anatomy and
the principal of leverage…

Leverage!
the truth!
So the strength of the opponent can be used against him
Jujitsu or juju magic charms
to be thrown at the spirits of greed wormed hate
Juliana returns to sugar beets

as I sink in mustard flowers
she holds lavender
I throw stones
she speaks in tidal waves
I use infixes to reach justice
maybe God, like the Arabic iq-ta-riba 'to come nearer'
some sort of loose pedantry
to lie
voir dire
to a tribunal
a society that would see me guilty when I am innocent
but too poor to defend myself

I tell the world I hope when Juliana awakens
I am
drowned in the North Sea

REVIEWS

A MAN FROM THE *BANLIEUE*

Suhel Ahmed

As prison dramas go, one immediately sees why Jacques Audiard's *A Prophet* has garnered so much praise, not to mention a flurry of prizes, since it hit the big screen in 2009. It picked up the Grand Prix at Cannes, the Best Foreign Language Film gong courtesy of the US National Board of Review, plus the Best Film award at the London Film Festival. Technically superb with its fluid camera work and chiaroscurist compositions, the film draws you into a claustrophobic world in which the Darwinian notion of survival operates, a world that becomes a rite of passage for the film's lead protagonist. *A Prophet* is a classic that aims to provide an insight into the world of Maghrebi immigrants in France.

Malik El Djebena, magnificently played by Tahir Rahim, a scared nineteen year old, is sent down for six years for assaulting an officer – a crime to which there is only ever a vague reference. He enters the prison a 'petit Arabe' but learns the skills to survive and prevail against all the odds. In this regard, the film could be read as a coming-of-age story. However, this 'coming-of-age' narrative alludes to an education that does not lead to a reformation, but makes him an expert in the world of crime. *A Prophet* might fall into the same bracket as movies that follow the rise of the anti-hero gangster, and indeed the film has been compared to genre classics such as *Scarface* (1983) and *The Godfather* (1972). However, such comparisons were probably drawn and spread by the film's marketing team to help the movie gain traction in the mainstream. Audiard's film has greater intelligence; for the most part he eschews Hollywood's need for gloss, finesse and cool and instead anchors his film to the conventions of social realism. In doing so he offers a grim but revealing insight into the state of French prisons. It's a moral responsibility the director is fully conscious of, having gone on record as claiming that France's 'social-cultural reality has been ignored by contemporary cinema'.

His vision of creating a film that boasts a greater degree of sociological accuracy has reaped its reward. *A Prophet* casts a sobering light on the plight of those relegated to the lowest rung of the French social order, which in this case happens to be the Arab-Muslim inmates. The prison is coldly lit and oppressive; Audiard shows that all spaces are small, sequestered by thick concrete, opaque glass and metal bars, the severe lines joining at right angles creating a boxed-in effect. The visuals are complemented by corridor echoes in which doors are frequently closing, keys jangling and locks turning. The roving, hand-held camera presses the viewer's gaze as close as possible to the realities of prison life and to those who occupy that space. Such was Audiard's desire for authenticity that he visited a number of jails so that he could recreate the harsh environment in a disused factory. Audiard even added ambient sounds recorded in a real prison to the film. The rendition of the prison setting is undoubtedly one of the film's finest achievements, so affecting, in fact, that at a private screening for prison workers, an official heralded it as the country's first great film about French prisons.

A Prophet directed by Jacques Audiard, produced by Martini Cassinelli et al, screenplay by Jacques Audiard, Thomas Bidegain, Abdel Raouf Dafri and Nicolas Peufaillit. Released by UGS Distribution.
In French, Arabic, and Corsican. France, 2009

What the viewer ascertains very early on is that the penal system depicted in the film isn't a place for reformation, and prisoners do not come out the other side primed to fit neatly into the national community. No, this prison gives off the odour of a dumping ground (or a camp, if one wishes to adopt a more post-colonial reading) which appears to be filled by two minority factions: French-Arab Muslims (mainly young, second generation immigrants) on one side, and those of Corsican descent on the other. Yet it is the Coriscans who rule inside the walls of this correction house, who behave as if they own the place, who can smuggle in contraband, and who have corrupt officials in their back pocket. This leaves the Arab prisoners at the very bottom and exposed to the prejudices of the Corsican mob. The dumping ground analogy in relation to French-Arab prisoners isn't perhaps as hyperbolic as it sounds when one considers that, according to sociologists, 60 to 70 per cent of inmates in the country's prison system are

Muslim, the majority with Maghrebi ancestry Algerians, Tunisians and Moroccans. The prison officials blame the high numbers on crimes associated with poverty perpetrated by people who have emigrated from these North African countries in recent decades. The consequence of France's inability or unwillingness to absorb this influx into its social and economic fabric is that the new generation of youths find themselves with little opportunity for self-betterment. They are the ones stuck in the ghetto neighbourhoods, the *banlieues*, which house a disproportionate number of broken families and are characterised by financial hardship, crime, violence, and gang culture with an emphasis on territoriality.

In Malik, Audiard has created a character who perhaps represents that lost generation, a generation caught between and betwixt, without a definite national identity or a sense of belonging; Malik is under-educated, a neglected orphan who has had to fend for himself for much of his life. Audiard offers the viewer a glimpse of his back story in a scene where the prison teacher evaluates his level of education. Asked about his mother tongue and whether growing up he spoke to his parents in French or Arabic, Malik is silent before shaking his head and saying that he was not with them. The reaction is odd but revealing. It is as if he is jolted by the thought that parents might have featured in his life at one time.

Belying this, of course, is an intense vulnerability, and this is captured in the opening scene. The image fades in to introduce Malik inside a keyhole effect somewhat reminiscent of the old silent movies. He is unshaven, dishevelled, sporting a cut under one eye. His hands are resting on his lap. They are cuffed. He is waiting to be met by the guards and can hear their aggressive voices directed at another prisoner; his eyes are wide, his shoulders stooped, his body language that of a schoolboy waiting outside the headmaster's office. He is alone with his thoughts and staring down the barrel of a future that's bleak with no kin or kith for support.

However, Malik's sense of isolation runs deeper. Not only has he been flung to the margins of society but appears also to be cut off from his Arab heritage. When the official processing Malik into the penitentiary asks him about his religion and whether or not he goes to prayer or eats pork, Malik shrugs his shoulders and shows complete ambivalence. Raised by various state agencies, he has not picked up any traditional religious or cultural values. In this respect, Malik's character is a departure from the typical *beur* protagonist – *beur* is a play on the word *Arabe* invented in the 1980s by second-generation French Muslims in an attempt to escape the negative connotations associated with being Arab. *Cinéma beur* was a term coined in the 1980s with the rise of French films dealing with the effects of immigration from the perspective of members of the second-generation North African community in France. Malik is not tormented by his fragmented identity and neither is he too concerned about trying to integrate into French society. No, Malik's character is all about the rise of the individual. He is quietly shrewd and has a capitalist's intentions, signposted from the very beginning when he tries to sneak money into the prison inside a hole in his trainers. When his lawyer asks him to sign a document so that he can apply for legal aid, Malik is perturbed that the lawyer will be getting all of the money. The most telling moment attesting to this character trait comes later on in a seemingly irrelevant image. Seconds before engaging in a gunfight in a shopping mall, Malik catches a glimpse of an expensive pair of shoes behind the window of a Parisian boutique. For Malik it is an arresting sight which briefly halts the flow of action allowing the viewer a naked view of his ambitions. The day he can fill those shoes is the day he can finally walk away from his humble beginnings which have been blighted by maltreatment and discrimination. This is in keeping with Audiard's treatment of the male lead in his other films, namely, *A Self-Made Hero* (1996) and *Read My Lips* (2001). Typically, the character operates on society's margins, and redemption comes once he cuts loose from those who have been exploiting him. Cynical it may be but in *A Prophet* freedom can be earned only through the accumulation of wealth.

For Malik, any association with a collective is relevant only insofar as it helps him achieve his own ends. While the state apparatus interprets his name and ethnicity to pigeonhole him into the French-Arab-Muslim demographic, Malik will soon learn that in order to succeed in 'business' it is best to be a chameleon and align himself with those with power, which in prison happens to be the Corsicans. In fact, he keeps a foot in each camp and straddles the divide masterfully throughout the film. In time he will become polyglot: French, Arabic and Corsican will roll off his tongue with equal fluency and eventually play a pivotal part in his ability to engage with all and carry out his Machiavellian schemes.

However, although Malik may seem largely unaffected (though he does lose his cool one time when an inmate calls him a pig), there is no denying that the environment he is incarcerated in is a racist one. The Arabs are referred to as animals by the Corsican gang leader Cesar Luciani. Upon seeing Malik for the first time he labels him a dirty Arab and this becomes an oft-repeated insult, a means by which Cesar reminds Malik of his station. From the outset Audiard sets up a racial hierarchy and it becomes one of the director's preoccupations to keep emphasising the racist vitriol to which the Arab faction is subjected. None is more offensive than the exchange between Cesar and a fellow countryman in the yard. Casting his beady stare at a new group of Arab inmates he asks whether the Arabs keep multiplying as if they are some kind of virus, and the other responds by calling them a dumb lot who always 'think with their balls'. (This is something Malik repeats to Cesar later on, but his tone is ironic and becomes an aside, a warning that Cesar's prejudice will ultimately prove to be his downfall.) This exchange typifies the kind of racist ideology that reduces the other to a sub-human level. It is one of Audiard's skills that he manages to make these acute commentaries about France and its troubled relationship with generations of Arab immigrants without laying it on too thickly. Precedence firmly lies with the storyline. It is not surprising that there is a finely tuned balance between social commentary and storytelling when one considers that Audiard spent years refining the script with the original screenplay writer Abdel Raouf Dafri.

The first thirty minutes of *A Prophet* make for compelling viewing and are arguably the most gripping section of the film. The tension is as taut as a snare drum, as we see the naïve Malik being initiated into the adult prison. (Up until now he has been in and out of juvenile centres.) Malik soon realises that prison is more dangerous than the outside world. On his first day out in the yard he is attacked for his pair of trainers and is left lying in a heap. Next, a fellow Arab inmate asks for a sexual favour in the communal showers in return for marijuana. But this scene isn't an incidental part of Malik's initiation. The inmate happens to be Reyeb, a key witness passing through the state prison who is to testify against Cesar's Italian mob boss on the outside, and of course Cesar sees this as his best opportunity to silence him for good.

Since Reyeb keeps himself confined to the Muslim wing of the prison, Cesar decides that the only way it would be possible to kill Reyeb is to get one of his 'own kind' to commit the act. It is at this juncture that his unwanted attention falls on Malik. A couple of henchmen summon Malik who is duly ordered by Cesar to carry out the murder: 'If you do not kill him, I will kill you,' he says, exercising a despot's sovereignty over Malik and establishing the terms of their relationship. Thus, on pain of death, Malik begins preparing himself for the act.

This set up leads to the film's most viscerally affecting scene, and the fulcrum on which Malik's character turns to find its new trajectory. Watching Malik learning to hide a razor blade in his mouth – with which he would attack Reyeb – is harrowing in itself: a montage of him practising shows the cuts he endures to his tongue as he tries to worry the piece of metal out of his mouth. The killing scene is brutal, completely unaesthetic, the camera refusing to turn away and forcing the viewer to avert their stare instead. Yet, the build-up to the murder is tender, with Reyeb expressing genuine care and sincerity – qualities that are in short supply in the film. In the moments leading up to the killing, an unwitting Reyeb advises Malik to learn to read and to leave prison a little smarter.

After the killing Malik does heed Reyeb's instruction, who will return as a kind of spiritual guide during the rest of the film, appearing to Malik both in his sleep and while awake, these visitations preceded by a chapter heading and marking out the passage of time in prison. This device gives the film its operatic flourishes, and serves to underscore Malik's status as the eponymous prophet. Indeed, he is referred to as a prophet later on in the film when, aided by a vision of Reyeb, he is able to use this otherworldly third eye to avert a deadly car collision. I remain a tad uncertain about these quasi-theatrical set pieces. Sure, they add a deeper and more esoteric layer to the film. For instance, Reyeb appearing before Malik to underscore the importance of education by recounting the story of the first Qur'anic revelation to the Prophet Mohammad is powerful, not least because of the obvious parallel. But for everything that is robust about the film, there is something contrived about these clairvoyancy scenes. They seem a little forced at times. One wonders what the film would have lost had some of them been consigned to the cutting room floor.

Forced then into becoming Cesar's errand boy, Malik earnestly plays the Corsican's Man Friday, silently enduring the bullying, but he uses his private time to enroll in prison school and begin his education. Any suggestion that Cesar's treatment of Malik might soften and he might turn out to be a paternal influence is thwarted from the start. Arestrup presents his character without a single sentimental fibre. Gruff, unkempt and hirsute, he is a menacing presence who regards Malik as little more than an instrument to achieve his own 'business' ends. Malik is often subjected to his beatings as a reminder of his non-human status. In the end, Cesar represents the monstrous figure Malik needs to break away from to earn his freedom. And this of course gives the film's narrative arc its impetus, as we watch Malik leading a double life, striving to learn and forge his own drug-dealing connections while masquerading as Cesar's dog's body. If there is one thing that Malik learns from Cesar, it is that people are there to be exploited and friendships formed only for personal gain. Even his supposed friendship with Ryad (Adel Bencherif), another French-Arab prisoner, who is later released, becomes a means by which to carry out his own drug deals and surreptitiously invest in building a trafficking network whilst still in prison. Having said this, the film's final scene suggests that Malik does have a conscience and there was perhaps a brotherly dynamic between him and Ryad.

Tahir Rahim gives an incredibly controlled performance as the impoverished young man who arrives in prison, unschooled both as a respectable citizen and a criminal mastermind, but who undergoes a transformation. The camera seldom leaves him. It is often right in his face, yet his performance remains unaffected; he never quite sheds the boyish quality in spite of all his cunning; he is calm yet ruthless in his capacity for aggression. There is nothing flashy about him, nothing that emblazons him with a star quality, and it is this everyman aspect that keeps the viewer believing in the character even when he's in the midst of another vision or overcoming the most unlikely obstacle.

Once Malik is granted day leave and the film moves outside of the prison walls, it loses some of its psychological intensity and its adherence to gritty verisimilitude appears compromised. The violence is ramped up and the film slips into gangster thriller mode, moving at a brisk pace as Malik uses the twelve hours to cut deals, shift drugs, engage in shootouts, collect bags of money and pave the way to become the cartel boss once his sentence is up. During this final third part of the film, Malik becomes a character serving the plot rather than a storyline for further character development. The cold palette of colours used to paint the prison is replaced by warmer tones while the camera is forced to pan back a little to accommodate the action. It's as if the viewer is denied the same proximity to Malik once he is out in the open air. Malik becomes involved in a number of gangs, acts as their go-between, and ultimately plays them off against each other in his bid to scale the underworld ladder in their wake.

Whether or not Malik's experience reflects the problems faced by second-generation French-Arab youths is certainly a moot point considering the high-octane nature of the crime capers during the second half of the film. However, *A Prophet* makes one thing clear: if you designate an individual as socially, racially and economically inferior than you should not be surprised if he ends up leading a life of crime, particularly when he inhabits a world that is ruled by tyranny, violence and corruption.

A GIRL FROM SAUDI ARABIA

Samia Rahman

Saudi Arabia killed my father. There was no violence. No Frank Gardner-style hail of bullets. There was no sound of shrill sirens. Crowds did not gather to witness robed figures dancing in the shadows. The wound was not visible to the eye. His was a murder of the heart. A silent, unseen weapon that twisted and killed without pity or remorse. It was the death of a dream.

My dad had been brought up to hold a deep reverence for the 'Land of the Two Holy Sanctuaries' – Mecca and Medina. As a youngster growing up in Allahabad, India, he resolved to one day make the pilgrimage to Mecca. It was the land that witnessed the birth of Islam, where all Muslims could feel that they had come home. Saudi Arabia was a concept he cherished. Ultimately, it broke his heart.

He was already in his fifties when he had an opportunity to work in Jeddah, Saudi Arabia's gateway to Mecca. There was much hand-wringing, family conferences were held, but he was convinced the positives outweighed the negatives. He had travelled to England as a 20-year-old in 1960, leaving behind everything and everyone he knew in the hope of securing a better future. He had faced loneliness, racism and untold challenges. This would be an altogether different dislocation. We would all benefit in the long term. It was decided. He would embark on this wonderful new life that would bring him as close to his faith as was possible. It would be a privilege. His wife and three teenage children would stay in the UK with the promise of frequent visits to allay any misgivings.

Wadjda directed and screenplay by Haifaa al-Mansour, produced by Gerhard Meixner and Roman Paul. Released Koch Media In Arabic. Saudi Arabia, 2013

A friend of my dad's – an Egyptian doctor with a family similar in age to my brother, sister and I – had spent a number of years working in Saudi

Arabia. He warned dad that he would be deeply disillusioned. 'The Saudis despise other nationalities. It's bad enough as an Egyptian but Indians and Pakistanis have it even worse. Don't be under any illusions that they will welcome you because you are Muslim. You will be shocked to see that you're treated better here in the UK than you will ever be there.' Within eighteen months of arriving in Jeddah, my father had his first heart attack.

The level of racism, corruption, archaic – often spiteful and obstructive – red tape and social ills overwhelmed him. Such maladies are not exclusive to Saudi Arabia by any means. There are a host of countries around the world that boast such winning attributes. But Saudi Arabia is the direction towards which all Muslims face when they offer their prayers five times a day. It is the birthplace of the Prophet, the site of the 'House of God'. Surely, the protector of Islam's most sacred sites would therefore be an upholder of basic Islamic virtues. How opposite the reality proves.

I don't associate Saudi Arabia with culture – any culture. It's a desert in the real sense of the world. So I was astonished to hear that a film has come out of Saudi Arabia – indeed, its first ever film, *Wadjda*. And, I wondered what my father, if he were still alive, would have thought about it. Wadjda is a young Saudi girl on the cusp of adolescence who wants more than anything in the world to possess a bicycle so she can race the neighbour's son Abdullah. To raise the money to buy a bicycle she incongruously enters a Qur'an recitation competition. Her desire to ride around on two wheels is met with horror by her mother and teachers who feel a female cyclist represents the epitome of indignity. Her mother even exclaims that bicycle-riding could render Wadjda infertile. There seems to be a Saudi obsession with the impact of various modes of transport on women's gynaecological health. One of the country's so-called clerics, Sheikh Salah al-Luhaydan, declared in September 2013 that there was medical basis for the ban on women drivers. He is quoted by Al Arabiya.net as saying: 'Physiological science and functional medicine studies have found that driving automatically affects ovaries and rolls up the pelvis. This is why we find women who continuously drive cars – their children are born with clinical disorders of varying degrees.' You couldn't make it up if you tried!

Gender segregation is policed socially, culturally and by law in Saudi Arabia. Writer-director Haifaa al Mansour, determined to film within the Kingdom for authenticity, was forced to direct from the back of a van.

Issuing instructions to the actors from the vehicle while watching the action on a screen was the only way she could avoid falling foul of regulations forbidding non-relative mixing of the sexes in public. The chronic fear and hysteria surrounding male-female interaction permeates *Wadjda*. In one scene the youngster and her schoolfriends are shooed away from an area within the school grounds because, despite wearing the hijab, they are in view of construction workers. Al Mansour alludes to the (usually South Asian) foreign labourer as mythical in his supposed lewd and libidinous prurience. He represents the worst of the everyman. He is the reason women must be veiled, remain invisible and unheard lest they unleash the innate beast within him. Indeed, there is an evil beast within every man. My dad told a story about a colleague who one evening was drawing his curtains when a fully-veiled (that is, niqab-wearing) woman happened to be exiting his apartment block. Very briefly, as he was at his window, their gaze met. Both quickly turned away but either someone observed the fleeting moment or the woman complained because the incident became the subject of malicious and feverish gossip. Other residents viewed him with suspicion and he became so uncomfortable he moved out and eventually returned to his home country, Pakistan.

Wadjda is alive with strong female characters. It occurred to me that for many of the viewers who packed cinema houses across the world, this may well be the first time they have ever seen recognisably Saudi woman unveiled. Such is the powerful symbolism of the *abayah*, particularly when worn with a *niqab*, that the women beneath the layers of black cloth become literally invisible, unfathomable and unknowable, yet so much is assumed about them. On one return visit to Saudi Arabia I sat amongst a group of Saudi women covered from head to toe in black. As the plane approached London, I saw one after another enter the toilets, only to emerge devoid of all black, wearing glamorous, designer attire and meticulous make-up, dripping bling and labels the way only new money knows how. *Wadjda* gives a voice to these women. It humanises them and no doubt assuages the curiosity of many a viewer.

Our quirky protagonist exerts personal freedom with an innocence that only a child could possess in such an oppressive environment. She is constantly reminded she must not laugh or talk too loudly in case a man may hear. Wearing nail polish is immoral, her trainers should be replaced by black shoes, and she must begin wearing the face-veil. In many ways she could be the blithe non-conformist of any coming-of-age film grappling with family strife, lectures on her fashion sense and choice of music. Wadjda's mother, unable to bear more children, is afraid that her husband – possibly due to pressure from society to produce a son – is seeking a second wife. Her character is complex, tragic yet ultimately empowered. She is a reminder to her daughter that they live in a deeply misogynistic society where a woman is valued, ironically, for her beauty. She seeks to protect by discouraging Wadjda's spiritedness. Unable to disconnect from the suffocating moral code that defines private lives, she judges her friends and neighbours, despite recognising the injustice of social conventions, and is constantly gossiping on the phone with her friends about other people. So much of her life is beyond her control and she has few outlets for self-expression. At times, she perpetuates the essentialised female – make-up, clothes shopping and revelling in the transgressions of others. Tempted to follow the example of a friend to apply for a job in a mixed-gender environment, a hospital, she backs down at the last moment. Her frustrations are channelled by passing judgement on her friend instead of supporting her. Unfortunately, the film seems to imply that free-mixing will lead to moral lasciviousness, as we see her friend flirting giddily with her male colleague. Ultimately, though, Wadjda's mother realises that working within the system need not mean the system cannot be subverted.

During one trip to visit my dad in Saudi Arabia, I met the female members of his landlord's family. A kind Saudi man, and a reminder to me not to generalise about the male members of Saudi society, he and his sons had saved my dad's life by rushing him to hospital after discovering him on the steps of the apartment block, which they owned and in which he lived. Naturally, dad and my brother met the male members of the family in one room in their apartment and me, my mum and my sister met with the women in a separate section. Just as Wadjda and her mother remain out of sight while Wadjda's father entertains his friends, leaving food by the door for them, I observed this gender segregation dance with our hosts. Great lengths were taken to prevent any accidental interaction between the two parties. I found it very stressful. Even upon entering their apartment in the same building I was compelled to stuff my unruly hair into the black hijab that, of course, kept gradually slipping down and I was constantly tripping over the hem of the too-long-for-me *abayah*. Wearing it was truly exasperating. The family were very sweet, and intensely curious about our lives in the UK. They were filled with preconceptions about life in Britain being decadent, deviant and dangerous. I was amazed by the prejudices that were brought into the open by us all and which, from the other's perspective remained true. The oldest daughter was recently divorced, having been married at a young age to a husband who was described as lazy, uncivilised and violent. She told us she had become the subject of gossip among family and friends these days so kept a low profile. Her three sisters were still studying and had lofty ambitions for their futures. From time to time I wonder how their lives played out.

While the portrayal of Wadjda's mother focuses on the way in which women's lives are curtailed within the domestic realm, her head teacher represents public social conditioning. She is a state-appointed moral guardian of the girls in her charge. Authoritarian and strict, she dresses luxuriously in designer heels and haute couture. She is beautiful and forbidding, preaching the Saudi official line – that the harsh and at times humiliating treatment of the girls is carried out with only their best interests at heart. Just as driving a car or riding a bicycle is the first step to the corruption of standards and the degradation of society, similarly the minutiae of the life of pre-teens must be scrutinised for the slightest deviance and punished severely and publicly, to be made an example to all. As dogmatic as her veneer appears, it soon becomes apparent that she is also conflicted. Rumours abound that she has a lover and she tells Wadjda that she reminds her of her young self. Perhaps her own personal frustrations and contradictions cause her to weigh down so heavily on the budding youngsters. By stamping out any inclination to err among the upcoming generation she can absolve herself of her own hypocrisy and save the innocent souls from a similar fate. It is in this way that Al Mansour refrains from any demarcation of her male and female characters into good guys or bad guys. Everyone is flawed. Even Wadjda's father, despite omitting her name from a family tree because she is female, and taking a second wife, loves his wife and daughter deeply. His choices are those of a weak man, cowing to the rumour mill that demands he has a son. Reference is made to his mother searching for a wife, not him. Perhaps we are once again seeing the maintaining of the status quo by women, keeping women in their place.

As women are unable to drive, they often employ men from the Indian sub-continent to chauffeur them around, not only for long distance journeys. Women do not walk anywhere in Saudi Arabia as I and my family found out one day while dad was at work. The sight of women attempting to go for a walk is an oddity that will cause taxi drivers to constantly stop their cars in the middle of the road and honk their horns in disbelief that anyone would voluntarily choose to subject themselves to a non-vehicular meander.

The plight of these migrant workers is touched upon in *Wadjda*. The film hints at the tension that arises when a society is both patriarchal and racist. Women are devoid of many rights in Saudi Arabia but the migrant worker, often working without proper documentation, is in a far more precarious and vulnerable position. Wadjda's mother is reliant on her Pakistani driver who has a young family 'back home' he barely sees. There is no camaraderie between these two marginalised individuals. Instead a power struggle and loathing defines their interaction as each attempts to garner an iota of respect in a society that affords them little. At one point the driver refuses to chauffeur Wadjda's mother any longer – or has Wadjda's father stopped paying him to do so? – leaving her unable to travel to work. When Wadjda and the neighbour's son Abdullah threaten to report him to a powerful relative if he does not resume his duties, he is rendered powerless. Even with the correct paperwork migrant workers are at the mercy of any local who decides to make trouble for them. Even a professional with all the correct legal documentation and a citizen of the UK as my father was, never felt his status was secure.

Al Mansour's film is enchanting and beautiful, but it is not without imperfections. The narrative, viewed through Wadjda's child's-eye perspective, is superbly played out but I wonder whether at times it is weighted by its own social consciousness. The innocence and simplicity of a young mind, not yet ground down by the incomprehension of her world, gives way to a series of fragments that do not reveal the true hypocrisy of Saudi Arabian society. At what point does journeying through the Kingdom's manifestation of misogyny – and there is an endless list to choose from – detract from the pace and cinematography of a story about a young girl? There are so many issues and while *Wadjda* overlooks some it does manage to navigate quite a few skilfully. The air of hypersexual paranoia leads to two female schoolmates being erroneously accused of inappropriate touching.

Wadjda is in a position to absolve them but she is reticent, fearful of jeopardising her chance to win the prize-money. Nevertheless, Wadjda is lauded as a beacon of hope for women's rights in Saudi Arabia. Her friend Abdullah offers a glimpse of the Saudi man of the future who is not intimidated by a strong woman. Yet, is Abdullah really a pioneer of his sex? Both he and Wadjda conspire to blackmail the Pakistani driver, albeit well-meaningly, compounding this highly vulnerable guest worker's already precarious position. Most tellingly, when Abdullah declares to Wadjda that he will marry her, it seems an endorsement of the notion that men and women are incapable of a relationship that is anything other than romantic or sexual.

I am quite sure my dad would have been saddened if he had lived to see the commercialisation of Mecca, the Ka'aba now dwarfed by vulgar luxury hotels. *Wadjda*, however, while providing much resonance, may have provided him with some hope for the future of a country that taught him the pain of unrequited love.

SAQI

www.saqibooks.co.uk

The Sultan's Sex Potions

Arab Aphrodisiacs in the Middle Ages

Naṣīr al-Dīn al-Ṭūsī

A Critical Edition, Translated and Introduced by Daniel L. Newman

The first in a series on classical Arabic erotic literature

This manual for self-healing was written by Nasir al-Din al-Tūsī in the 13th century – the historian Ibn Khaldun considered al-Tūsī to be the greatest of the Muslim scholars

Available in English for the first time, will provide an invaluable insight into sexuality in mediaeval Middle Eastern society

January 2014 • £17.99 • 978-0-86356-747-6

'Essential reading for anyone who wants to know where the future of Yemen lies after the toppling of Ali Abdullah Saleh' CHARLES SCHMITZ, American Institute of Yemeni Studies

'An up to date and wide-ranging guide to what is arguably the Arab world's least known and most misunderstood state' MICHAEL WILLIS, University of Oxford

February 2014 • £21.99 • 978-086356-777-3

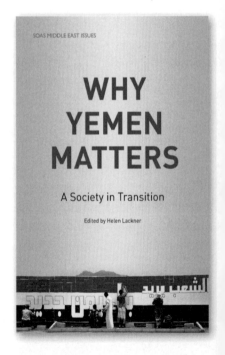

SOAS MIDDLE EAST ISSUES

WHY YEMEN MATTERS

A Society in Transition

Edited by Helen Lackner

ET CETERA

TEN MOROCCAN ODDITIES

Morocco, the land of bougainvillea, snow-capped mountains, ochre pise' walls, water sellers in hats with fuzzy red guy-ropes, sticky black soap, pointy shoes and leather trilbies, is perhaps unique in the Muslim world. It's the only Muslim country with both Atlantic and Mediterranean coastlines, the only one to keep much of its historic cultural property intact, including the only fully functioning classical Islamic city, Fez, and the only one with a King who claims to be *Ameer al-Momineen*, or Commander of the Faithful. Unlike its eastern neighbours it never became part of the Ottoman Empire. And while the king claims descent from the Prophet's family, Morocco is perhaps the least 'Arab' country in ethnic terms – Marrakesh, Meknes and Tarroudant are capitals of a specifically Berber culture. Endlessly diverse, Morocco has generated figures of cultural worth from the great fourteenth-century globetrotter ibn Battuta to the taboo-busting twentieth century novelist Mohamed Choukri. It is a country at once of the twenty-first century and the eleventh, the First World and the Third, shaken not stirred. A society horizontally divided into layers that slide across each other like wet fish on a fishmonger's slab, of extraordinary wealth and extraordinary poverty, where goats climb trees and sheep ride motorbikes. The country's rich history has left some strange traces, a fascinating nest of conundrums and contradictions. So here are ten of our favourite Moroccan quirks.

1. Multilingualism

Former Prime Minister Abbas el-Fassi famously claimed that he spoke *fusha*, or classical literary Arabic, with his wife and family, a claim that instantly became a joke. Nobody anywhere in the Arab world speaks *fusha* at home, and particularly not in Morocco, where the predominant dialect of Arabic – Durija – is a melting pot language brewing Berber rhythms and intonations alongside French and Spanish borrowings. An embarrassment for purist Arabists, a delight for cosmopolitans, Durija carries within it the history of North African polyculture. Added to this richness, almost half of Moroccans also speak one of three Berber languages – Tamazight, Tamarift or Tashelhit. After years of postcolonial struggle, the Berber languages are now broadcast and taught in school; in other Maghreb states the struggle continues. French is widely used in bourgeois life, and Spanish is spoken in the north and far south. Moroccans slip between languages as between the waves of the ocean, smoothly, hardly noticing the transitions.

2. Diabetes

The comedy film, *Elle est Diabètique 3* (2012) is one of the biggest hits of recent times. *Trois?* You mean there have been two previous instalments on this rock about theme? Yes, indeed. *Elle est Diabètique 3* is directed by two brothers who go under the joint name of Imad Noury Swel. Their father, Hakim Noury, made *She is Diabetic, Hypertensive and Ready to Die I* (2000) and *She is Diabetic, Hypertensive and Ready to Die II* (2005). In Morocco diabetes is both big and a big business. The country has a dangerously high rate – in the range of 7.6–8.3% of all adults – but this places it only seventy-fourth in the world, far behind the UAE (second), Saudi Arabia (third), Bahrain (fifth), Qatar (sixth), Kuwait (eighth) and Oman (twelfth). Sugar consumption comes in the form of viscous mint tea with cataclysmic quantities of sugar poured in. Once a cheap form of instant energy for manual workers, tea is now drunk at every opportunity, everywhere in Morocco. In its heyday the loaf sugar came from the British West Indies and the Hyson tea from China, both via London in British ships. As for the mint, well that just grows wherever you let it. And what is it about those Gulf countries? Sedentary or something?

3. Gymnastics

Wherever you go in Morocco, you will find gymnasts doing their thing. Gymnastics is one of the many specialties of Morocco's brotherhood of Sufi acrobats, the followers of the sixteenth-century master, Si Ahmed Ou Moussa, who brought Sufism to the Anti-Atlas and founded semi-mystical guilds of archers and gymnasts. The gymnasts, who wandered from *moussem* to *moussem*, the religious and commercial fairs, giving highly symbolic displays of athleticism, stand in a direct line of ancestry to the street and artistic troupes which still ply the trade and are often to be seen in spectacular rehearsal on Morocco's beaches. More secular now, and perhaps less symbolic, they still invoke Si Ahmed before a difficult routine. The old boy would no doubt be supporting a big grin while resting under his mausoleum. By the way, mausoleums are as common in Morocco as diabetes and Sufi gymnasts.

4. Hoopoes' Blood

The hoopoe, for the uninitiated, is a beautiful, colourful bird with a distinctive crown of feathers. Though currently common in North Africa it could become extinct – thanks largely to the Moroccan tendency to drink the noble creature's blood. Supposed to guarantee academic success if drunk in sufficient quantities, it's a magical remedy on sale in all good Moroccan witches' outfitters. With a first-round baccalaureate pass rate this year of only 37 per cent, there clearly isn't a glut of the stuff on the market. Moroccan witches are highly esteemed across the Arab world, though consulting them is not a widely admitted habit, and they tend to be flown off to appointments in the Gulf in private jets with their supplies of wax, lead and hoopoes' blood. The pass rate went up to 53 per cent on the baccalaureate resits, so perhaps stockpiles were released in time.

5. Tablecloths

If they're not selling you leather goods in the medina, then they're urging you to buy one of their fine tablecloths made of plant – cactus – silk. No tourist has ever left Morocco without a tablecloth in their luggage. But the tablecloths have a more subtle use than the obvious. One of the greatest risks of Moroccan dinners is the relentless quantity of food that comes in wave upon wave like advancing infantry – salad, *bastilla*, roast lamb, chicken, fish and fruit on even quite a modest occasion. If you miscalculate and eat too much too early you can be really stuck well before the end of the meal (a risk intensified by the curious habit of serving sticky cakes before it). So count the tablecloths. In the old days, when the cloth was changed between courses, diners surreptitiously riffled through the cloths with their fingertips, to count how many courses there were going to be, and paced themselves accordingly. Mind you, if you go for a second helping of *bastilla*, the exquisite sweet pastry envelope of almond paste, pigeon, cinnamon and icing sugar, you are doomed anyway. We recommend a quick test for Diabetes before they release *She is Diabetic, Hypertensive and Ready to Die IV*.

6. Eels and Eggs

On the edge of Rabat is a splendid walled enclosure called the Chellah, which is perhaps the site of the first Punic settlement, and certainly that of the Roman port, Sala Colonia, whose forum is still to be seen there. In one corner there is an old basin, perhaps a Roman cistern, long inhabited by giant eels. It is the habit of the barren ladies of Rabat to visit the eels, and to feed them a hard-boiled egg (conveniently available from a vendor by the pool). The symbolism is obviously lubricious, the efficacy unknown. But the ministry placard by the pool used to say, until it faded away in the sunshine, that this was a *lieu de culte* (religious site), an unusual statement to find in a Muslim country, and an excellent symbol of Morocco's syncretism.

7. Oral Tradition

The average Moroccan is said to read for two minutes a day, or three pages a year. So they are very slow readers taking 122 days to read a page! Literacy, according to the World Bank's figures is 56 per cent, but a good deal of this is still 'signature literacy'. On the whole, Morocco remains in many ways an oral culture with remarkable facility of memory: the number of Moroccans who memorise the Qur'an (and other religious texts) by heart is much higher in absolute and proportional terms than any country of North Africa. In many areas of education and life memory remains king, which is not the strongest of bases for building cultural capital in the twenty-first century.

8. The Shehonk Calendar

The Berber calendar begins in 943 BC when Pharaoh Sheshonk I, a seminal figure in Amazigh history, seized the throne of Egypt. The calendar was actually invented by Berber exiles in Paris in the 1960s, so that although it is now 2963 by this After-Shehonk reckoning, the first 2903 or so New Year's Days (every January), passed the world by entirely uncelebrated. Morocco's Berber newspaper *Le Monde Amazigh* (also known as *Amadal Amazigh*) bears the Anno Domini and the After-Sheshonk dates, but pointedly omits the Hijra year. And as you may have noticed, 2963 actually starts the clock at 950 BC, so the pharaoh's accession date may itself be a bit of a guess.

9. Black Shoes

When the Alaoui Sultan Moulay Ismail (1634–1727) captured the harbour town of Larache in northern Morocco in 1689 he decided in his usual impetuous way to lay down the law. He started by banning black shoes, which he regarded as an abominable emblem of Christianity, imported and encouraged by the Spaniards. Thenceforth only Jews could – and indeed must – wear black *babouches*, the strange, flat, lightweight Moroccan slippers with pointed toes. The God-fearing Muslim was to wear the gorgeous canary-yellow ones that every respectable Moroccan sports to this day.

10. Bowler Hats

The Jews of Mogador, a city in western Morocco on the Atlantic coast, used to be famous for their bowler hats. It acquired its name when it was seized by the Portuguese and turned into a fortress in the sixteenth century. Nowadays it goes by name of Essaouira – the 'Beautifully Designed'. In 1900 Mogador was still a Jewish majority city – probably the only one in the Muslim world – and the focus of the city's commerce was the Manchester cloth trade. It used to be said that Mogador was closer to Manchester than to Marrakesh, and its Jewish traders would often seek to be naturalised as British citizens – a quick trip to Gibraltar would do the business. And when Mogador's Jews came home as newly-minted Brits, they cast off the black turbans which the Sultan's Jewish subjects had to wear, and began to flaunt their bowlers, as signs not just of their British citizenship, but of protection. A tradition that lives on! Brollies of course were more problematic in Mogador's extraordinarily windy conditions.

ON WIN–WIN WORLD

Ziauddin Sardar

'CLOSED to vehicular traffic'.

The sign at the entrance to St George Street is unexpected. In a culture given over to the automobile, where atomised individuals in their private, insulated space, drive up to cash dispensers, fast food counters, and to the heart and top of perpendicular offices and dwellings, a sign discouraging the car is unique. But then St Augustine, Florida, itself is quite a unique town.

'It is the oldest town in the United States.' That was Hazel Henderson, grand matriarch of a generation of Americans seeking positive change, doyenne of alternative economics, and adopted elder sister. 'In St Augustine, past and present merge to produce a visible, contemporary synthesis. I moved here because it provides an antidote to the globalised, consumerist culture, a vision of a positive future.'

It was 1979. I was taking my first steps towards becoming a 'futurist'. Having spent most of my youth looking for love, peace and goodwill to all humanity, as well as the end of Civilisation as we know it, and failed miserably, I had come to the conclusion that I was looking in the wrong direction – a common enough practice amongst us Muslims. I was looking backwards rather than forwards in the future. The future is undoubtedly the best place to find whatever you are looking for simply because you can't change the past. You can interpret it, rediscover it, draw lessons from it, but you can't change it. Neither can you change the present. Change is not instantaneous; it takes time. By the time the present has been changed, it is already the future. So to change the present you need to start in the future.

My first, tentative steps towards becoming a futurist son led to an obvious discovery: I discovered that the future is all things to all people. Most people perceive the future, when they think of the future at all, as though it is computer code divided into ones and zeros, optimism and pessimism.

The optimists look at the future from the perspective of the past and the present and extrapolate into the future. The past was good and wholesome; the present, despite a few problems, is thriving. So it follows that the future will, in most cases, be the same – only better, faster, bigger, smaller, cheaper. A typical optimistic future may look something like this. Technological developments will mean that our houses will be automated, computers will be so small that they will be integrated into everything from our walls to the very clothes we wear. Medicine will have tackled some of our most persistent health problems, largely on the back of the same advances in genetics that will revolutionise food production. Indeed, genetic engineering will transform us and we will become 'transhumans' with super power, able to live for decades, if not forever. Science will take giant leaps forward and we will have a 'Theory of Everything'. Cheers; and trebles all round!

The optimists tend to be scientists, technocrats, and business-oriented folks who work for corporations or the government – and neo-liberal types who believe science is Truth but deny that there is such a thing as climate change, let alone that it has been caused by human actions. When they think of the future, dollar (or Yuan, Rupee or whatever currency you choose) signs magically appear in front of their eyes. For the future is a commodity. It's big and lucrative business – and they are in the business of selling us the future they have chosen for us.

The pessimists also extrapolate the past and the present but reach diametrically opposite conclusions by concentrating on the downside of technology and focusing on destructive trends. The past was full of horrors, the present is a disaster, so the future is a calamity waiting over the horizon. All pessimistic perceptions of the future essentially boil down to the *Blade Runner* or *Terminator* scenario. Here, runaway technology produces a dark, dreary and dingy future. The world is controlled by a megalomaniac corporation, privacy has evaporated, and cyborgs police the streets.

Hazel taught me to think beyond this absurd dichotomy. In between the cheerleading optimists and banal pessimists, there is a wide range of other options, she told me. As the title of her first book, *Creating Alternative Futures*

(1978), which had just been published, suggests there is not one but countless futures. And, as I was to write some years later, the very act of putting the definite article in front of future is to colonise it. Moreover, Hazel suggested that future is not something that is inevitable, *a priori* given, but it can be invented and shaped in a positive direction.

Both of us eventually realised that the duel between optimistic and pessimistic futures is a confidence trick. It has little to do with the future and a great deal to do 'the market'. Both optimistic and pessimistic futures are consumer items sold either as developments in technology or cultural products (films, novels, television series) or both. This is why, even though prediction is a hazardous business – the chances of getting one's prediction totally wrong are quite high – the business of forecasting has spread like a global fire.

I noticed that unlike many American cities, St Augustine has no multi-storey buildings and there were very few cars on the road. Moreover, it has real history. The sort of history that goes back centuries and can be touched. We were walking on St George Street, a bit touristy, but with several lovingly restored buildings – Grist Mill, the Spanish Inn, Episcopal Church, Fatio House, Arrivos House. Moreover, many of these buildings were inhabited by families who had been there for centuries. The Greek Orthodox Church contains not only a display of the history of the local Greek community, but also a chin whisker of grandfathers and grandmothers in attendance ready to relate that history as they lived it. For a moment, I thought I was breathing the Mediterranean air. Street names reinforced this feeling. Cordoba Street, Seville Street, Valencia Street. Occasionally, I became slightly confused, unsure whether I was north or south of the Straits of Gibraltar. While St George Street and the parallel Cordoba Street are very Spanish, on King Street, hidden just behind Auggies Corner Café, I came across a Moorish house, complete with exquisite tile works — a hallmark of the Maghreb. My confusion was further compounded when I was invited to buy an armadillo from an adjacent shop. A few steps along King Street we visited the old Alcazar Hotel, now the Lightner Museum. It could easily be mistaken for a *riad*, the traditional Moroccan house, complete with a courtyard and – well, there must have been a fountain where now stands a small bridge encrusted with gaudy shells. Inside, I found a fascinating collection of nineteenth-century musical instruments and a complete *hammam* distinguished by a rounded dome. I remembered seeing a similar museum in Fez but instead of musical instruments it had beautiful wood furniture and artefacts. From the museum we walked towards Montanzas Bay.

'Imagine if the entire world consisted of small, enchanted communities with local economies, their own thriving cultures and living history,' said Hazel; and after a pause, added with some determination, 'we can change the world you know.'

Hazel and I have been trying to change the world for decades; one could say we have accumulated more blueprints of alternative futures than are lodged in the St Augustine Planning Department. Change is, of course, the only constant left in contemporary times. Everything changes, but few things change for the better. Positive change requires effort, real sweat and labour variety, and has to be worked towards. What this means from the perspective of the future is not simply breaking away from the banal self-fulfilling prophecies of the optimistic and pessimistic modes of future gazing, characterised by a vast array of forecasting techniques, but also opening up the future to democratic, dissenting and pluralistic possibilities. No matter how sophisticated the techniques of forecasting, and they are becoming more and more refined and complex, they simply end up by projecting the (selected) past and the (often-privileged) present on to a linear future. So the best thing for people who want to change the world is to bother less with predictions and forecasting (they are distinct and different things) and concentrate more on the future as an arena of all imagined and unimagined potentials. As such, an awareness of the future can empower people and open up possibilities where none existed before. That's where futures thinking and social activism join hands.

'This time', Hazel said, 'let's start from where the world is, as it is, not as we would like it to be. Just because we accept the world as it is does not in any sense weaken our desire to change it into what we believe it should be. I am tired of standing on the periphery shouting "foul". It's about time we got where the action is and sorted out the ruffians. That means working in the system.'

We turned into Charlotte Street. In the shadow of the statue of Ponce de Leon – who arrived in the new found land with Columbus on his second voyage in search of the fountain of youth – a local watering hole. I admired Plaza de la Constitution. A covered arcade sported a wall plaque: 'From 1605 to 1765 there stood on this site a grand house and tower. Under British rule it became the market and place of public auction ever since called the slave market.'

'Working in the system is like changing the world in three acts', I mused. 'The first act only introduces the characters and the plot. In the second act the plot thickens to grab the audiences' attention. In the last act, good and evil have their final confrontation and sort each other out. We have been trying to go right to the final act, skipping the first two; this is why there had been no play, only rootless confrontation. A quick flash and fade to black. Changing the world is not about revolutions; it needs a slow build-up. Not just shouting "shoot the referee" and expecting him to drop dead from fright.'

Hazel laughed and shook her head vigorously in agreement. From the market we crossed the Bridge of Lions to Anastasia Island and walked towards Hazel's new colonial mansion. 'People won't step abruptly out of the security of familiar experiences; they need a bridge to a new lifestyle. What we have to do is to construct this bridge.'

Being an inquiring, investigative sort of chap, I couldn't help asking: 'Just how do we build the bridge?', thereby plummeting headlong into a well-set trap.

Hazel took a deep, self-satisfied breath. 'In consumerist, high-tech cultures', she declaimed, 'there are a lot of people who are extremely confused. As old cultures break down, there is nothing to take their place. There is a massive dislocation as we move towards a global economy. We all have to realign and restructure ourselves on a new global roller coaster. As industries close down, computers take over, everyone chases their own tails with no sense of direction. They can see the political process everywhere is corrupted by money. We have, in all democratic societies, the best democracy that money can buy. Or, the golden rule of politics is those who have gold, rule. No wonder half the population of any country never makes it to the polling booth. And if they do they have to choose between two evils. So what do these people do? More and more of them are taking things into their own hands. That's why citizens' movements and voluntary organisations have grown so much in the last decades. What we have to do is to channel their accumulated energies towards positive change. This is the bridge we have to build.'

As we arrived beneath her portals, she turned and said, 'In the first act, we meet the characters just as the floods begin to undermine the edifice of their beautifully laid town centre.'

She opened the door and a gush of water cascaded out.

'Win-Win World. You win, we win, the world wins. Everybody wins – and the world wins too. Win-Win World.'

The flood of chorus greeted me as I entered Hazel's magnificent abode, lasting several minutes. When the place returned to normalcy, a rare event in this household, Hazel introduced me to the gathering saying 'meet the cast of characters playing to change the world'. We walked over to the swimming pool and sat round a table.

Scanning the faces, I found myself in a postdiluvian matriarchy. Apart from the tall, dominating blonde figure of Hazel Henderson, there was the ethereal, exquisite presence of Barbara Max Hubbard, futurist and mystic, former candidate for the Vice-Presidency of the United States, current lynchpin of citizens promoting cooperation and peace between – well, between anyone who is engaged in a conflict, and mother superior to countless idealists who throng to listen to her powerful, moving orations for internal and external change. What does she do for an encore, I wondered. She flew past me like a levitational express to answer the phone. She was preoccupied with the issues of the Foundation of Conscious Evolution, of which she was a founder. In her slip stream, Connie Buffalo, half (red and gentle) Indian, half (tough and rugged) Sicilian, half Zen, half city businesswoman, abundantly holistic mother. She too was busy on the phone – half negotiating a business deal, half administering household affairs with her children. Next, Margaret Lloyd, a Mother Theresa without the religion, completely devoted to serving others and changing lives, and fully supplied with the means to do so. Last, and definitely not least, the token man: Carter Henderson, ex-husband, present lover, former *Wall Street Journal* hack, now enjoying the success of his book, *Winners*. He reclined in the sun with his extraordinarily long legs sprawled towards the table. I leaned against him in unconscious alignment against the matriarchy.

'You see Zia, we are a civilisation of binary logic. You immediately gravitate towards chauvinist solidarity', Connie admonished me.

'Indeed', said Hazel, 'the whole culture is based on yes-no, win-lose logic. Every game we play is about winning or losing. And, as we all know, it is only the few who win. The vast majority of humanity consists of losers. Take conventional economics. Its driving force is oppositional competition, it does not concern itself with moral values or what kind of behaviour will leave a healthy planet for our children and grandchildren. It is concerned with winning now; by any means necessary. But people are beginning to realise there is something wrong with this logic of self-interest. Even while politicians are urging us to be more and more "competitive", people are moving in a different direction – consuming less, living more simply, trying to realign their lives, joining citizens movements to save the environment, investing in socially responsible funds which avoid companies involved with military contracts, nuclear energy, with bad pollution control records, bad labour relations or human rights records, as well as those producing unhealthy products like alcohol and tobacco.'

'But the market mechanism is a natural system, after all half the eco-system does operate competitively, species do compete with each other', reacted the suppressed Wall Street instincts of Carter.

'But our market economic theory now focuses only on the competitive half,' Margaret jumped in.

'That kind of thinking is based on the western notion of fallen man, the Hobbesian war of all against all', I intervened. 'It's a vision of the natural world that has no place for cooperation and working together. It's a colonial notion that has no place in an interdependent, interconnected world.' My *volte face* took them all aghast.

Hazel adjusted her hair in agreement, and followed through.

'When we realise that this is one planet and think globally the market turns into a "common" – and a different logic takes over. In fact, the rule becomes exactly the opposite of the conventional marketplace, such that if you don't cooperate, you destroy each other and the resource base from which you are working. We find that the world's oceans are common and we can no longer treat the seas as if we were pirates, competing with each other and polluting. Under the new logic, the game changes and the perception is that we are all going to have to take care of the oceans or the oceans will be destroyed for everybody. And, of course, it's the same with air and water and this interlinked, global economic system itself. Right now, each government is trying to preserve its so-called competitive advantage and sovereignty right to the brink of financial collapse. We are filling the whole planet with the junk products of our aggressive and competitive activities. We need to galvanise all those people who have seen through the phony logic and are looking for another way of living.'

Then Barbara made her sublime contribution. 'The new logic is in fact a primal logic. It is the logic of the ancient wisdom. It has different names in different systems. It is none other than the logic of *shura* (cooperation) in Islam. Or the logic of *jnana* (awareness) in ancient Hindu thought. The essence of the logic is not win-lose but win-win.'

At this cue the whole assembly rose in unison, even Carter levitated himself into an exultant lamp post, to chorus their endorsement: 'Win-Win World. You win, we win, the world wins.'

'So what do you think?', queried Hazel. 'Are you with us?'

'Humm', I said, reflecting that I could hardly be against them and in favour of sin and noting with some relief, 'You can have a free lunch without toxic side effects.'

'It provides us with an opportunity to find what we are looking for – love, peace and goodwill to all humanity', Hazel said.

'And a bit of laughter, beauty and poetry', I mused.

'And a chance to land a well-targeted blow and do some irreparable damage to the reproductive organs of the macho, competitive world structure', Margaret added.

After the round table discussion, and my initiation into the group, Hazel decided to reward me by showing me her latest discovery. 'Come on', she said, 'we are going to Fort Mose.'

'Fort Mose? What and where is that?' I was as intrigued as surprised by the sudden announcement.

We left the mansion, jumped in Hazel's old, very old, Citroen and drove out of St Augustine.

'Keep an eye open for the old city gates', she said, and began to explain the significance of Fort Mose. 'It is believed to be the oldest settlement of free blacks in North America. The story goes that Fort Mose was inhabited by runaway slaves from the British colonies who found sanctuary in Florida under the protection of the Spanish King. Long before slaves followed a northward underground railroad out of the South, their forebears risked hardship and death to find passage from the British held Carolinas to the promise of freedom in the Spanish colony. At Fort Mose, the runaway slaves regained the savour of being masters of their own destiny. Are you looking out for the city gates?'

Without waiting for an answer, Hazel continued: 'These slaves defended the fort against the British; in fact, they knocked the shit out of the British colonial army. The Fort was abandoned in 1763 and along with it a chapter of black history, a chapter of courage and epic struggle by the first measure of self-sufficiency and self-determination, was lost. Keep your eyes open for the old city gates. Conventional history tells us that blacks were a rather docile and subservient lot. But now with the discovery of the remains of Fort Mose by a team of archaeologists from the University of Florida, this interpretation of black history can be thrown in the trash can. Fort Mose is a symbol of black freedom in colonial North America, an image we don't get much of in history books. Have you spotted the old gates yet?'

Partly because I was fascinated by the story and partly because there weren't any real gates to be spotted, I totally failed to find the landmark. We had actually driven several miles past the spot where we were supposed to leave the main road and had to turn back. Eventually, Hazel spotted the 'old gates'. The gates turned out to be statues of Spanish soldiers – one raising his sword ready to defend (or attack?), the other leaning on his sword standing guard – on either side of the road. We took the next turning, drove for a quarter of a kilometre and parked the car on a side road.

'We are two miles north of St Augustine on the banks of North River. From here on we walk.'

I rolled up my trousers and trailed behind Hazel. We walked along a twisted creek in a salt marsh. It was low tide but the banks of the river were muddy enough for my feet to sink almost ten centimetres. As we approached the Fort Mose island, we were greeted by a colony of baby crabs. For a moment I thought they were some kind of mutation as one of their claws was disproportionately large; huge in fact. But Hazel assured me they are a natural species in this part of the world. 'Like the crabs, the grass in this region is also special. Its technical name is *halophijtes*, and there are over two thousand native varieties. Its ability to grow in salty water means that some varieties can be used for greening the deserts. It's an idea that has not occurred to many people.'

Eventually, after making our way through knee-deep rapidly flowing water we arrived at Fort Mose. Hazel suggested we stand still and observe two minutes of silence in remembrance of black slaves who died here defending their freedom. But it was difficult for me to stand still with gale force winds gusting against my body.

We began to examine the site. Even though the excavation had only just begun – only three small areas had been opened, the largest dig was covered with thick cellophane and was slightly water-logged – the remains of Fort Mose were showing through distinctly. Once the two centuries of mud and soil had been removed, the rotting timber of Fort Mose was there to be seen. I jumped inside a partly excavated site and looked at the remains.

'You have been awfully quiet for some time', Hazel finally broke the silence.

'For some reason', I said, 'I feel very close to this place. I am trying to work out the connections in my mind.'

'What connections?'

'The slaves who lived here were obviously very good fighters. It is likely they were from some Maghrebi tribe; or, perhaps, from the Mandinka tribe of Senegal. We know both the Spanish and British took Muslim slaves from North and West Africa. Probably, in all but name, Fort Mose was a Muslim settlement.'

'But I have checked the roster of their names in the Town Hall. They all had Christian names; they had converted to Christianity', Hazel was ready with an immediate answer.

'The colonial missionaries followed a policy of forced conversion. That the Africans had converted is not surprising; but originally they were Muslims. Just as Alex Healey traced his *Roots* to Muslim Gambia, the roots of the slaves of Fort Mose belong in North Africa. The real name of this place is not Mose, which is a meaningless word, but Musa, the Qur'anic name for Moses. As they had converted, it was natural for these Africans seeking their freedom to call their settlement Musa. This is Fort Musa.' I said that with some conviction and felt as though I was absorbing the history of my own civilisation, meeting some long lost relatives. Hazel too shared my experience and joined in the joy of discovery.

'Now that we have drawn inspiration from the battle of Fort Musa and the struggle for freedom that took place here, let us return to the struggle we face today. Let's go and change the world', she said, slapping my back.

'Right on, sister', I said as we navigated our way through the water-logged marshes.

CITATIONS

Introduction: Dusklands by Robin Yassin-Kassab

I am indebted to Susan Gilson Miller's bright and informative, *A History of Modern Morocco* (Cambridge University Press, Cambridge, 2013). For more on the Glawi family and other southern warlords, the indispensable book is Gavin Maxwell's classic *Lords of the Atlas: The Rise and Fall of the House of Glaoua 1893-1956* (Eland, London, 2004). A devastating critique of Hassan II's tyranny is provided by Gilles Perrault, *Notre Ami Le Roi* (Our Friend, the King). (Editions Flammarion, Paris, 1993), in French. The hashish metaphor is worked through in Naguib Mahfouz's *Adrift on the Nile* (Bantam Doubleday, New York, 1994); and the guidebook I refer to is the *Lonely Planet Morocco: Country Guide*' (Lonely Planet, London, 2011).

See also: Barnaby Rogerson, *Marrakesh Through Writer's Eye* (Eland, London, 2006); Peter Mayne, *A Year in Marrakesh* (Eland, London, 2002); and Walter Harris, *Morocco That Was* (Eland, London, 2007)

A brilliant deconstruction of the new constitution, its contradictions and deceptions, is provide by Ahmed Benchemsi at: http://ahmedbenchemsi. com/hello-world/; a list of Berber personalities can be found at http:// tamazightinou.blogspot.co.uk/2012/05/list-of-berber-personalities-in-history.html; and information on the revived Tifinagh script can be found at: http://en.wikipedia.org/wiki/Tifinagh

Mystical Ibn Khaldun by Robert Irwin

The *Muqaddima* has been translated into English by Franz Rosenthal as Ibn Khaldun, *The Muqaddimah: An Introduction to History*, 3 vols. (London: Routledge and Kegan Paul, 1958). Because of the meticulous, even pedantic quality of this text, Rosenthal's English text is a better guide to Ibn Khaldun's thinking than the various and variable Arabic versions. There are no English translations of the *'Ibar* or the *Ta'rif*, though there is a partial translation into French of the *'Ibar* and a translation of the *Ta'rif* by Abdesselem Cheddadi in Ibn Khaldun, *Le Livre des Exemples*, 2 vols. (Paris, Pléiade, 2002, 2012). For some aspects of Ibn Khaldun's approach to Sufism, see Alexander D. Knysh, *Ibn 'Arabi in the Later Islamic Tradition: The Making of a Polemical Image in Medieval Islam*, (New York, State University of New York Press, 1999). See also Allen James Fromherz, *Ibn Khaldun, Life and Times*, (Edinburgh, Edinburgh University Press, 2010); Muhsin Mahdi, *Ibn Khaldun's Philosophy of History*, (London, George Allen and Unwin, 1957); Robert Brunschvig, *La Berberie orientale sous les Hafsides*, (Paris, vols. 3 and 11, 1940 and 1947 of 'Publications de l'Institut d'Études Orientales d'Alger': Michael W. Dols, *The Black Death in the Middle East*, (Princeton, N.J., Princeton University Press, 1977).

The quotations from Ibn Khaldun are from *The Muqaddimah*, Rosenthal translation, vol.1, p.64 and vol. 3, p.81; and from Ibn Khaldun, *Ta'rif*, in *Le Livre des Exemples*, vol.1, p.151 and p.162. Other quotations are from Toynbee, *A Study in History*, vol.3, p.322; Gellner, *Muslim Society*, pp.88–9; Brunschvig, *La Berberie orientale*, vol.2, p.393; and Fromherz, *Ibn Khaldun*, p.115.

For modern assessments of Ibn Khaldun, see Aziz Al-Azmeh, *Ibn Khaldun in Modern Scholarship: A Study in Orientalism* (London, Third World Centre, 1981); Arnold Toynbee, *A Study in History*, 12 vols. (Royal Institute of International Affairs, London, 1934-61); Ernest Gellner, *Muslim Society* (Cambridge University Press, Cambridge, 1981).

On Ibn al-Khatib, see Emilio, Molina López, *Ibn al-Jatib*, (Editorial Comares, Granada, 2001).

Frank Herbert's epic science fiction novel, *Dune*, which contains many Islamic elements, came out in 1965, and is widely available. It is the first novel in the Dune saga, which includes *Dune Messiah*, *Children of Dune*, *God Emperor of Dune*, *Heretics of Dune*, and *Chapterhouse: Dune*. Don't bother with the 1984 film; read the novels! Bruce Chatwin's *Songlines* was published in 1986 and is available in Vintage Classics.

Poetry in the Maghreb by Marcia Lynx Qualey

The translation of Abdellatif Laâbi's 'In Vain I Migrate', by Andre Naffis-Sahely, can be found in a dual-language chapbook, *Abdellatif Laâbi: Poems Poèmes* (Poetry Translation Centre, London, 2013) or downloaded from its website http://www.poetrytranslation.org/poems/404/. Laâbi's 2001 interview with *Double Change,* translated by Omar Berrada, can also be found online at: http://doublechange.com/issue3/laabi.htm. Quotes from Mohammed Bennis from an interview with *Banipal* issue 29 are also online at http://www.banipal.co.uk/selections/56/80/mohammed-bennis/ and 'Dans le dialogue', in *Les nouveaux enjeux de la francophonie au Maroc, acts of the colloque* (du 23 février 2001, Rabat), p. 59. The Words Without Borders special section on Libya, edited by Khaled Mattawa, can be found at http://wordswithoutborders.org/article/preface-to-the-libya-issue-of-words-without-borders-july-2006.

Several poems and quotes, including 'Saddle Up, O Warrior!', 'Guardian Shadow 1', 'Counsel for My Family After my Death', 'The Will', 'Of solitude and a few other matters', and 'Mother Tongue' come from Pierre Joris and Habib Tengour's indispensable *Poems for the Millennium* (University of California Press, Stanford, 2013). Rachida Madani's poetry comes from her *Tales of a Severed Head,* translated by Marilyn Hacker (Yale University Press, New Haven, 2012).

Other works mentioned in the essay include Helen Metz's *Algeria: A Country Study* (Federal Research Division, Library of Congress, Washington, D.C., 1994), Ilan Pappé's *The Modern Middle East* (Routledge, London, 2005) and Salma Khadra Jayussi and Christopher Tingley's *Trends and Movements in Modern Arabic Poetry* (Brill, Leiden, 1977).

I conducted interviews with Algerian linguists and literary scholars Nadia Ghanem and Lameen Souag, Tunisian poet Inas Abbassi, Tunisian critic Mohamed-Salah Omri, and Libyan poet and journalist Ghazi Gheblawi for this essay.

Invisible Interzone by Julia Melcher

The quotations from William Burroughs are from *Interzone* (Penguin, New York, 1989), pages 119 and 58. *The Naked Lunch* was published in 1959 (Random House, New York). Paul Bowles novels include *Let It Come Down* (Random House, New York, 1952), *A Hundred Camels in the Courtyard* (City Light Books, San Francisco, 1962), and *The Sheltering Sky* (Vintage Books, New York, 1977). Jane Bowles' works include the novel *Two Serious Ladies* (Alfred Knopf, New York, 1943) and the play *In the Summer House*, which was first performed on Broadway in 1953. Tahar ben Jelloun's *Leaving Tangier* was published in 2009 by Penguin.

See also: Ralph Coury and Kevin Lacey, editors, *Writing Tangier* (Lang, New York, 2009); Iain Finlayson, *Tangier: City of the Dream* (Harper Collins, London, 1992); Greg Mullins, *Colonial Affairs: Bowles, Burroughs and Chester write Tangier* (The University of Wisconsin Press, Madison, 2002); and Millicent Dillon, *A Little Original Sin: The Life and Work of Jane Bowles* (University of California Press, Berkeley, 1981).

Berber Springs by Hicham Yezza

In his important study on the origins of the Muslim reformation movement in Algeria, *Le reformisme musulman en Algerie de 1925 a 1940* (Editions el hikma, 1999), Ali Merad revisits the now-forgotten battle between indigenous partisans of European assimilation and those arguing for a revival of the region's ties with the Arab-Islamic Orient. The quotation from Robert Hugh is from 'Co-opting identity: the manipulation of Berberism, the frustration of democratisation and the generation of violence in Algeria' (Working Paper No 7, Development Research Centre, LSE, December, 2001), which can be downloaded from http://eprints.lse.ac.uk/28311/1/WP7HR.pdf. Said Sadi's *Askuti* is published by Imadyazen (ed.), Paris, 1982, in French.

See also: Ernest Gellner and Charles Micaud, (eds), *Arabs and Berbers: from tribe to nation in North Africa* (Duckworth, London, 1972); Patricia M.E. Lorcin, *Imperial identities: stereotyping, prejudice and race in colonial Algeria* (I.B. Tauris, London, 1995); and Michael Willis, *Politics and Power in the Maghreb:*

Algeria,Tunisia and Morocco from Independence to the Arab Spring (Hurst, London, 2012).

Background information on the Amazigh campaigns can be obtained from: www.amazigh-voice.com and www.amazighworld.org

The Jews of the Maghreb by Louis Proyect

Ibn Warraq's review of Paul B. Fenton and David G. Littman's *L' Exil au Maghreb* (P U De Paris, Sorbonne, 2010) can be found at: http://www.jihadwatch.org/2011/09/review-of-paul-b-fenton-print.html.

David Littman's introduction can be read at Dhimmitude.org, a repository of articles designed to support the idea that Jews suffered oppression under Islamic rule and maintained by Gisèle Littman, David Littman's widow: http://www.dhimmitude.org/archive/littman_jews_under_ muslims_19thcent_wlb_1.pdf.

Report of the protests at Georgetown University can be found at: http://en.wikipedia.org/wiki/David_Littman_%28historian%29

The quotations are from: S.D. Goitein, *Jews and Arabs: a Concise history of their social and cultural relation* (Dover, Mineola, N.Y., 2005), p. 124; Richard Hull, *Jews and Judaism in African History* (Markus Wiener Publishers, Princeton, 2009), p. 48; Maurice M. Roumani, *The Jews of Libya : Coexistence, Persecution, Resettlement* (Sussex Academic Press, Portland, 2008), p. 14; Daniel J. Schroeter's article 'The Shifting Boundaries of Moroccan Jewish Identities' appeared in *Jewish Social Studies*, New Series, vol. 15, no. 1, Sephardi Identities (Fall 2008); the quotation is from p. 155; Mark A. Tessler and Linda L. Hawkins' article 'The Political Culture of Jews in Tunisia and Morocco' appeared in *International Journal of Middle East Studies*, vol. 11, no. 1 (Feb, 1980); the quotation is from p. 60; and Arye Gelbaum's article appeared in *Ha'aretz* (Tel Aviv, 22 April 1949); it is cited by Meyrav Wurmser, 'Post-Zionism and the Sephardi Question', *Middle East Quarterly* (Spring 2005).

See also: David Shasha, 'Sephardic Judaism and the Levantine Option', *Critical Muslim 6: Reclaiming al-Andalus* (Hurst, London, 2013), p.91–104.

Revolution in Maghrebi Cinema by Jamal Bahmad

The quotations from Nouri Bouzid are from his article, 'New Realism in Arab Cinema: The Defeat-Conscious Cinema', (translated by by Shereen el Azbi) *Alif: Journal of Comparative Poetics*, 15 (1995), pp. 242-250; the quote from Youssef Chahine is also taken from this article. Habib Bourguiba quote is cited by Nouri Gana, 'Bourguiba's Sons: Melancholy Manhood in Modern Tunisian Cinema', *The Journal of North African Studies* 15.1 (2010), pp.105–126; and Bouzid comments on Bourgabia appear in Jeffery Ruoff, 'The Gulf War, the Iraq War, and Nouri Bouzid's Cinema of Defeat: It's Scheherazade We're Killing (1993) and Making Of (2006)', *South Central Review* 28.1 (2011), pp.18–35; Ben Highmore quotation is from *Everyday Life and Cultural Theory: An Introduction* (London, Routledge, 2002), p.148; and Michel de Certeau quotations are from *The Practice of Everyday Life* (translated by Steven Rendall) (University of California Press, 1984), pages 239 and 40.

Nouri Gana's *Signifying Loss: Toward a Poetics of Narrative Mourning* is published by Bucknell University Press, Lewishberg, PA, 2011. See also: Roy Armes and Jamal Bahmad, 'Casablanca Unbound: The New Urban Cinema in Morocco', *Francosphères* 2.1 (2013), 73-85; and David Murphy and Patrick Williams, *Postcolonial African Cinema: Ten Directors* (Manchester University Press, Manchester, 2007).

Inside Mauritania by Anita Hunt

Ould Aggat's programme is available form Radio Mauritanie webpage: http://www.radiomauritanie.mr Details of Nouakchott's Assalamalekoum Festival can be obtained from: http://www.assalamalekoum.com/ Both Waraba 'The Lion' Brahim Fall and Ewlad Leblad can be found on YouTube. Many Mauritanian bloggers can be read in French, including: Abbass Braham http://tedwinatarim.blogspot.com; Abdellahi Med Abderrahmane http://abdallahimaur.blogspot.com/; Ahmed Jedou http://ahmedjedou.blogspot.com/; 'Canal H' collective http://canalh.blogspot.com/;

Djigo Souleymane http://djigosouleymane.blogspot.com/; Elhadj Brahim http://rightpencil.blogspot.com/; Mouna Mint Ennass http://maurichronique.blogspot.com/; Salek Najem http://saleck-najem.blogspot.com/ and Sidi Tayeb Ould Moujtaba http://moujtebarim.blogspot.com

See also: David Robinson, *Paths of Accommodation: Muslim Societies and French Colonial Authorities in Senegal and Mauritania, 1880-1920* (James Currey, London, 2001); and Noel Foster, *Mauritania: The Struggle for Democracy* (First Forum Press, Boulder, Colorado, 2011).

Last Word: On Win-Win World by Ziauddin Sardar

Hazel Henderson's *Creating Alternative Futures* is available in revised fourth edition (West Hartford, CT., 1996); her latest book, with Daisaku Ikeda, is *Planetary Citizenship: Your Values, Beliefs and Actions Can Shape a Sustainable World* (Middleway Press, Santa Monica, 2004). Barbara Max Hubbard's main work, written with Barry Weins and Wabun Wind is *The Evolutionary Journey: A Personal Guide to Positive Future* (Evolutionary Press, New York, 1993). Ziauddin Sardar's *Future: All That Matters* has just been published by Hodder Education, London.

See also: Ziauddin Sardar, 'Colonising the Future: The 'Other' Dimension of Future Studies', *Futures* 25 (3) 1993; and *Rescuing All Our Futures: The Future of Futures Studies* (Adamantine Press, New York, 1998).

CONTRIBUTORS

Suhel Ahmed has just published his first novel, *Broken Path* • **Naziha Arebi** is a British photographer and film-maker now living in Tripoli and rediscovering her Libyan roots • **Lina Sergie Attar**, Syrian-American architect and writer, is co-founder of Karam Foundation, a non-profit organisation that focuses on delivering humanitarian aid to Syria • **Jamal Bahmad**, a native of Morocco, writes on North African and postcolonial cinema and popular culture • **Sarra Hennigan** writes poetry and aims to produce her own food and share the abundance • **Anita Hunt** is a freelance writer who blogs about human rights and civil activism, with a special focus on Mauritania and Western Sahara • **Aamer Hussein** is incredibly well known as a short story writer • **Robert Irwin** is the author or editor of seventeen works of fiction or non-fiction, of which the most recent is *Memoirs of a Dervish* • **John Liechty** is looking for a literary agent • **Julia Melcher** is writing a blockbuster thesis on 'Literary Voices of the Muslim Diaspora in Postcolonial London' • **Cécile Oumhani**, poet and novelist, lives in France; her latest novel is *L'atelier des Strésor* • **Louis Proyect** is a journalist, blogger, and non-Jewish Jew in the spirit of Isaac Deutscher • **Marcia Lynx Qualey** writes daily about literature, authors, publishers, and translations at arablit.wordpress.com • **Samia Rahman**, Deputy Director of the Muslim Institute, is finally writing a book on Muslim misogyny • **Barnaby Rogerson**, writer and publisher, loves dogs and souks in equal measure • **Ziauddin Sardar** was Editor of *Futures*, the primary journal of futures studies, from 1999 to 2011; now relegated to the status of Consulting Editor, his latest book is *Future: All That Matters* • **George Szirtes** has just published two collections of poems, *Bad Machine* and *In the Land of Giants* • **Robin Yassin-Kassab** is writing a novel set in the Syrian revolution • **Hicham Yezza**, an Algerian writer and researcher, is Editor-in-Chief of *Ceasefire*, a UK-based magazine concerned with politics, culture and activism.